JC INC
NOVEL

ALSO BY JOHN CLARKSON

DEATH COMES DUE

JOHN CLARKSON

A John Clarkson Inc. Book
Brooklyn, NY

DEATH COMES DUE

This is a work of fiction. All the characters, organizations, and events portrayed in this novel are either products of the author's imagination or used fictitiously.

First Edition published 2020 by John Clarkson Inc. 11 Schermerhorn Street, Suite 6WB, Brooklyn, NY 11201

www.johnclarkson.com

ISBN 978-0-9992155-8-6   hardcover
ISBN 978-0-9992155-9-3   softcover
ISBN 978-1-7356335-0-3   e-book

Subjects of this book.
Crime – Fiction
Ex-convicts – Fiction
Murder – Fiction
Suspense – Fiction
New York – Fiction

Cover and interior design: Design for Writers

ACKNOWLEDGMENTS

Special thanks to my wife, Ellen, for her support and encouragement. Thanks to Dermott Ryan and Brooks McMullin for providing feedback on this novel. You made this a better book and me a more diligent writer. And finally, deep appreciation and thanks to my readers for their interest and enthusiasm. If it weren't for you, there would be little point in writing this series.

For the victims of mass incarceration

Demarco Jones asked, "Where's Manny?"

James Beck looked up from his book and said, "On the pier. Fishing."

They were in Beck's bar on the first floor of his renovated building in Red Hook, Brooklyn. Demarco stood behind the hundred-year-old oak bar that dominated the first floor, reading the manual for a new coffee maker. Beck sat on a barstool at his usual spot, reading a new history of the United States he'd been absorbing in chunks.

Neither of the men looked like devotees of the written word.

Demarco Jones stood six feet four, head shaved, linebacker physique. He was a hardened criminal, ex-con, and an exceptionally efficient killer.

Beck was less imposing, but he was sturdy, fearless, and had survived more life-and-death situations than he cared to remember.

Beck asked, "What was wrong with the old coffee maker?"

Demarco kept reading the manual and muttered, "Lots."

"That one looks like it should be in a chemistry lab."

Jones didn't bother to respond.

Beck persisted.

"I'm not sure it fits in with the décor."

Demarco looked up from the manual.

"You mean this Iceman Cometh turn-of-the-century dive bar look?"

"Painstakingly executed."

"You think it should be in the new kitchen upstairs."

"I do."

"But this is where we take our morning coffee."

Beck made a small sound of concession and looked back at his history book.

Demarco dropped the manual on the back bar and began filling the coffee maker with freshly ground coffee. He said, "I'm glad Manny went out."

Beck closed the eight-hundred-page book and said, "You're noticing it, too?"

"About the only time he goes out is to shop for food."

"You think it's because he's getting older?"

"Partly. Mostly it's all the time he spent inside. It's wearing on him. And that mess with his niece didn't help."

Beck said, "The shooting or the betrayal?"

Demarco's answer came without hesitation. "Both. She was the last of his family far as I know."

"There's still us."

"Hmm."

Beck took another sip of his coffee. The last cup made with the old coffee maker. He said, "Doesn't change the past, I guess."

"What?"

"Having us. And this place."

"You can't change the past, James. Maybe tone down the effects. But Manny is Manny. The original OG. The tats, work clothes. He's not gonna change. Still got one attitude – stay the fuck away from me."

"Yes," said Beck. "No illusions." He tapped his knuckle against his book. "History of this country is pretty clear."

"America loves locking people up."

"Or just killing whoever is in the way."

Demarco turned on the coffee maker, shaking his head.

Beck said, "What?"

"Even you."

"Even me what?"

"Even you got nailed. White, no priors, no history – and they still locked you up."

"I killed a cop, D. Powers that be couldn't let that go."

"Well, you beat it. And you got paid."

"After eight years of hell and Phineas moving mountains. Any particular reason you decided to bring all that up this morning?"

"I don't know. Talking about Manny, I suppose. He was locked up longer than any of us. What is he? Sixty-two, sixty-three? Forty-five years in the system. What that does to you is permanent, James."

"It's all permanent, brother. I remember the feel of the handcuffs that first time. And every time after that."

Demarco leaned against the back bar and watched the steam rising from the new coffee maker.

"When I was a kid, I had an operation on my eyes. I think it was pretty standard. To tighten the muscles or something, but I had bandages over my eyes for maybe two weeks. My Aunt Ethel was with me when they finally took the bandages off. I remember opening my eyes."

"And?"

"First thing I did was close them."

"Really."

"Everything was too bright, too disorienting. Aunt Ethel kept tellin' me to open my eyes, but I just wanted to sit in that chair. Go back to the way it was until I could get a hold of myself."

"Like the guy who gets out of prison and wants to sleep in a closet."

"On the floor."

"Yeah."

Demarco said, "It's good Manny has this place."

"And us."

"And his fishing buddies, I guess."

Beck said, "Ramon and Eduardo. I think it's Eduardo."

"They ex-cons?"

"Maybe some small-time stuff. I think Manny would've told me if either of them had done hard time. They're just neighborhood guys."

"But Hispanic."

"Yes. Not Dominican like Manny. Puerto Rican, I think. I'm not sure. I suspect the common denominator is they all like rum."

Demarco smiled his killer smile. "Come to think of it, I don't remember Manny ever bringing home any fish."

"Nah. Manny Guzman is not going to eat anything out of New York Bay."

Beck looked at the bottle of dark Dominican rum on the back-bar shelf that Manny sometimes sipped with his morning coffee – Matusalem Gran Reserva 18. He thought of pouring a bit for himself but decided against it. Maybe when Manny got back.

Demarco warmed a small pitcher of milk in the microwave on the back bar and placed the pitcher next to Beck. He replaced Beck's half-full coffee cup with a clean cup, then poured in steaming coffee from his new machine. Beck added just the right amount of warm milk. Despite the chilly March morning outside, the rich aroma from the fresh hot coffee made the old barroom feel like home.

2

A little over a mile from where Beck sat, NYPD Deputy Inspector Dianne Brennan stood in the bowels of the massive Red Hook Grain Terminal – a dangerous, derelict structure, abandoned for nearly fifty years. She stared at a burned and twisted corpse made lurid by the unforgiving glare of police emergency lights.

Brennan, a tall redhead with an athletic figure, wore a tailored gray pantsuit, white shirt, and black round-toe pumps, her Sig-Sauer riding high on one hip, her police radio on the other, and her Deputy Inspector insignia on her lapel. Brennan looked like a confident commanding officer, but she felt like a disoriented bystander dropped into a surreal hellhole and immobilized by a gruesome specter of death.

The abandoned grain terminal was a vast labyrinth of massive crumbling concrete pillars and walls, corroding metal staircases, giant rusting metalworks, and creeping black mold marred by patches of garish, ugly graffiti. The corpse lay in a blackened alcove at the end of a hundred-foot-long corridor, its ceiling supported by gigantic circular pillars with massive concrete conical tops. Most of the clothing had burned away, all the skin had turned black. The body looked like a filthy, misshapen statue that had fallen into a pile of ashes – the remains of several wooden pallets that had fed the fire. Brennan knew that for the rest of her life, two things would haunt her: the expression of pain and absolute terror fixed forever on the face of the victim, and the sickening smell – a combination of burned gasoline, scrap wood, and human flesh.

The two patrolmen from the 76th precinct who had found the body knew enough to sidestep the usual procedure and call in the discovery by cell phone. That kept the information off the radio frequency monitored by news organizations and other trawlers looking for excitement. The desk sergeant on duty had the presence of mind to report the finding directly to the precinct commander, Captain Nicholas Fernandez, who made sure to keep the investigation off the grid. All the necessary NYPD personnel – crime scene unit, medical examiner's office, precinct homicide detectives from the Seven-Six, and FDNY investigators – had filtered into the location in unmarked cars or vans discreetly parked on side streets surrounding the abandoned grain terminal.

Brennan stood with Fernandez facing the murder scene, forcing herself to look at the burnt and twisted remains despite how queasy the sight made her feel. It was important to her that she did not show any weakness to Fernandez. Brennan was aware of her standing among her fellow officers. Particularly male officers. Brennan worked directly with the commissioner of the New York Police Department. She was his eyes and ears. She investigated crimes that could become P.R. problems, attract media attention, foment protests. Usually, higher-ranking cops would defer to someone with her rank, but they knew that Brennan had no power of her own. No real command authority. She had a measly squad of four detectives, nothing more. She did, however, have the ear of the commissioner, so NYPD command staff were careful around Dianne Brennan. That didn't mean they respected her. In fact, far too many resented her, particularly those assumed that a woman as young and attractive as Brennan had earned her rank by sleeping her way to the top.

Brennan's response was to ignore the bullshit, keep her cool, and do her job. A job Commissioner Warren Roth had made clear to her: "Make sure I'm never the second person to know something that will affect the department."

Brennan's job was to gather information. Which, at this moment, meant following protocol – check in with the highest-ranking cop on the scene, Captain Nicholas Fernandez.

After greeting Fernandez and shaking his hand, Brennan skipped the small talk and asked, "How did your guys find this?"

Fernandez pointed up to the blackened ceiling. "The fire in here ran along the ceiling and out that opening facing the bay, scorching the wall outside. My guys were rolling on Bay Street. Regular patrol. They saw the scorch marks. Normally, we don't come in here. It's too dangerous. This place is twelve stories high, seventy-feet wide, five-hundred-feet long. No lighting. Open holes everywhere. Everything falling apart."

Brennan said, "But they came in to investigate the fire."

"There wasn't any fire by the time they were within sight. Just the signs of a fire."

"Enough to come in."

"Yes. They found the body. Called it in Kept it off the radio. Here we are."

"Well, Captain, you and your people did a good job keeping this off the grid. This is one of those cases we'd like to get a handle on before the press swarms all over it."

Fernandez turned to Brennan, literally sick of looking at the corpse. "Just so I know, Inspector, are you going to be taking command of this investigation?"

"No. I report what I find to the commissioner." Brennan made sure to add, "He might ask my opinion, but it's his call who does what."

Fernandez nodded. "I'm assuming this will get bumped up at least to the borough level."

"Probably. But you should keep doing what you're doing until you hear otherwise."

Fernandez nodded but didn't say anything. Brennan could tell he didn't like getting any kind of direction from her. Tough shit, she thought. You don't want to hear what I have to say, don't ask me. Brennan dropped her collegial act.

"Tell your guys to stick around until I can talk to them."

Fernandez gave Brennan a half salute and moved off to talk to his precinct detectives.

Brennan did a quick circuit of the area gathering people she wanted to talk to: the detective in charge of the crime scene unit, the head technician from the medical examiner's office, and a fire marshal from the FDNY Bureau of Fire Investigations. They walked to an open area facing the bay to get away from the smells and sights of the brutal murder. Brennan had received the first report shortly after she had arrived at her office in One Police Plaza at 8:32 a.m. Overnight, warm air moving across the cold water in the bay had created a layer of fog, now mostly dissipated in the morning sun.

Brennan knew the CSU detective, a large man with an easy-going, confident manner named Gerry Austen. He'd been on the job eighteen years but had never seen a murder as grim as this one.

"Gerry, nice to see you again. Despite the horrible circumstances."

"Likewise, Inspector."

"What's your take?"

Austen stared out at the bay for a moment, considering what to say. "Ah, I'd say this is about as bad as it gets." Austen nodded back toward the body. "Obviously, the body was doused with a flammable liquid. My nose tells me it was gasoline."

Austen looked at the fire marshal, who nodded but didn't say anything.

Brennan asked, "How much gas would it take to do that?"

"I don't know. Four or five gallons. But it was those wooden pallets that kept it going. I assume the pallets were already here. The gasoline burned long enough so that the skin split open and the body fat fed the wood. The fat and wood kept everything burning.

"The only other significant thing, it looks like there was a trauma to the left side of the skull. Blunt force. Hopefully, the blow either killed the victim or knocked him out before the fire."

The fire marshal chimed in, "The autopsy will confirm that."

Brennan asked, "How?"

"If the victim was breathing, there'll be residue in the lungs. Irritants, carbon monoxide, and particulate matter from the accelerant. And damage from the super-heated air."

Austen said, "Even if he was conscious after the first few lungs-full, there'd be massive edema to his airways. That would cut off the oxygen, and he'd pass out."

The medical examiner investigator said, "I concur. At the most, ten or twenty seconds of pain and panic, and that would be it."

Thirty seconds thought Brennan. She knew what a drop of cooking oil splashed out of a frying pan onto her hand for a split second felt like. She couldn't imagine the eternity of pain and agony of a body covered in burning gasoline for twenty seconds.

Austen continued, "Obviously, this one is going to be tough. No weapons on the scene, no blood, no prints. The one thing we have going for us is the teeth are intact. First line of investigation would be dental records. We could use them to confirm the identity. Of course, after we get a name. Maybe we get lucky with Missing Persons, and that gives us some direction. Honestly, Inspector, we have an awful long way to go."

Brennan nodded. She asked the ME investigator, "You think there might be any blood in the internal organs?"

"Doubtful. We can get DNA from the teeth, but again that's only good if we get a name to start with like Detective Austen says. Otherwise, we have nothing to compare it to. Same thing with dental records. I took a quick look at the teeth." The technician grimaced and shrugged. "He's had cavities filled. No bridges. I don't think there are any implants. We may get some fractures once we x-ray the skeleton. But again…"

Brennan interrupted. "We need a name, something to start with." She turned to the fire marshal, "Any estimate on when this fire was set?"

"Body is still warm. The wood ash is somewhat intact. The concrete underneath is still warm. I'd estimate six, seven o'clock this morning."

Brennan asked the men around her. "Anything else you want to tell me?"

There wasn't.

Brennan looked past the group and saw two of her detectives approaching. Good, she thought. These guys aren't going to be much help any time soon.

3

Beck came down into the first-floor barroom, his hair still wet from his after-workout shower. He had a daylong to-do list in his head, and it was already past noon. Before he made it halfway to his front door, he heard a familiar knock – a heavy one-two pounding that Beck knew meant Willie Reese was outside his door.

Reese had become a peripheral member of Beck's crew after he had come to Beck's building looking to extort money from Beck for the privilege of living in his neighborhood. Willie had just been released from a two-year stint in Sing Sing and needed to start earning.

Willie was big enough and strong enough to put down a man much larger than James Beck. He'd also brought along four of his gang, just in case. But Willie Reese had made a mistake. Beck had outsmarted and outfought Willie, rendering a brutal beating. Manny Guzman and Demarco Jones ran off the others with shotguns pointed at their heads.

After the fight, Beck called on his friend and personal physician, Brandon Wright, to put Willie Reese back together, and then further tested Willie by making him an offer to see if Willie could learn from the experience. Willie Reese had been smart enough to accept Beck's proposition. When Wille ended up making much more money than he would have made extorting Beck, he became Beck's neighborhood protector, a job he was well-suited for since he ruled over just about every gangbanger and bad boy in Red Hook. Beck took Willie into his tight-knit crew, and their mutual loyalties had grown stronger over the years.

Beck unlocked his front door and stepped aside for Willie to enter.

"What's up, big guy?"

"Cops is what's up."

Beck took a quick look outside, scanning Conover Street. "Where? Why?"

"Unmarks been sneakin' into the neighborhood last couple hours or so. They parkin' over in the lots off Columbia and walkin' past the park and gravel pits into that abandoned grain terminal."

"Why?"

"Not sure. But from outside, it looks like there was a fire in there. I drove around and spotted a fire department SUV stuck in there between some empty truck trailers."

"No other equipment?"

"Nah. Nothing's burning now."

Beck thought about it for a moment. "If the cops are investigating, might be somebody burned up in there."

Willie said, "That shithole would be a good place for it."

Beck walked toward the end of the bar and called out for Manny Guzman, thinking he would be in his small kitchen behind the bar. No answer. Manny's absence frustrated Beck, but he had other concerns. He walked behind the bar, pulled out a gun lockbox holding his Hi-Power Browning, and placed it on the bar.

"Willie, you strapped?"

Willie reached under his 4XL Brooklyn Nets pullover hoodie and extracted a Desert Eagle .50 caliber pistol he'd been carrying in the waistband of his heavy denim jeans.

"Jeezus, how can you carry that cannon around with you?"

"Easy."

"Easy for you. If we have cops crawling around the neighborhood, you don't want to be on the streets with that."

Willie put the gun on the bar as Beck pulled out a Benelli M3 shotgun from under the bar top and laid it down next to his gun box and Willie's Desert Eagle.

"Hang on, let me get Manny's Winchester out of the kitchen."

"Where's Demarco?"

"Out for a run. When he gets back, tell him to add his Glock to the pile and lock up whatever else we don't want the cops finding if they come barging in."

Beck went into the kitchen behind the bar. He came back with a beautifully maintained double-barrel Winchester shotgun and a large blue Ikea shopping bag. He placed the lockbox, Willie's Desert Eagle, and the shotguns into the bag.

"Demarco's gun will fit into this bag, too. After he stores everything in the safe, tell him to lock up and make himself scarce. You, too."

"Where you goin'?"

"To find Manny."

"Where is he?"

"Probably shopping at Fairview."

"Or maybe down by the pier fishin'."

Beck muttered "maybe" as he headed out the door. He didn't want to tell Willie that Manny had already left at dawn to catch the high tide. Or that he should have been back by now. Nor did Beck want to tell Willie that Manny's fishing gear wasn't in the storage closet near the kitchen. And he sure as hell didn't want to tell him that there was no way Manny would go food shopping with the goddamn stinking five-gallon bucket he uses to carry his bait.

Beck headed toward the supermarket anyway, trying to convince himself that Manny might have left his gear with his buddies while he made a run to the grocery store. And then he saw the flashing red and blue police lights parked near the foot of Pier 44 where Manny and his buddies fished. He broke into a run.

4

Dianne Brennan waved a hand to get the attention of Alphonse Grimaldi and Dave Metuchen, both First Grade NYPD detectives. She walked back toward the crime scene and met them near the body, giving them a few moments to see what they were dealing with. They exchanged looks, but nobody said anything. Brennan led them away from the scrum of activity so that their conversation would remain private.

Alphonse Grimaldi was a big man with a large nose who grudgingly wore his baggy suits and outdated ties. He only buttoned his suit jacket and the top button of his white shirts for weddings, funerals, and court appearances. He had a perpetual five o'clock shadow and would never lose the bags under his eyes. Grimaldi had spent years on the Major Case Squad investigating kidnappings, high-end robberies, and burglaries. He believed he was the best investigator in the room, had plenty of New York attitude, and fit in well with NYPD cops and detectives who naturally accepted him as one of their own and treated him like the veteran detective he was – something Brennan found useful because the rank and file kept their distance from her. She was management.

Dave Metuchen was Grimaldi's opposite. Metuchen's 38 regular suits fit him well and looked like they had just come from the dry cleaners because they had. Metuchen had other skills that Brennan needed. He had a nonthreatening manner that put civilians at ease. He'd spent years in the NYPD Robbery Division working on task forces that regularly involved the ATF and FBI, so he was good at dealing with outside law enforcement agencies, navigating fiefs, and overcoming distrust, even though he personally trusted no one. Metuchen always figured the angles and calculated the politics in any situation.

Brennan quickly filled them in on what had happened. Grimaldi didn't hide his disgust. Metuchen showed no reaction.

Grimaldi got to the point.

"So, what's the plan, boss?"

"Find the monster who did this and lock him up. Fast."

Both detectives understood what "fast" meant. Before the local precinct homicide detectives cracked it, and before the higher-ups took over.

Dianne Brennan was the most ambitious person either of them had ever dealt with. She'd been plotting her moves to the top in the NYPD from the day she entered the police academy. She'd used her looks, her brains, her work ethic, and her blue-collar Irish-kid-from-Queens background to get assignments in precincts where she could earn her gold shield and get to where she wanted to be. Without even knowing the details, Grimaldi and Metuchen both knew that a homicide case drawing this much attention was exactly the kind of case that could keep her on the rise.

Metuchen spoke first.

"What do you figure, twenty-four, forty-eight hours?"

"Tops. Roth will move on this quickly, but it will time for the chiefs to gear up and get moving. Forty-eight hours max, we'll be shunted aside."

Grimaldi said, "And so far, we got no ID on the vic, no motive, no weapons, no suspects, no witnesses."

Brennan said, "So what's that leave us with?"

Grimaldi said, "Well, by the looks of it, we have a fucked-up, horrifying MO. Phil is good at running through all the databases. Let's see if we can find anything like it. What's he doing?"

Phil Harris was the third detective on Brennan's four-man squad.

Metuchen said, "He's on that bullshit thing about the mayor's campaign contributor."

Brennan said, "That bozo who owns a bunch of pharmacies. The media is making a big deal out of it. The commissioner wants to know how dirty he is."

Metuchen said, "I would assume very."

Brennan said, "Obviously. We're trying to figure out if he's going to get indicted."

Grimaldi asked, "For what?"

"Take your pick. Illegal campaign contributions, tax fraud, conspiracy. I'll pull Phil off that and put him on this for now. It's a base we have to cover, but if anything like this has been done before in our area, I think we'd already know about it."

Metuchen said, "Agreed. First job is to identify the victim. Start with the basics. There's no magic to it. Canvas the area for witnesses. What's Jerome doing? Is he still undercover on that extortion thing?"

Brennan said, "Yes. He's in Fort Greene on a construction site. We have to find out whatever there is to find out long before I can free him up."

Grimaldi said, "So, it's basically us."

"And whatever the Seven-Six homicide guys do."

The two detectives knew horning in on the investigations would piss off the local precinct guys, but they'd stopped caring about that sort of thing.

Grimaldi said, "The other angle is Missing Persons. Couldn't tell much by looking at that mess, but I assume the victim is an adult male?"

"According to the CSU and ME guys."

Metuchen said, "Going through the missing persons squad will take too long, and anybody missing long enough to be on their list probably isn't our vic."

Grimaldi said, "I agree. Someone missing recently, family or somebody will go to the local precincts. We could give it a shot there and hope we get lucky."

Brennan said, "What's the best way to do that?"

Grimaldi said, "Go straight into the precincts. Find the detectives who have missing persons on their to-do list and talk to 'em. Any other way, they'll avoid us."

Metuchen shook his head slightly. "Lotta footwork for a long shot. We don't have any kind of description of this guy. Is he white? Hispanic? Black? Height, weight, features. Whoever did this took all that out of the picture."

Brennan said, "I know it's a longshot, but if the ME comes up with dental work, fractures, anything that might identify the victim, we'll need a name to match it to."

Grimaldi said, "We can't wait for the ME."

Brennan said, "No, we can't wait."

There was a pause as everyone thought about options. There weren't any good ones. Brennan made the decision.

"All right, forget missing persons for now. Start canvassing the area. Maybe somebody saw something."

Grimaldi said, "Not much around here."

Brennan said, "Then it won't take long. Start close and keep expanding the radius until you hear from me or tap out. Try not to bump into the local homicide guys. They'll be doing the same thing. I'll get Phil going on the MO."

Metuchen gave Grimaldi a look that said this is awfully thin.

Grimaldi shrugged.

Brennan had pulled out her cell phone to call Phil Harris when the voice of her driver, William Jablonsky, crackled over the police radio on her hip. She had recruited Jablonsky fresh out of the police academy. He had finished a B.A. in Criminal Justice at John Jay while in the police academy and was about to start Fordham law school at night.

"What's up, William?"

"Report just came in of a dead body in the water near a pier about a mile from where you are. Cops from the Seven-Six and harbor patrol are on the scene."

"Shit. You still parked on Columbia?"

"Yes, ma'am."

"I'll be there in a minute. Anything else?"

"That's it."

Brennan speed-dialed Phil Harris's number on her cell phone. Grimaldi and Metuchen stepped away so that they didn't have to listen. They had heard Jablonsky's report over Brennan's radio.

Grimaldi said, "Another body."

"I don't believe in coincidences." Metuchen nodded discreetly toward Brennan and said, "She's gonna run hot now."

Grimaldi said, "No shit."

Brennan finished her call and joined her two detectives.

"Dave, start canvassing this area. Call me if anything pops. Alphonse, come with me."

Metuchen watched Brennan and Grimaldi rush off. Grimaldi turned, mimicked phoning. Metuchen nodded and made the same motion. They both wanted to know whatever the other one found out.

5

Beck saw three police cars in the supermarket's auxiliary parking lot and another parked at the foot of Pier 44, blocking entrance to the pier where Manny and his buddies fished. The jetty extended about 200 feet into Red Hook Channel, which led to the Gowanus Flats and eventually into New York Bay.

A handful of people were standing around the parked patrol car.

Beck didn't pause for even a second as he made his way through the small crowd, around the patrol car, and out onto the pier. Halfway out, yellow police crime scene tape strung across the width of the pier stop him. Two uniformed cops stood guard, preventing anyone from getting closer to the crime scene. Beck went right up to the tape. One cop was white, the other Asian. Both were young. The white cop, the larger of the two, held up his hand and told Beck, "Hold on."

Beck looked past him and could just make out the shape of a body under a blue tarp near the northwest corner of the pier. An NYPD harbor patrol pontoon boat bobbed in the water about five feet from the pier's stone foundation. A CSU van was parked near the scene. Beck couldn't see much because too many personnel were surrounding the corpse, but even from a distance he could see a large amount of blood staining the rocks near the end of the pier.

The thought that the blood might be from Manny Guzman, that he might be dead under that blue tarp, sent a dizzying wave of rage, remorse, and dread surging through Beck. He realized he had lived with the possibility for years while he and Manny were in prison together. And on some level, after they had gotten out of prison. It was part of the ever-present cloud of uncertainty and powerlessness they had to endure because they were ex-cons. But that hadn't prepared Beck for what was happening now.

The cop put his right hand on Beck's chest. His partner came over to add his presence, feet widespread, hands on his belt. Beck had to muster enormous effort not to shove the cop's hand off his chest.

Beck moved back.

"Do they know who it is?"

"Off the pier, sir. They're looking into it."

"What happened?"

"We don't know." The cop raised his voice. "You'll have to go back off the pier."

Beck couldn't risk getting arrested, but he had to find out if that was Manny. He backpedaled a couple of feet and moved over to the railing on the north side of the pier. He leaned out as far as he could. It was impossible to tell who was under the tarp.

The cop decided to be more aggressive.

"C'mon, pal. Off the pier. Now."

Beck moved back from the railing to the center of the pier. He looked at the uniformed cop. He gave Beck the impression that he relished his size and position of authority. The patrolman was unshaven, adding to his menacing look. His bulletproof vest gave him extra bulk. Beck took in all the equipment on his belt: a semi-automatic handgun, leather case for extra ammunition, police radio, collapsible steel baton, handcuffs, flashlight, pepper spray, Taser. A patrolman. A cop at the lowest rank but with the power to make Beck's life miserable. To disable him. Maim him. Even kill him if it came to that.

The white cop came out from behind the crime scene tape, his Asian partner backing him up with a hard look. Beck stood his ground. He kept his hands at his sides. He made sure to look the cop in the eyes without expression, without saying anything but maintaining eye contact to show the cop that he wasn't going to back away. Fuck that.

The cop came toward Beck, looking ready to teach this guy what was what, just as an unmarked, black Chevy Tahoe turned onto the pier, its grill light silently flashing red and blue.

Grimaldi sat next to William Jablonsky in the front passenger seat of the SUV. Brennan sat behind him on the bench seat. Jablonsky was a tall, trim young man just twenty-one. He wore slim-fit suits made for someone his age. His hair was neatly trimmed. He wore Ray-Ban sunglasses. Grimaldi liked him because Jablonsky seemed to respect his elders, but he knew Jablonsky belonged to a generation he was long past understanding.

Brennan asked, "What are you picking up on the radio feeds, William?"

Jablonsky turned slightly to answer her. "Not much. They think the victim might have been down there fishing. He was half in the water, half lying on the rocks. I heard comments about damage to his head and multiple stab wounds."

The cop about to go after Beck stopped when he saw the big SUV coming his way. He knew it had to be carrying NYPD brass. When the patrolman paused, Beck turned and walked away, still fuming about the uniformed cop.

As Jablonsky drove slowly past Beck, Brennan asked, "Who's that guy?" even though she knew nobody had an answer.

Brennan said, "Hold on, William."

Jablonsky stopped the SUV.

Brennan said, "Alphonse, go check him out. Might not be the first time a doer returned to the scene."

6

Monster-Boy watched the streaming feed from his remote-controlled surveillance camera. The camera had 4K resolution, 20X zoom, and a 360° turning radius. He'd tracked Beck from the moment he emerged from his bar on Conover Street. The feed was less than a second slower than in real-time.

The camera had been mounted on the roof of a warehouse building on Beard Street, carefully hidden and connected to the Wi-Fi feed of one of the commercial tenants on the Beard Street pier. It provided a 180° view south, east, and west that included Beck's building and the fishing pier before the roof obstructed its view.

Beck's movements had been predictable. Everything had gone well except for maybe Worm's excessive work with his shiv. That, too, had been predictable. When the Worm got to work, he couldn't stop. Monster-Boy recalled the sound of the shiv tearing into the body, splattering blood. He didn't have time to see the blows, but he heard the sounds – whap, whap, whap. The screams. The Worm stabbing over and over in a frenzy to get the work in before the prison guards stopped him. Dumbass. There were no prison guards this time. At least the Worm had remembered to avoid stabbing the head. Less chance of breaking the blade. The fucking degenerate still insisted on using a homemade shiv. Could've had a real combat knife. Something a hell of a lot harder to break. But Worm remembered the most important thing – cut the man's throat. Ear to ear. *Slice him open,* Monster-Boy had told the greasy little slave. Didn't want anybody surviving a bunch of stab wounds. He'd seen lots of losers survive dozens of stab wounds punched into useless places like the chest and arms and back.

Monster-Boy had watched Beck run out onto the pier and almost get arrested. Good thing dead-man, asshole Beck had been smart enough to back off and avoid that. But now it looked like someone with more rank had shown up. An unmarked SUV stopped to check out Beck. Monster-Boy couldn't see who was in the vehicle. The guy getting out had to be a detective. Slightly less dense than a uniformed cop. Fucking Beck had better hold it together, thought Monster-Boy. Getting arrested wasn't part of the plan. Can't have no fun if they haul your ass off, shitbag.

7

Alphonse Grimaldi raised a hand and said, "Hey, buddy, hold on."

Beck turned and saw the detective approach him as the SUV continued toward the crime scene. Relaxed. Playing it like he was going to ask him an innocuous question. Right, thought Beck. Something simple so he could ask another question and another until Beck made a mistake. Then it would be turn around, hands behind your back.

Beck turned and smiled, concentrating, thinking ahead, trying to come up with a path that wouldn't lead to being held for questioning, or worse – getting arrested.

The detective approached with a sorry-to-bother-you look. This wasn't a rookie. And he'd stepped out of an unmarked NYPD SUV that clearly belonged to someone higher in rank. Certainly above the precinct level.

Had they come from the grain terminal? Likely. What the hell was going on?

Beck turned and smiled back at Grimaldi, not fooled one second by the cop's Columbo act.

Beck's instincts were to go on the offensive, but not right away.

"What's up?" Beck asked.

Grimaldi held up a wallet displaying his detective shield and ID. "Can I ask you a couple of questions?"

"Sure."

"You live around here?"

He got right to it, thought Beck. If I say no, that leads to – what brings you here? And that leads to more questions he won't have a good answer to. And checkmate. Handcuffs. If not an outright arrest, being detained.

Fuck it. Gotta take control of this, now.

"I'm here off and on, officer. I'm a real estate developer." Beck pointed vaguely in the direction of Conover Street. "I own a piece of property over there I'm developing. I spend a couple of days a week here. But I also have two other residences. Sorry for being nosey about what's going on. I kinda have an interest in what happens around here." Beck nodded toward the crime scene. "That sort of thing isn't good for property values, if you know what I mean."

"No. What do you mean?"

"Officer, c'mon, even from here, it looks like a dead body out there. You got cops everywhere. Harbor patrol. What happened?"

"Do you mind if I see some identification?"

"Of course not," said Beck.

He pulled out his wallet and dug out a New York State driver's license.

Grimaldi carefully examined the license.

"Thomas Eaton. New Paltz?"

"Yes. I have a house up there."

"Where is that?"

"New Paltz is just west of Poughkeepsie."

"And you own property around here?"

"Yes." Beck waited to see if the detective was going to grill him on that, figuring out how to respond, but Grimaldi took another tack.

"Looked like you were getting into it with the officer over there."

Beck hardened his attitude. "I'd say it was the other way around. If you ask me, he was a little aggressive. Unnecessarily aggressive. I'm a property owner. I live here. I work here. I was polite." Beck pointed behind him. "There wasn't anything that said I couldn't go up to that crime scene tape. Did you see him

25

put his hand on my chest? I thought that was out of line. Tell you the truth, when he did that, I thought about calling my lawyer and finding out how to lodge a complaint. Not that I think it would do any good. But there might be someone I could talk to in the NYPD who would give me an ear."

Grimaldi's attitude hardened. "You thinkin' about that now?"

"No. I don't want to be the rich asshole making empty threats. I just don't like getting hassled. What is it you want from me, officer?"

Beck watched the detective carefully. He had played all his cards. He had money, owned property, had a lawyer, wasn't afraid to lodge a complaint.

Grimaldi took out his notebook and carefully wrote down the information on Beck's Thomas Eaton license. He handed the license back to Beck and asked, "Which place is yours over there? What's the address?"

Beck told him the address without hesitation. He knew he wasn't going to be at the address for the next few days. He knew his lawyer Phineas P. Dunleavy had acquired the property in the name of an LLC that would make it extremely difficult to identify the LLC's limited partners: James Beck, Demarco Jones, Manny Guzman, and Ciro Baldassare.

Grimaldi wrote down the address. "Okay. What I want you to do, Mr. Eaton, is leave here and let us do our work."

Beck smiled and said, "No problem."

He'd avoided the worst, but it had cost him. He'd have to stay away from his building for the time being. He'd just burned an ID that had taken a lot of effort to set up. He still didn't know if that was Manny lying dead at the end of the pier. He had no idea what had happened in the Red Hook grain terminal, and he couldn't risk going over there to try to find out now.

As he walked toward his building, Beck seethed. Cops. Goddamn, fucking cops. They presented a constant danger to him and those he cared about.

And then, just before he reached the end of the pier, he felt his smartphone buzz in his pocket and emit a sound that signaled he'd received a text.

He stopped and pulled out his phone.

The readout on the screen said UNIDENTIFIED CALLER. He opened the text, and a picture came into view. A picture of a human body engulfed in flames. There was an arrow in the middle of the screen indicating it was the first frame of a video. Beck felt a churning in his stomach as he punched the arrow to play the video.

It took five seconds to download the file. Beck stood immobilized but then had the presence of mind to walk forward in case the detective was still watching him. And then he stopped as the video began to play a horrifying, sickening scene of a man screaming, writhing, burning to death. Beck recognized the location, the grain terminal. Was that Manny?

Beck stopped, closed his eyes, and bowed his head. He felt a searing pain rising from his gut like acid indigestion, but it felt cold instead of hot.

He had no idea how or why this was happening.

He could not look at the video again to decide if it was Manny, his friend, his partner, his comrade in arms.

He typed a response: *Whoever you are, you're dead.*

And then he stopped. He methodically erased each word, letter by letter.

James Beck refused to let whoever sent the text know that he was coming to kill him.

8

Monster-Boy watched Beck staring at his phone. He smiled and nodded. He zoomed in to get a closer look at Beck typing on his cell phone.

"Yes, yes. Send it. Send it, you piece of shit."

Monster-Boy held his phone, looking at the screen for the text message to appear. He waited. And waited. He looked back at the video feed. Beck had disappeared.

Monster-Boy felt the black rage climb up into the base of his skull. He gripped his smartphone with enough force to crack the screen. He looked at the screen. It didn't matter. The phone wouldn't be used much longer. He forced himself to calm down, concentrating on turning the phone off.

He closed his eyes, picturing James Beck strung up, imagining himself shaving off a nice wide strip of skin from Beck's back. He wondered how sharp the knife would have to be. Then realized Beck couldn't be hanging. He would squirm and writhe too much. It would be impossible. He'd have to tie him down. How? How could he tie him down so tightly he couldn't move?

But wait. So what? So what if he moved. He could still make a couple of deep slices into the skin, grab the flap of skin with pliers, and tear it off. That would hurt even more. Pull off a chunk of skin and burn the bloody muscle and fat underneath. Torch it with one of those big cigar lighters. That's what he would do.

Monster-Boy realized he had stopped breathing. He opened his eyes and took a deep breath. He blinked, trying to come back. He took another deep breath, bent down, and picked the phone's

SIM card out of the rubble. He twisted and broke the small piece of integrated circuitry that identified the phone.

Monster-Boy talked himself down, keeping his voice low, speaking slowly.

"That's fine. That's fine. No problem. Be smart, Mr. Beck. It won't matter."

Monster-Boy forced himself to smile, revealing a mouthful of misshapen teeth. The legacy of a methamphetamine habit. A crudely repaired meth mouth. Monster-Boy's smile faded, and his rage returned.

9

Beck hurried toward his bar, moving quickly in between and around the onlookers who had gathered in the small garden park at the foot of the pier.

He walked into the ground-floor barroom just as Demarco came up from the cellar where he had stashed guns, computers, and hard drives in a hidden safe. In Beck's basement, a fake section of the wall behind moveable shelves concealed an entrance to the building next door. Beck had a net lease on that property, but his identity as the leaseholder was hidden behind another LLC. He rented the upper floors to the garden supply company on the corner for storage, keeping the basement for his own use. Built into the foundation wall was a safe tall enough to store long guns and wide enough for anything else Beck wanted to hide from a police search.

When he emerged from the basement, Demarco was still wearing his running clothes. He stood near the cellar door. Willie Reese sat at the bar, talking on his cell phone. He hung up and turned toward Beck.

They both saw the concerned look on Beck's face.

"What did you find out?" asked Demarco.

"Two dead. One of them could be Manny. But I'm assuming he was with his fishing buddies. Ramon and Eduardo. If one of the dead is Manny, either Ramon or Eduardo should be around, but they aren't. Unless they're both dead."

Demarco asked, "Where are the bodies?"

"One is at the end of the pier. The other inside the grain terminal. Set on fire."

Willie Reese said, "What the fuck?"

Beck said, "Cops will be canvassing soon. They'll definitely come here. I got braced by a detective out on the pier. Had to use a fake ID and give him this address. At some point, they'll find out Manny lives here and show up. I don't want any of us to be here when they do. I don't want to get into a fight about letting them in for probable cause or some other bullshit they make up. Is everything locked up?"

Demarco answered, "Guns, ammo, hard drives, weapons. Cash, passports, IDs were already in the safe. What do you think is going on, James?"

Beck's answer was to place his phone on the bar. "You have to see this."

He replayed the video, letting Willie and Demarco witness the horror for themselves. Willie Reese's brow creased, and a frown etched itself on his broad face. A frown that looked permanent.

Demarco turned stone cold. He stepped back and said, "Insane. But that is not Manny."

Beck said, "I couldn't look at it closely. How do you know?"

"The shoes. Manny wears those black Timberland things, look like heavy-duty sneakers. With the steel toes and a bright orange seal in the middle of the soles. The shoes haven't burned completely in that video. Those shoes look like regular white sneakers. That's not Manny."

Beck nodded. "So it's Eduardo or Ramon."

Demarco said, "And it's either Eduardo or Ramon at the end of the pier. If it was Manny, why send you that video?"

Beck said, "I agree. It's a threat. Whoever killed Eduardo and Ramon is telling me they have Manny, and he's next."

Willie pointed to the phone and said, "Next to be burned up like that?"

"Or worse," said Beck. "But right now, we have to assume he's alive."

31

Demarco said, "He is. They're using Manny to get to you. Why else send you that video?"

"Which means anybody close to me could be in the crosshairs."

Willie asked, "How'd the one on the pier die?"

"From halfway out on the pier, I saw a hell of a lot of blood where they found the body. Had to be a knife."

"Where was that?" asked Demarco.

"On the rocks near the water's edge."

"What the fuck is going on? Who's doing this?"

Beck said, "Somebody with a score to settle."

Demarco nodded. "Lot of people could be on that list, James."

"True. Right now, we don't have time to guess about it. We have to get the hell out of here. It's not just the cops we have to worry about. It's whoever did this. D, grab whatever you need. Willie, you should leave now. See if you can get a couple of your guys to hang around by the grain terminal. See if they can find out what happened there. You stay clear of that place. I don't want you getting locked up. Stay in the neighborhood. Keep eyes and ears on this place. I'll call you later."

"Got it."

"And Willie…"

"What?"

"You watch yourself. Somebody got to Manny, and he's not easy to get to."

Willie Reese gave Beck a deadpan stare and nodded slowly.

Beck turned to Demarco, "D, as soon as you're ready, get the car."

"Where're we going?"

"Alex's place in Greenpoint. We're going to need his skills and a place to work. I'm going to call Ricky and Jonas. Whoever did this put in the time to figure out how to snatch Manny. We have to find out how they pulled it off."

Demarco said, "We gotta call Ciro, too. If we're going to war, he'll want to be with us."

"I know."

Demarco saw the concerned look on Beck's face. "What?"

"Going to be hell trying to control Ciro."

"Be worse if we don't tell him now."

"I know."

10

Grimaldi caught up with Brennan at the end of Pier 44 as she was finishing up with a sergeant from the 76th precinct. The March morning had turned crisp and clear, the sun shining brightly on the congealing blood still oozing from the corpse.

Grimaldi waited until the sergeant moved away and asked Brennan, "What's the story, boss?"

"Brutal. The homicide team stopped counting at twenty-two stab wounds. Plus, the throat is slashed. A sergeant from the Seven-Six is in charge here. They retrieved identification on the victim that says he's Eduardo Ramirez. Address in the Red Hook projects. Looks like he was out here fishing with a couple of other guys." Brennan pointed to the railing at the end of the pier. "Three fishing poles, a bucket of bait, and tackle are over there. Plus, a cooler with a half-bottle of rum, orange juice, and beer."

Grimaldi asked, "Three poles?"

"Yeah."

"Well, we've got two dead bodies. Think this guy is connected to our body in the grain terminal?"

"Could be."

"If so, that leaves one more, figuring three poles, three guys."

Brennan said, "There's no sign of a third victim." Brennan pointed to the rocks between the pier and the water. "Somehow, that victim ended up half in the water, half on the rocks. Nobody seems able to figure out how. Maybe the third one ended up in the water."

Grimaldi leaned over the pier railing and looked at the landfill surrounding the pier. "What do you figure, those rocks go out about six feet?"

Brennan looked with him. "About."

"Hard enough to get one body half in the water from up here. Much less all the way."

"Maybe. Harbor patrol called in divers to search."

"Good luck."

Brennan said, "So we have two dead. One here, one in the grain terminal. One missing. Unless one of the vics brought two poles."

"I guess guys fish with more than one pole, but that's a lot of drinks for two guys."

"Not for some people."

Grimaldi said, "So we have three fishing buddies getting drunk. One of 'em, the missing third guy, goes off his nut. He stabs the shit out of one, cuts his throat, and throws him over the railing almost to the water."

"With super strength."

"Uh-huh. While he's doing that, the other guy stands around until crazy fisherman number three knocks him out."

Brennan said, "Assume he knocked him out before he stabbed the other guy."

"Okay, fine. Nut job then transports the second body to the grain terminal, a mile away, where he just happens to have enough gasoline to set the corpse on fire. And then our super-man killer disappears. You sure you want to go with that?" said Grimaldi.

"No."

Grimaldi said, "More likely two guys killed two other guys. Why? No clue."

"What about the third pole?"

"Okay. Two guys killed three guys, although one body is missing."

Brennan said, "Or one guy stabbed one guy to death, then went to the grain terminal and set himself on fire. And the third guy just went home."

Grimaldi snapped his fingers and said, "Even better."

"Okay, I get it. We don't know much of anything. So what do we know? We know this is a goddamn mess. We can keep a lid on the body burned in the grain terminal for a while." Brennan gestured toward the corpse. "But this one is laying out here for the whole neighborhood to see. It won't be long before the two murders are discovered. One thing I know for sure, Roth is going to want this figured out. Fast."

Brennan's concern about the police commissioner annoyed Grimaldi but didn't surprise him.

"So Roth can put a lid on it. Fast."

Brennan said, "Right. Let's stop fooling around and start investigating. We have almost zero chance of identifying the burned-up corpse any time soon, so we go with what we know. We have an ID on this victim. We track down his family, his friends, find out who he is, why he was down here, who he was with, and go from there."

"Which might also lead us to the third guy."

"Correct."

"How do you want to play this? Should we work with the Seven-Six homicide detectives?"

"No. We keep this in the squad. I don't want to get bogged down working through Fernandez."

"Okay. If we bumped into the Seven-Six detectives, we'll act nice and keep going."

Brennan pulled out her police radio. "Exactly." She located Dave Metuchen and told him she'd meet him at his car. Then she asked Grimaldi, "What happened with that guy I told you to stop?"

"He said he's a real estate developer. Said he's working on a property over on Conover, where he has an office and an apartment. Spends a couple of days a week in the neighborhood. He made sure to let me know he has money and lawyers and all that shit without being too obnoxious about it. Said he came onto the pier to see what was going on. Didn't like crime happening around here. Not good for property values."

Brennan said, "Yeah, well, then maybe he should go gentrify someplace else."

Grimaldi tapped his large nose. "Yeah, but my bullshit meter was going off."

"Why?"

Brennan listened carefully. She trusted Grimaldi's instincts.

"He was saying all the right things, but it seemed off."

"How so?"

"He had ID that puts him living in New Paltz. Said he owns a house up there. Don't exactly fit with him working down here."

"Fits with a rich asshole trying to avoid city taxes."

Grimaldi said, "True. But the guy just didn't look like a real estate developer."

"Why not?"

"Too rough around the edges. Unless he started out in construction and moved on up to his own projects. But I don't like it when I'm filling in facts to make a story plausible."

"Okay."

Grimaldi said, "I think he was conning me. I think he was good at it. Tell you the truth, he gave me the impression he was someone who did time."

"Really?"

"Yeah. He wasn't like a civilian, you know? Normal people usually go overboard when a cop questions them. If they're assholes, they get overly aggressive. If they're normal John Q's, they try too hard to be helpful. Or, if they've done something wrong, they get nervous. This guy was different. He went on the offensive but played it right. If anything, questioning him made me nervous. You know, like I had to watch in case he wanted to take a swipe at me."

Brennan thought back to when she had told Grimaldi to check out the guy.

"You know, Alphonse, thinking about it, I thought I was having you check out a perp who might be returning to the scene."

"I figured."

"But a perp who comes back to the scene, he doesn't make a fuss. Hangs back in the crowd. Stays unobtrusive. That guy walked past everybody and came out to the middle of the pier. I think you're right. There's something off about him."

Grimaldi nodded. "Yes. He had an interest." Grimaldi nodded toward the shape under the blue tarp. "Like maybe he knew the victim."

Brennan nodded. "Okay. Where did he say he lived?"

"He pointed over to Conover. On the block right across from the empty lot."

"You get an address?"

"I did."

"You think he gave you the right address?"

Grimaldi shaded his eyes and looked at the block. "I'll find out."

"All right. I'll meet Dave and head over to the projects to run down our stabbing victim, Eduardo Ramirez. You go over to Conover and find your guy. What's his name?"

Grimaldi didn't have to check his notes. "Thomas Eaton."

"Okay. You find Thomas Eaton and bring him in for questioning."

"One PP?"

"Yes. This is our investigation. If Dave and I get a line on Ramirez, I'll head back to One PP and fill in the commissioner. You bring in Mr. Eaton. If we identify the victim and get a person of interest, Roth will keep us on the case."

Grimaldi nodded. It irked him that Brennan made decisions based on whether the commissioner would keep her involved. No surprise. Dianne Brennan didn't get to be where she was without pushing her agenda.

Brennan said, "Keep me posted, Alphonse. Keep the momentum going. Find Mr. Eaton. Bring him in."

11

Demarco Jones sat in Beck's customized Mercury Marauder parked in front of the bar waiting for Beck to come out. He looked at his watch. 1:10 p.m. Jones was not the nervous type. He'd learned long ago survival depended on never showing fear. Or tension. Or any sign of nerves. All showed weakness. Predators could smell weakness from across the room.

But Demarco knew that survival required more. He grew up in a Bronx neighborhood where the choices were grim, knowing from the age of twelve that he was gay, and that decent housing, a stable family, and a good education weren't going to be part of his life. Out of necessity, crime became Demarco's path forward. By sixteen, he was big enough and smart enough to be formidable. But it took time to develop and burnish himself into living without fear. That part of Demarco Jones was hard-earned through a gauntlet of fights, never backing down from an enemy, and hard time in New York State's maximum-security prisons.

When it came to crime and violence, Demarco Jones had turned pro long ago. Fear might pulse at some level, but for Demarco, whatever fear resided in him acted as a catalyst that sharpened his instincts and performance.

That's why Demarco was surprised at the discomfort he felt waiting for Beck. Why was he anxious? Because Manny Guzman had been either killed or captured. And that unnerved him. Manny was a calm, focused, dangerous man. He had survived plots and assaults aimed at him from a spectrum of enemies. He never left the safety of Beck's headquarters without at least one gun, usually his six-shot Charter Arms .38, a weapon Demarco knew Manny would not hesitate to use. Manny Guzman would shoot first and deal with the aftermath second. Yes, Manny was getting older, but Manny Guzman was far from a target.

And yet, somehow, someone had gotten to Manny and killed two men while doing it. Not just killed them, mutilated and murdered them in violent, horrible ways.

So, yes, Demarco Jones was anxious for Beck to emerge so they could get going, find out what the hell was going on, and deal with it.

Finally, Demarco saw Beck and Willie Reese step out onto Conover. Beck turned to lock the front door while giving Willie last-minute instructions.

Out on the pier, Grimaldi had just walked past the crime scene tape when he spotted the black car parked in front of the building on Conover Street. He had an unobstructed view across the small park at the end of the pier and the empty lot fronting Beck's building. He increased his pace.

Movement in his peripheral vision caught Demarco's attention. He looked to his left and saw Grimaldi hurrying in his direction. Even from fifty yards away, Demarco knew the big man in a baggy suit was a cop. Probably the detective who had stopped Beck. Apparently, Beck's bullshit hadn't quite done the job.

Demarco turned toward Beck and tapped the horn. Beck looked over. He saw Grimaldi. Beck said to Willie, "Disappear, brother. I'll be in touch. Watch yourself." He headed toward the Mercury.

Demarco turned back to watch Grimaldi. Their eyes locked. Demarco already had the Mercury in gear. He heard the passenger door shut.

Grimaldi yelled out, "Hey! Hold it."

Demarco acted like Grimaldi was invisible and pulled away while Grimaldi ran across the empty lot towards Beck's building. Willie Reese had already turned the corner down the block.

Demarco said to Beck, "That was the cop?"

"That was him."

"Didn't take him long. How much you think he figured out?"

"Apparently enough to come after me."

"Now what?"

Beck said, "Let's see if we can get out of the neighborhood without being stopped."

Grimaldi chased after the Mercury trying to see the license plate number on the black car. He stood in the middle of Conover Street, slightly out of breath.

"Real estate developer, my ass."

He pulled out his police radio and switched from the frequency used by Brennan's squad to the frequency shared by the two nearest Brooklyn precincts, the Seven-Six and the Eight-Four. He alerted all patrol cars in the area to stop and detain the occupants of an all-black sedan, license plate ending in two-seven.

There was no insignia on the back of the car, so Grimaldi said, "Look for a black sedan, Crown Vic or Mercury Marquis. Stop and hold occupants for questioning."

Grimaldi doubted anybody would spot the car before it got out of the precinct, but it was worth a try. He shoved his radio in the side pocket of his suit jacket.

Brennan would not be happy that he'd lost Thomas Eaton. He peered around the area. The buildings looked even less residential than from the pier.

Fuck it. Time to knock on doors.

12

Monster-Boy hadn't moved from his computer monitor. Once Beck had gone back to his building, he'd kept the camera trained on the cop who had questioned that soon-to-be-exterminated animal, James Beck. He'd swiveled the camera from its hidden perch on the warehouse building on Liberty pier across from Pier 44, tracking the detective talking to his boss. A fucking woman. Unbelievable how cunts were taking over everything. At least she looked hot. From a distance, anyhow. Clearly, she'd fucked her way to the top. She'd be on the list with Beck as the idiots who would have no idea what was going on.

Monster-Boy told himself – you knew there'd be a lot of cops on this. Just keep to the plan. Even cops in the dark would serve their purpose.

Monster-Boy saw the male detective head back toward Conover Street. Maybe the bitch wasn't completely stupid, sending him to check out Beck.

Monster-Boy swiveled the camera to follow Grimaldi and saw Beck's car parked in front of his building. He zoomed in. The bald-headed nigger was at the wheel. And then Beck came out with another nigger. Another big fucker. Who was he? Jeezus Beck loved to hang with the mud people. Niggers and spics like Manny Guzman. The old shot-caller. Fucker had gone for his pistolero awful damn fast. Made it a close call. But too late, pendejo.

Monster-Boy pictured how it had gone down. Reliving it was almost the best part. Learning from it. Going over it again and again. Making all the links stronger. Making everything come true. Picturing it, imagining it. Creating an alternate reality like he'd learned to do in prison.

So far, the plan had worked. It would all work. Putting the Worm out on that pier had been the key. Getting that sniveling, cock-sucking slave in place. The Worm would do anything because he was so needy and disgusting. Too bad he talked too much once he got going. Always trying to con everybody. Ingratiate himself. Fucking slaves can't help doing that.

It was so perfect. The four of them lined up like that at the end of the pier. As willed by me. From left to right, first Guzman. Then the other two spics. Then the Worm. If Guzman had been next to the Worm, it wouldn't have worked. But Monster-Boy knew he had put in the required effort. Watching, planning, imagining, willing it. Effort ordinary human chattel couldn't expend. And worth every fucking second. All of it adding to his power and control.

Monster-Boy watched Beck get into his car. He laughed at the cop running after Beck's car. What a dolt.

Monster-Boy swiveled the camera back to the end of Pier 44 and saw the redhead get back into her SUV and drive away. He kept watching until they loaded the cut-up spic into the meat wagon. Nobody had found the body of the dipshit maintenance worker. A brown-skinned mongrel riding around on his stupid garbage cart. They weren't going to find him for a long time unless they dug through that mountain of gravel near the grain terminal. It was fun killing him. Smacking him in the back of his head, then trying to twist it off. Breaking everything in his neck. Funny look of surprise on his face.

The garbage cart was perfect for getting Guzman and his pal off the pier and over to the van. Only thing not perfect was wearing the mongrel's stanky-ass shirt, which was way too small. If they do find him and his broken neck, it'll add to the fun. Assholes.

Monster-Boy turned off the monitor.

Time for the next step.

43

13

Grimaldi knocked on Beck's door just to make sure nobody was inside. No answer. He went to look through the front window. The bottom section was covered in flat black paint. Even on his tiptoes, Grimaldi couldn't see into the barroom.

He went to the door and knocked again. Waited. Same result. Then he pounded on the door. Then Grimaldi beat on it just because he was pissed off.

Out of the corner of his eye, Grimaldi saw a short, sturdily built man in his thirties standing down the block to his right. He had come out from an open space bordered by a chain-link fence shading his eyes as he stared at the stranger in front of Beck's bar. He wore gray overalls, a flannel shirt, and work boots.

Grimaldi turned away from Beck's front door and headed toward the corner. He waved at the guy trying to appear friendly.

The workman didn't return the wave but waited for Grimaldi to come closer.

"Uh, if I were you, I wouldn't pound on that door too much."

"Why's that?"

"I don't think those guys would like it. Actually, I don't think anybody would like it."

"What guys?"

"The guys who hang out there."

"Hang out?"

"Yeah."

"Live there or hang out?"

The workman shrugged. "Both, I guess."

"What do you know about them?"

"Not much. Just see 'em coming in and out. Not too often."

"How many guys we talkin' about?"

"I don't know. Three or four."

"Can you describe them?"

"Not really."

"Is one of them white, around forty. Dark hair. Solid looking."

"Yeah." The workman balled his fists and flexed his arms in front of him. "Looks like he can take care of himself."

Grimaldi said, "Who else you see coming in and out of there?"

"One of them is black. Tall. Bald. Built like a pro athlete."

"Anybody Hispanic?"

"Yeah. He's shorter. Older. Hair going gray. I think I've seen him once or twice."

"Anybody else?"

"Not really."

"What's that mean?"

Again, he shrugged. "Other people come and go. I don't keep track."

Grimaldi looked left at the setup behind the fence.

"You work here?"

"Yes."

"What kind of place is this?"

"Storage for a gardening business."

Grimaldi nodded. He took note of racks holding young plants in plastic trays. Bags of soil and mulch stacked in piles. Terracotta pots in different sizes. A small greenhouse stood at the back end of the lot. Grimaldi turned back and noticed the stains on the knees of the man's overalls and the dirt under his fingernails.

"How long have you worked here?"

"Couple of years."

"Can I ask your name?"

"Can I ask yours?"

"Sure. Alphonse Grimaldi. Detective Alphonse Grimaldi." He pulled out his NYPD ID. Announcing he was a cop didn't seem to surprise the workman.

"So, what can you tell me about the guys who live there?" Grimaldi bent toward the workman waiting to hear his name.

"Zeke."

Grimaldi repeated the name. "Zeke."

"Not much. They keep to themselves."

"How so?"

"You know," Zeke shrugged. "They just keep to themselves. Don't say much to anybody."

"Why is that?"

"I guess they like their privacy."

"Uh-huh. Any particular reason for that?"

Zeke knew the cop wasn't going to give up until he found out everything he knew about the men who lived in that building. He regretted trying to warn the cop about pounding on the door. Finally, he decided to tell the detective what he knew, and next time keep his nose out of it.

"Rumor is they're ex-cons or something."

"Really. You know any of their names?"

"No. No way. People around here know to keep away from those guys."

"Why?"

"For one thing, word is they were involved in a shootout that killed a bunch of people. It's like you hear long-time residents in this neighborhood say stuff like, 'don't fuck with those guys. That's where the gunfight took place.' Or 'they were in the middle of that shootout.' Like that."

"Really?"

"Yeah." Zeke pointed to his right. "Before they built that restaurant, there was nothing there. Just an empty lot. That's where the shootout took place. Rival gangs or something. Cops showed up. They opened fire. It was in the papers. Cops wounded. Four or five guys shot."

Grimaldi nodded toward Beck's building. "And how were those guys involved?"

"No idea."

"When was that?"

"I don't know. Three, four years. Before my time."

"You live here?"

"No. Just work here. I live in Carroll Gardens."

"Just work here?"

"Yes."

"Know anybody else who lives around here?"

"No. This isn't really a residential block. Listen, mind if I get back to work?"

"Not at all. Thanks, you've been very helpful."

Zeke headed toward the storage lot, then stopped and turned around.

"Hey, do those guys have anything to do with the murder out there on the pier today?"

"Who said it was a murder?"

Zeke shrugged. "I don't know. Couple of people."

Grimaldi noted that word had already spread. Thankfully, this guy hadn't heard about the burned corpse in the grain terminal. He gave Zeke a blank look and said, "I don't know."

Zeke nodded and went back to work.

Grimaldi looked at his watch. Of course, he'd lied to Zeke. He was convinced that Thomas Eaton had something to do with the murder on the pier. He just didn't know what.

He also remembered hearing about the gunfight in Red Hook about four years earlier. Something about rival factions of Russian mobsters shooting it out. Didn't recall hearing anything about neighborhood ex-cons being involved.

Grimaldi checked his notes to confirm the address Thomas Eaton had given him for his building. It matched. If Thomas

Eaton had been involved in getting cops wounded and Russians killed, he sure as hell intended to find out why. And what his real goddamn name was.

14

Beck and his crew sat around the long kitchen table in Alex Liebowitz's renovated townhouse in Greenpoint, Brooklyn.

Liebowitz, another ex-con in Beck's crew, was the group's tech guru, research maven, and Beck's investing partner. His Greenpoint house had been built in 1842 in the style of a Dutch canal warehouse. An old iron beam, once used for hauling bulk to the top floor, still hung out over the sidewalk. After he bought the building, Liebowitz left the old paint on the façade so that it fit in with the neighborhood. But the windows on the old building told another story. Although they were in the original style, they were custom-made using UV-tinted Thermopane. Inside, Liebowitz gutted the building down to the bare walls and rebuilt it to his specifications.

Liebowitz had acquired the property and paid for the renovation with money earned working with Beck, mostly from a major score involving a hedge fund and an arms dealer. Part of Liebowitz's job during that caper was to make sure there wasn't a trace of where that money had come from. He did the same thing regarding ownership of his building. Anybody trying to find out where Alex Liebowitz lived, or who lived at his address on West Street in Greenpoint, would find nothing but LLCs that would be virtually impossible to connect to him.

Liebowitz had also scrubbed or altered all the public records on sites like Property Shark, StreetEasy, Trulia, Zillow, and on all the New York City brokerage company sites that might have had information on his property. He'd also fudged the info on all the NYC property records and sales data on government websites.

Demarco and Beck had entered through the ground-floor door that led to a secure man-cage entrance hall. The front door locked behind them. A second door kept them locked in the space until Alex checked them out through his security cameras.

They passed quickly through the ground floor – an open space decorated with dark gray couches, indirect lighting, wide plank floors, and floor-to-ceiling glass doors that opened onto a rock garden bordered by a wall of bamboo.

On the second floor, which Alex had turned into an open-plan workspace with a spacious modern kitchen, Beck and Demarco followed Alex into the kitchen where they could sit and wait for the others.

The first to arrive was Ciro Baldassare, a powerfully built man who had survived the dangerous life of a mafioso, including during the time when the FBI prosecuted the ruling echelon of the Bonanno crime family. They followed the usual strategy – make deals with underlings and work their way up.

That strategy didn't work with Ciro Baldassare. He had refused to rat out his superiors to make a deal. He ended up in a federal penitentiary, maintaining and enhancing his reputation as a man of honor, and as a man not to be challenged or confronted. If Ciro Baldassare decided to be loyal to someone, his loyalty was unshakeable. He expected the same in return. Few met his criteria, particularly among the members of the corrupted version of the current Mafia. As a result, Baldassare generally went his own way within the mob. He'd earned the right. Even the most reckless mobsters gave Ciro Baldassare a wide berth. Outside the organization, one of the few men Baldassare trusted was James Beck. Beck had gained Ciro's trust when he saved Baldassare's life in a chaotic fight between black and white inmates that broke out in Dannemora, the maximum-security prison in Clinton, New

York. Ciro had accepted Demarco Jones and Manny Guzman as part of Beck's crew, but he remained reserved and wary of everybody else.

Generally, Baldassare maintained a relaxed demeanor. However, Beck knew what always hummed under Ciro's calm exterior – the potential for terrifying, unrelenting violence.

Alex asked about coffee or drinks. Everybody politely refused. Beck looked around the table. Alex sat to his right at the head, Demarco at his left. Ciro Baldassare sat opposite him. Beck realized how different and unnatural everything felt without Manny Guzman at the table.

Ciro asked, "We waiting for anybody else?"

Beck said, "Ricky and Jonas."

As if on cue, the downstairs buzzer rang. Alex left the kitchen to let them in.

As with the others, Beck had met Ricky Bolo while in prison. This time at the Eastern Correctional Facility near Ellenville, New York. Ricky was hyperactive, talked non-stop, always seemed to be enjoying himself, and determined to continue enjoying himself, even in the confines of a maximum-security prison. His brother, Jonas, who had been convicted of the same crimes as his brother, was kept in a separate facility. The DOC had no intention of housing them in the same prison at the same time. Jonas was much the opposite of Ricky. Smaller than his older brother, low key, terse, and inward.

The brothers were master thieves. Experts in security systems, technology, safes, locks, surveillance. They knew every security company and supplier in the Tri-State region, all the latest equipment and systems for sale, and were familiar with the software those systems used. At one time or another, the Bolos had hacked into most of the major security companies in the United States and Europe. After serving their prison terms, the Bolo brothers (a name based on the bolo Ricky wore) had retired from doing active break-ins. Now they made their money setting up high-end heists for top crews, taking a non-refundable fee up-front and a negotiated percentage of the profits. On their own, they ran the occasional, complicated long cons on select wealthy individuals and organizations.

Ricky and Jonas entered the kitchen. There were silent nods and greetings. Even Ricky was subdued. They knew why they had come to this grim meeting.

Beck started by saying, "Manny has been missing a little over eight hours."

That simple statement set the tone. Every man at the table knew that even if their friend and colleague wasn't dead, he'd probably suffered an immeasurable amount of pain in that amount of time.

Beck continued, carefully explaining everything, from the moment Willie Reese walked into his bar until he had arrived in Greenpoint with Demarco.

He finished by asking Alex to download and play the video he had received by text. In less than a minute, Alex had it up running on a 55-inch LCD screen mounted on the bare-brick kitchen wall. The men viewed the gruesome scene of a man burning to death without comment. None of them had anything to say.

15

As Grimaldi drove to the 76th precinct, he checked in with Dianne Brennan via cell phone. She asked, "What's up, Alphonse?"

"Inspector, I tried to run down that guy Thomas Eaton."

"And?"

"Just missed him. He was getting in a car with a black guy. They pulled out when they saw me coming."

Brennan said, "I guess that's evidence of something."

"Yeah, evidence that Thomas Eaton is full of shit. Get this, I nosed around the neighborhood. A guy who works down the street knows Eaton, or whatever his name is, and said he's an ex-con. Lives with other ex-cons in that building."

"Really?"

"Yeah, really. He also told me some kind of gunfight occurred at that address. You remember that thing with Russian gangs shooting it out in Red Hook."

"Yes, I remember something. Four or five years ago. At that address?"

"In the empty lot behind Eaton's building. Eaton, or whatever his name is, ain't no real estate developer. He was living in the building during that shootout. I'm heading to the Seven-Six to see what I can find out about it."

"And who Thomas Eaton really is."

"Absolutely."

"Was his driver's license real?"

"The new licenses on polycarbonate and layers and all that shit make 'em pretty much impossible to fake. It was his face on that license, but I don't believe Eaton is his real name."

"So that means Eaton has the resources to construct an alternative identity."

"Yep. And that same neighborhood guy said he's seen a black male and an older Hispanic male with graying hair come in and out of that address."

"You think the Hispanic might be our third fisherman?"

"I'd bet money on it. Explains why Eaton was on the pier trying to find out what happened. As opposed to that bullshit about being worried that crime is bad for the neighborhood."

"Okay, find out what you can, find Eaton or whatever his name is, and bring him in."

"I'm on it. Anything useful at your end?"

"Despite my crap Spanish, we tracked down Eduardo Ramirez. He's part of a big family unit all jammed into one apartment in the Red Hook Project. I don't know how they get so many people staying in one NYCHA apartment."

"Nobody's keeping track, that's how."

"We ran into three generations. Lots of hysteria. Made it hard to get straight answers, but I suppose that's the point. These people don't like interacting with the law."

"Not even a sympathetic woman and a non-threatening guy like Metuchen?"

"Not even. But we got what we needed. Mr. Ramirez is, was, on Social Security Disability. So plenty of time for fishing."

"Better he should've had a damn job. Stay off that fucking pier."

"The family denies any criminal record, but I've got Nina confirming that. Nobody had any idea why someone would want to harm him."

Grimaldi asked, "What about the second fisherman?"

"They gave us a name, Ramon Escobar. I don't know if that's the Hispanic guy living at Eaton's place or our second victim in the grain terminal. I've got Dave looking for the Escobar family. Finding out if Ramon is missing. If he is, he'll try to get medical and dental records that might match our burned-up corpse. The

54

good news – Escobar's family also lives in the Red Hook Project. In the east section. Bad news – nobody in the Ramirez family knew the exact address."

Grimaldi said, "How many Escobars you think are in that place?"

"More than one."

"So, if Escobar is the guy in the grain terminal, that leaves the mysterious third fisherman unidentified but likely connected to Thomas Eaton."

"Correct."

"What did the Ramirez family tell you about the third fisherman."

"Nothing. And now it makes sense. Obviously, Eduardo didn't want his family knowing he was hanging out with an ex-con, someone associated with a gunfight in the neighborhood."

"So, what do you think? Maybe the third fisherman was the doer."

Brennan said, "As far as I'm concerned until he shows up dead, he's a suspect."

"I guess we're making progress."

"We got a possible suspect. We got when, where, how. Now all we need is why. I'm about to go into headquarters. Don't get bogged down in that shootout four years ago. You're looking for information that will help us find Mr. Eaton and his Hispanic friend. Keep me posted."

"Will do."

Grimaldi turned onto Union Street, heading for the precinct house. Brennan was right. Mostly. The third fisherman had to be considered a suspect, but he couldn't imagine why a guy who goes fishing with two buddies on a regular basis would become enraged enough to kill both of them by stabbing and burning. Not to mention single-handedly heave one of the dead almost ten feet off the pier and transport the other victim a mile to that grain terminal. It didn't add up.

Grimaldi shut down his unmarked and put his NYPD identification on the dashboard. He grimaced and shook his head. Everything had mushroomed in the last hour. He had to identify fisherman number three. Figure out who committed those murders. And find an ex-con hiding under the name Thomas fucking Eaton.

"Shit."

16

Silence descended around the Liebowitz's kitchen table when the video stopped.

Alex turned off the screen so that they didn't have to stare at the frozen image of a human being engulfed in flames, silently screaming and writhing.

Demarco broke the silence. "Just to be clear, that isn't Manny."

Ciro asked, "How do you know?"

"This is the second time I've seen this. Those aren't Manny's shoes."

Alex said, "You sure?"

"I'm sure."

Ciro said, "All right. But whoever sent that to James is telling us they're going to do that to Manny."

Beck said, "I agree. My phone said Unidentified Caller, but the caller's phone number is on the screen. Can it lead us to whoever sent the video?"

Liebowitz said, "We'll check the phone number, but I can't believe the bastard didn't use a burner phone. The best we can do is find out where the phone was bought."

Beck asked, "You can text a video over a prepaid phone?"

"There are some with MMS capability. Actually, I imagine he could even use a burner app on his smartphone. Shoot the video. Send it via a burner number."

Jonas Bolo said, "Give us your phone, James. We should download that file and the number where it came from. There are ways to hack into those files and extract information that might be useful."

"For how long? I want to have the phone if he tries to contact me again."

"Fifteen minutes tops if Alex lets me use one of his computers."

Liebowitz nodded toward the work area. "Go for it."

Beck handed Jonas the phone.

Ricky said, "We'll unpack those files. For sure we ought to be able to find out which cell phone network he's on. It's a start."

"How long will that take?"

"Two, three hours."

"Good."

Demarco spoke up. "Maybe we should start trying to figure out who might be behind this."

Alex said, "Feels like James is the target. Somebody took Manny to get to James."

Beck said, "If they're after me, why not just come at me? Why use Manny?"

Ciro said, "Who the hell knows why. Maybe it's somebody who wants to get to all of us. This is just a start."

Ricky Bolo said, "I'd put the Vory in Brighton Beach on the list. Those people hold grudges for generations. Maybe even the Bosnians."

Beck knew the name Bolo hid the brothers' ethnicity. They were Albanians. They had deep contacts in the Eastern European criminal underground.

Beck said, "Ricky, you and Jonas should tap into your sources. It's a possibility."

Ciro said to Beck, "Both you and Manny were together at Clinton for what? Four years? Gotta figure there could be some assholes from prison still looking to settle a score."

Demarco said, "I don't think Manny got wind of anything."

Beck said, "He's good at keeping troublesome shit to himself."

"Not if it might have spilled over onto you, James."

Beck thought about that for a moment and said, "True. But he didn't say anything to me."

Ciro said, "Doesn't mean there wasn't somebody looking to settle a score. It's the ones that come out of nowhere that get you."

Beck fell silent, thinking about men in prison that he and Manny had gone up against. A handful of inmates came to mind. But he soon realized that connections to them could ripple out to include many more. There would never be enough time to run down just the first ring of possibilities before Manny suffered serious injury or death.

Demarco said, "Could be something more recent. That mess up in the Bronx. We took down a lot of fools up there. I'll reach out to Big Ben and some of the gang elders. See if anybody has heard anything."

Beck nodded, distracted by his thoughts. The more his crew talked, the deeper he felt himself being pulled into a quagmire. Hacking the text message would take too much time. The list of possible enemies was too long. Manny had already been missing for nine hours.

"Listen, we have to reach out wherever we can. But what do we know right now that can help us find Manny? Assuming he's still alive."

Demarco jumped in.

"Okay, assume Manny is alive. That tells me there had to be more than one person behind this. I can't believe one guy could take down Manny, cut the throat of one of his fishing buddies, take down the other fishing buddy, take him to that grain terminal, set him on fire, and get away with Manny."

Everyone around the table nodded and agreed.

Beck continued, "And somehow, they knew where Manny lived. They knew he fished at the end of Pier 44. They had some idea of how often he went down there. They knew the time of day he goes out..."

Demarco broke in. "Just before dawn. Which would be the best time to take out two guys and snatch Manny."

"Right. What else did they know? My phone number. So, how'd they find out all that?"

There was silence around the table while the others mulled over the question. Jonas Bolo returned from using one of Alex's computers. He handed Beck's phone back to him.

Ricky Bolo said, "Phineas hid the ownership of your building, but that mess with the Bosnians and the Vory made the papers. Police were all over the place. Lot of people knew about that shootout, James. Maybe that led someone to you."

Beck nodded, thinking about how Ricky's theory might lead him to his enemy.

Jonas continued, "So, clearly, they found you. Based on what they had to know to take Manny down, it's logical to assume they surveilled you. For a long time. Probably weeks."

Alex Liebowitz added, "I agree. But I'd say it's highly unlikely they did any surveillance with feet on the ground, especially over a long period. You would've spotted them, James. Or Demarco or Manny would have. Even Willie's guys might have spotted them."

Ricky Bolo said, "I agree with Alex. It would take too much manpower. Or, I'll say, if they had enough manpower to run weeks of around the clock surveillance, you have a damn big problem. My bet is they set up a surveillance camera on you. Tracked you from offsite."

Beck asked, "How?"

"How what?"

"How'd they transmit the image?"

Liebowitz said, "Piggyback on an existing Wi-Fi connection nearby. The neighborhood is filled with Wi-Fi routers now. Hack into a router and stream video surveillance twenty-four seven. It's not hard."

Jonas said, "Only way to do long-term surveillance."

Beck could feel the energy in the room pick up. He knew they'd cracked a part of it.

He said, "Okay. Ricky, Jonas, can you locate the camera? Figure out how it's transmitting? Maybe even where to?"

Ricky was already on his feet heading out of the kitchen, his brother following. "Hell yeah, we can."

Beck yelled after them, "Don't forget to check your sources on the Russians and Eastern European mobs." He turned back to the others at the table. "Alex, I think you should get online and see how far and wide any information about that night the Russians and Bosnians came at us got out."

"Definitely. We did a fairly good job of keeping our names out of it, but I'll find out if there's anything out there that could lead to you. And I want to see what's in the NYPD databases."

"Can you get into where you want to look?"

"Yeah. It's a sieve. The NYPD has a lot of information on public access sites. Most of it sourced from commercial databases. Getting through the bullshit firewalls between those sources and NYPD's databases isn't that tough."

"Good. Ciro, can you send the word out? See what's in the air?"

"What are you thinking?"

"Brighton Beach."

Ciro nodded. "I know guys who keep tabs on those Russian pricks. I'll see what I can find out."

Beck turned to Demarco. He was already on his phone talking to his connections up in the Bronx.

Beck sat back, thinking through everything. Of all the possibilities, his gut told him Manny's abduction had something to do with the night they were attacked by a Russian gang led by a Vory mobster named Ivan Kolenka working with a Bosnian gang of war criminals. After the battle in Red Hook, he and Demarco had tracked down and killed Kolenka, but the Bolos were right. Ivan Kolenka had lived the life of a criminal for a long time. His connections had to be extensive. Four years ago, Beck's goal was to make it too costly for whatever was left of Kolenka's Vory faction of the Russian mafia to come after him.

But if someone connected to Kolenka had decided on revenge now, they could have the manpower and tech resources to pull off Manny's abduction and the murders of his fishing buddies.

But would someone connected to Kolenka have the patience to wait four years? Maybe. If so, they had already shown more cunning than last time. Had Manny Guzman already become the first casualty? Or did whoever was behind this have the patience to keep Manny alive and use him as bait to get to the rest of them?

17

Monster-Boy and the Worm parked a blue and white, rusted-out, fifteen-year-old Ford Econoline van across the street from a restaurant on Reed Street. They had stolen it a week earlier in Weehawken, New Jersey. The sunny March morning had turned overcast. The streets were quiet. The restaurant was months away from its summer opening.

Monster-Boy and Worm were dressed in matching work clothes, dark green twill pants, and matching shirts. Monster-Boy almost looked like a workman except for his massive, steroid-built body. Worm looked like a flat-out criminal. Skinny, slouching, furtive, with prison tats visible on his neck and long dirty hair; everything about him said skel.

Monster-Boy pulled open the van's back doors and lifted out a Gas & Go polyethylene 25-gallon rolling fuel cart with an attached hose and nozzle. He quickly lowered the cart onto the street, even though it weighed nearly 168 pounds. Most of the weight came from twenty-five gallons of gasoline.

Once the gas cart was on the street, Worm reached in and pulled out a toolbox and a sixteen-foot aluminum extension ladder, struggling a bit to balance the eight feet of double ladder.

Monster-Boy and Worm fit a familiar pattern for a pair of workmen. One big and strong. The other small, more agile.

A casual observer wouldn't have done more than glance at them. A closer look might have raised questions. Were these plumbers? Exterminators? Heating contractors? Why were there no identifying marks on the van? Or their clothes? And why the hell were they hauling equipment between two ramshackle buildings that led to a rubble-strewn empty lot?

Anybody looking might have had questions but wouldn't have had time to ask them. Monster-Boy did not act with doubt or hesitation. Over the years, his psychosis had deepened and metastasized to the point where he lived in his own reality. Adding enormous doses of anabolic steroids and growth hormones made everything exponentially worse. But even in his delusional state, Monster-Boy operated with preternatural cunning and an exaggerated level of confidence. Monster-Boy believed he could get away with whatever he set his mind to. He believed in his own mythmaking. Rationality barely imposed on him. Monster-Boy acted as if he had every right to do whatever he was doing.

Once they made their way past the two buildings facing Reed Street, Monster-Boy and Worm entered a rubble-filled lot.

Worm asked, "How'd you find out that guy lives here?"

"None of your fucking business. I know people, all right. Think I'm fucking around in the dark here?"

"You sure nobody's here?"

"Of course, I'm sure. Stop asking me stupid questions."

Worm looked down. He had made a mistake questioning his master, much less questioning Monster-Boy while he had to lift and carry the heavy fuel cart over the uneven ground between two buildings.

Worm made his way in front of the big man, stumbling, struggling, but making sure to keep his mouth shut. He walked with the ladder resting on his right shoulder, the toolbox in his left hand, every move exaggerated by the swinging, dipping eight feet of double ladder. Monster-Boy enjoyed watching the Worm struggle. He believed the Worm had been born to suffer, that he needed to suffer. But everyone had their breaking point. That was the most fun, seeing someone crushed and broken. But you didn't want to ruin them too soon. Then the fun would be over. Monster-Boy thought about making the Worm suffer more when they finished this job. He would perform a sex act on the Worm. But how to make it more demeaning? He'd do it back here amidst all this filth. He'd make him get on his knees. But what could make it really disgusting? Monster-Boy distracted himself, thinking about it as they approached a small, cube-shaped building at the end of the lot. The structure was fifteen feet long, wide, and high. One corner of it butted up against an extension added to a warehouse on Beard Street. The two buildings bordered the small garden behind Beck's building on Conover Street.

Worm quickly set up the extension ladder and climbed up on top of the smaller building. Monster-Boy slowly followed him up the ladder, pulling himself up rung by rung as he carried the fuel cart. Monster-Boy weighed 278 pounds. Adding the fuel cart's weight exceeded the capacity of the rungs on the aluminum ladder, bending each one as he stepped higher and higher.

Monster-Boy muscled the fuel cart up onto the roof, then stepped off the ladder onto the flat surface. He stood back as Worm pulled up the ladder, walked it over to the other side, and lowered it into place behind Beck's building. Monster-Boy rolled the fuel cart across the roof, stepped onto the ladder, lifted the cart, and carried it down to the small patch of green behind Beck's building. Another feat of extraordinary strength. From there, it was only ten feet to a ground-floor window.

Worm dropped the toolbox next to Monster-Boy and opened it. The hulking man delicately ran a hand over a square pane of wire-mesh reinforced glass in the bottom section of a double-hung window. The presence of the wire mesh did not concern him. Monster-Boy knew that, contrary to what most people thought, the wire mesh did not make the glass stronger. If anything, it made it weaker. The purpose of the mesh was to make the window more fire resistant. Monster-Boy smiled. That wouldn't make any difference, either. The fire would be on the inside.

Monster-Boy examined the window to see if there was any security tape. There wasn't. There was, however, an alarm wire set into the horizontal sash, connected to the sash lock. If the window moved even a quarter of an inch, or the lock turned, an alarm would go off.

No problem. Monster-Boy didn't intend to open the window.

Worm handed Monster-Boy an SD-10 circular glass cutter and a small can of machine oil. Monster-Boy set the glass cutter's suction cup in the center of the lower pane. He set the cutter for a six-inch-wide hole. He oiled the surface of the glass, then carefully turned the cutter around until it came full circle and joined the beginning of the cut with a soft click. He removed the glass cutter from the window. The next step would be to carefully apply pressure from the other side of the glass to run a crack around the cut. But Monster-Boy couldn't get to the other side, so he took another suction cup and attached it to a section of the glass near where he had scored the glass and pulled. Then he moved the suction cup counterclockwise around the circle and pulled, moved it, and pulled, all the way around the score, running the cut through the glass. Now he pressed the score from his side all around the circle, opening the crack.

He scored the glass horizontally and vertically back and forth across the circle with a straight glass cutter, then softly tapped on the scored circle until pieces began to break free. The wire mesh held the glass bits together, but he snipped the wire with diagonal cutting pliers. Within two minutes, Monster-Boy had pulled out enough of the glass so that he could stick the nozzle of the fuel cart hose through the hole in the window.

Finally, Monster-Boy lifted the 168-pound cart onto the sill and held it in place, resting the rear wheels on the window-sill. Worm squeezed the nozzle handle enough times to get the siphoning effect going, sending the gasoline flowing into Beck's building. It took some time to empty the entire twenty-five gallons, but that was fine with Monster-Boy. He spent the time leaning against the fuel cart to hold it in place and removing more of the glass circle. It also gave more time for the gasoline to spread across Beck's ground floor.

When the fuel cart was empty, Monster-Boy placed it on the ground. Worm handed him an object from the toolbox. Monster-Boy had built a device to ignite the gallons of gasoline they'd poured into Beck's building. Monster-Boy had taken a 6-volt lantern battery and soldered the female prongs of an inexpensive plug-in timer switch to the battery terminals. Then he'd plugged in a four-foot piece of electrical lamp cord into the timer. He'd stripped the ends of the electrical cord and weaved the bare wires to a bundle of copper wool. When the timer switch turned on, the six-volt battery would send a charge through the electrical cord, creating a ferocious spark where the bare wires met the copper wool.

Monster-Boy stood behind Beck's building holding the timer, smiling to himself, imagining the ferocious flames that would burn in Beck's ground floor. Smoke and fire would rise and ravage the old building. He checked his watch. 2:48 p.m. Monster-Boy wanted the fire to start during daylight hours, but he needed time to get away. Not much. Although it might be fun to set it for later. Maybe catch Beck or one of his asshole friends coming back to the building.

Fuck it. Monster-Boy set the timer to go off in one hour. He peered through the hole, looking for a spot where the gas had puddled. Almost a gallon of it had pooled against the wall directly under the window. Monster-Boy's arm was much too big to fit through the hole in the window. He handed the ignition device to Worm.

"Get your fuckin' pipe stem arm in there and drop it down next to the wall, piss boy."

Worm did as he was told. He was able to get his entire arm through the hole. He lowered the timer about four feet above the floor inside. When he dropped it, the ignitor plopped onto a puddle of gas resting against the wall. Perfect.

Worm pulled his arm out. Monster-Boy said, "Good work, slave. Now for your reward. On your knees."

Monster-Boy hadn't come up with anything new to humiliate the Worm. He checked his watch. He didn't have a lot of time. He'd give it fifteen minutes. Not like when they were locked up together, and he could spend half the night tormenting the Worm. Oh well, I'll come up with somethin,' thought Monster-Boy as he unbuckled his pants.

18

Grimaldi entered the 76th precinct, walked up to the desk sergeant on duty, flashed his ID, and said, "Alphonse Grimaldi. I'm from the commissioner's office. Here to see Captain Fernandez."

The sergeant checked out Grimaldi for a moment. Grimaldi gave the sergeant a look that said, don't fuck with me.

The sergeant turned to a uniformed cop at the front desk and said, "Is the whip back?"

"Yeah. He came in about fifteen minutes ago."

The sergeant asked Grimaldi. "He expecting you?"

Grimaldi wasn't going to play the sergeant's game by answering any of his questions. "I was with him this morning. I need to talk to him. It's important."

To save face, the sergeant hesitated before he picked up the phone and called the precinct commander's line. He spoke carefully, making sure to lay the responsibility on Grimaldi.

"A detective from the commissioner's office is down here. He doesn't have an appointment but wants to speak to the captain. Says it's important."

Grimaldi didn't appreciate the bullshit about not having an appointment but let it go. He had to wait for ten minutes until a civilian employee came down to bring him to Fernandez's office on the second floor. Grimaldi assumed Fernandez had made him wait to make a point.

When Grimaldi entered the precinct commander's office, Fernandez was sitting behind his desk writing something. He didn't look up when he said, "What's so important? Something happen?"

Grimaldi didn't answer Fernandez or ask if he could sit. He took the chair opposite the captain's desk.

"I need to find out about an incident that happened over on Conover Street near where the second body was found today."

That got Fernandez's attention. He stopped what he was doing and looked up.

"What incident?"

"A shootout four years ago that injured cops and resulted in multiple deaths."

Fernandez said, "That was before my time."

"Be that as it may, anybody in the precinct still around who knows about it?"

Fernandez tossed his pen on his desk and sat back in his chair. Grimaldi watched him carefully. Grimaldi pegged Fernandez as being young for his position. Or was it just that nowadays, most people sitting behind a precinct commander's desk would look young to him? Whatever his age, Grimaldi hoped Fernandez was smart enough to cooperate.

He watched Fernandez thinking it through. Grimaldi was patient. Maybe that was part of being older. Knowing when to keep your mouth shut.

Finally, Fernandez said, "I have a detective in the house who was around back then. In fact, he was there the night it happened. It's been a sore spot with him for quite some time. Is it worth me pulling him off whatever he's doing to talk to you?"

Grimaldi took a deep breath and let it out slowly, staring at Fernandez, giving Fernandez time to understand that Grimaldi didn't appreciate the question.

Then he said, "Yes, Captain, it will be worth taking him off whatever he's doing."

"I presume it has to do with that murder in the grain terminal, too."

"Yes."

"So, the two murders are linked?"

"That's what it looks like at the moment."

"And how is what happened on Conover Street four years ago connected to the two murders today?"

Grimaldi's patience evaporated. He leaned forward, spoke softly and slowly.

"Captain, with respect, I'm not here to answer your questions. I'm here to find out answers to my boss's questions so she can answer the commissioner's questions. If I can't answer their questions because I spent my time answering your questions, I'm not going to be coy about what held me up. So, if you got questions, Captain, call Brennan or call the commissioner. Me, I got two questions – who's the guy who knows about the shit that went down in Red Hook near where the murders took place today, and when can I talk to him?"

Fernandez said, "All right, all right, don't get your balls in an uproar. What's Brennan's story anyhow?"

"Still with the questions?"

"Humor me. What's Brennan's story?"

"What do you think? She wants to be the first female NYPD Commissioner."

Fernandez smiled. "Think she'll make it?"

Grimaldi opened his hands wide. "Why the hell not? It's gonna happen sometime. She's been planning on it since the day she got out of the police academy. Probably before she went into the academy." Grimaldi sat back. "Look, you got an interesting command here, Captain. You got Carroll Gardens coming along nicely with its gentrification. Red Hook is right behind it. Got all the mobsters and bullshit out of the precinct. Nothing's perfect, you still got a couple of bumps over there in Red Hook with the projects and all, but you could look real good over the next couple of years. Position yourself for whatever you want. I don't want to jam you up. It's a waste of my time. Let me get done what I got to do, and I'll tell everyone how helpful you were. Make some goddamn friends in high places for yourself."

Fernandez pitched forward in his chair and said, "Why not? The detective's name is Esposito. First Grade. An old-timer. Good guy."

Grimaldi said, "Jeffrey Esposito?"

"That's the one."

"I know Espo."

"You do?"

"Hey, twenty-two years of this shit, I'm two degrees away from everybody."

"All right. Hang out with my assistant for a couple of minutes. I'll have him drop what he's doing and fill you in."

"Appreciate it."

Grimaldi left Fernandez's office and stood near the desk of the person who'd brought him upstairs. He pulled out his phone and checked his emails. This time, he waited only five minutes.

Detective Jeffrey Esposito showed up with a fat manila folder under his arm, walking fast. He waved at Grimaldi from across the squad room.

"Alphonse Grimaldi."

"Jeffrey Esposito." Grimaldi pronounced Esposito's last name in two parts. Espo. Sito. "How are you?"

They shook hands. Esposito said, "Same-o, same-o. And you?"

"As well as can be expected."

"I hear ya."

Esposito looked like the years hadn't treated him well since Grimaldi had first met him working on a complicated string of burglary cases in the diamond district in Manhattan.

Esposito said, "So you're looking into that shootout in Red Hook."

"Sort of." Grimaldi wanted to correct Esposito as quickly as possible. "I'm trying to get a lead on a guy who resides at…" He paused to pull out his notebook.

Esposito interrupted and recited the Conover Street address for him.

Grimaldi said, "Yeah, that's it. Guy goes by the name of Thomas Eaton, but I think that's a fake identity."

Esposito said, "You're right. His real name is James Beck. He's a fucking menace. Should be behind bars." Esposito looked around and lowered his voice. "Come on. The interrogation room is empty. Follow me. I'll fill you in. Something should've been done about James Beck a long time ago."

Esposito didn't wait for a response from Grimaldi. He turned and headed back across the detectives' squad room, Grimaldi hustling to keep up with him.

19

After the Bolo brothers left, Beck's men spread out on the second floor. Alex sat out in the main room, working on his computer. Demarco sat at a workstation talking on his phone. Ciro remained by himself at the large kitchen table, his feet up, conversing with one of his mob connections in coded mob-speak.

Beck stood in Alex's kitchen. It was nearing three o'clock. He had raided Alex's oversized Sub-Zero refrigerator for lunch and put together a large salad in an aluminum bowl, warmed up a plate of grilled chicken breasts in Alex's microwave, and assembled Ciabatta bread, slices of swiss cheese, cold bottles of Brooklyn lager, mustard, and a bag of Kettle chips.

Alex's well-stocked kitchen made the job easy, but it also made Beck realize he was doing the chore that Manny Guzman always took on. He'd seen Manny do it better hundreds of times. A feeling of dread and remorse made Beck feel clumsy and slow.

He brought everything out to the kitchen table. The spread attracted Alex and Demarco from the work area.

As he made a plate of food for himself, Alex reported his findings.

"I looked through a lot of sites from four years ago. Nothing on social media. A couple of mentions on local broadcast news. The Post had the most print coverage, but none of the papers had any of our names. The media pretty much went with the story the NYPD put out. Rival gangs. Russians versus foreign rivals. It played out in public the way you planned it, James."

"Okay."

Alex said, "Obviously, there's more information in NYPD records. I'll search around there next, but none of that would've been public. I'm betting they also downplayed it internally. Or maybe they never actually figured out what really went down."

Demarco took a seat. His plate held chicken and salad. No bread, no chips. He sipped from a glass one-third full of beer.

"I got hold of Pastor Ben up in the Bronx. I don't think he was especially happy to hear from me. But he came around when I told him Manny was missing. The man is a walking history book. Gave me a lecture on how Manny Guzman didn't leave tracks. Didn't leave people who could come back at him. Said he didn't think anybody from prison would be looking for revenge this many years later, although he couldn't completely rule it out. He also told me there's a lot of youngbloods in the Dominican gangs who would still be happy to give Manny the heads up if they heard something."

Beck said, "I think Manny would have told us if he'd gotten a warning."

Demarco's shoulder twitched. "Maybe. But it wouldn't be unlike Manny to keep it to himself. Particularly if he didn't take it seriously. Anyhow, Pastor Ben said he'd put some feelers out with the gangbangers in Bronx River Houses and around there."

Beck asked, "What about you, Ciro? Hear anything?"

Baldassare had just taken a bite out of thick sandwiches. While he finished chewing and swallowing, Ciro raised one hand and brought his fingers and thumb together and apart in the sign indicating talking.

"I made inquiries with guys who've been around. Not the low-level cugines. You gotta speak in code to these pricks, but they understood what I'm asking about. It's a simple question. A friend of mine is missing. You heard anything? I didn't bring up Russians or anybody else. Wanted to see what might come up."

"And?"

"Mob guys are always willing to spin out some theory. All of them knew about what went down between us and the fucking Vory. A couple of 'em brought up the Brighton Beach gangs, but more like asking me, you know."

"You think that was an indirect way of telling you?"

Ciro made a face. "Everything is always indirect with these guys. Especially on the phone. But what happened wasn't on their turf, didn't have to do with their businesses, so if they knew about someone coming after us because of that night, I think they would've made it clear to me."

Beck nodded. Restless. Frustrated.

Alex asked, "Do we still think it's connected to what happened that night?"

Demarco said, "Getting doubtful."

Alex said, "How about that guy Walter Pearce? Or those damn mercenaries working for that arms dealer? They knew our location. You think any of them are looking to settle a score? Or provide information to someone who wants to get to us?"

Beck said, "I don't think so. Pearce is an ex-cop. I can't see him having anything to do with two homicides and abducting Manny. Plus, he got paid. Handsomely. The mercs got paid twice and helped find the big pile for the government, which put them in a good light. Also, I don't think stabbing and burning people is their style."

Beck was about to pick up the phone and find out if the Bolo brothers had come up with anything when his phone buzzed. He saw their innocuous caller ID on his screen. ABC EQUIP-MENT RENTAL.

Beck said, "What's up?"

Ricky Bolo's voice came shouting over the phone.

"James! Your goddamn building is on fire."

"What?"

"Your building. It's on fire. We're standing in the lot across the street. You better get over here."

76

Everyone had heard Bolo's voice over the phone. Everyone was on their feet.

Beck yelled to the others, "It's them. They tried to burn us out four years ago and failed, but they're doing it now!"

20

Grimaldi hurried into One Police Plaza. He had two minutes to get upstairs and meet with Brennan. She'd called him back to fill her in before she was to meet with Commissioner Roth. He had to leave the Seven-Six before he'd finish with Esposito. The guy had a hard-on for James Beck. Based on what Esposito told him, it was easy to understand why.

When Grimaldi walked into the small conference room near Brennan's office, she said, "I'm seeing the boss in ten minutes. Talk fast."

Grimaldi dropped his notebook on the table and started talking before he sat down.

"Thomas Eaton is a convicted cop killer named James Beck."

"What?!"

"You heard me. But – his conviction on first-degree manslaughter was overturned. After he'd served eight years, so technically, he's got no criminal record. Plus, he sued the state for wrongful conviction and settled for almost two million."

"Where did you get all this?"

"From a detective in the Seven-Six who tried to serve an arrest warrant on Beck four years ago and ran into a gun battle with a bunch of bad guys."

Brennan gave Grimaldi a confused look.

"It's complicated. The main point, Esposito and his men walked into a shit storm. Esposito believes James Beck used the department to take out his enemies. It's always bothered him that Beck got away with it."

"This is the gunfight you were talking about?"

"Yes. And according to Esposito, it wasn't between two rival Russian gangs. It was between Beck, his men, and a Vory crew that had teamed up with Bosnians." Grimaldi looked at his notes. "Four men died on the scene. One found dead from wounds incurred while he was supposedly fleeing the scene. Subsequently, three more died of wounds. Four others ended up in the hospital. And, here's the most important part – four cops were wounded, one fairly seriously."

Brennan shook her head. "That's not how the department laid it out."

"Nope. Esposito said that was basically a cover-up. I didn't get a chance to hear why Beck was their target." Grimaldi paused again to check his notes. "The night the squad from the Seven-Six went to serve the arrest warrant, a retired cop named Walter Pearce tipped off Esposito that there might be armed criminals at the location who might interfere with the arrest. When Esposito arrived on the scene, the tip turned out good. He says the gangs tried to drive Beck and his crew out of that Conover Street building and shoot them down. When Esposito and his men arrived, there was a fire out front, gunshots out back. He called for reinforcements. Ended up in a full-scale gun battle. Cops killed all but one or two of the bad guys. Meanwhile, no sign of James Beck or any of the known felons he was supposedly associated with."

"How's that happen?"

"I don't know. Beck and his guys somehow got away during the shooting."

"And he's convinced Beck was behind it."

"Absolutely."

"Why wasn't more made out of this back then? Why did the department spin it?"

"Lotta reasons. The NYPD killed most of the dead on the scene. Some of them shouldn't have even been in the country. The shooting was justified, so why complicate it. The official version was that two rival gangs went at it. Police stepped in and stopped it. End of story. Again, Esposito had a lot more to say, but I didn't really want to hear it. I just wanted to get a lead on James Beck."

"You believe Esposito?"

"Mostly. I know him from working together like eight, nine years back. He's an experienced detective. Granted, he's all wound up about James Beck setting the cops up to be a death squad, and he bitched about pressure from above to shut it down. He lost me when he went on about a secret federal agency being involved. Oh yeah, he also claimed the battle in Red Hook was connected to a shooting near JFK later that night. An old Russian mafia guy got taken out. Apparently, before he could get on a plane. Esposito thinks Beck was involved in that, too, but admitted it could've been people from the other gang."

Brennan looked at her watch. "So, how does this help us with our investigation?"

Grimaldi had anticipated the question on his drive to One PP. He answered quickly.

"Even without getting Esposito's whole story, four things are for sure. One, Thomas Eaton is James Beck. Two, exonerated or not, James Beck is a criminal who associates with violent felons. Three, something off the charts went down in Red Hook involving Beck. Four, and most important, when you get that many dead and wounded bad guys, there's a good chance somebody is looking for payback."

Brennan didn't respond. She sat nodding to herself, thinking it through. Grimaldi watched her, doing his own calculation about how much of her thinking involved political considerations.

Grimaldi said, "Oh yeah, also important, Esposito gave me names to go with the descriptions I got of the felons living at Beck's address."

"From the guy who works down the street?"

"Yes." Again, Grimaldi referred to his notes. "One is Demarco Jones. Another is Ciro Baldassare. And the third is Emmanuel Guzman. All are ex-cons. Esposito gave me a top sheet on their records. My bet – fisherman number three is Emmanuel Manny Guzman."

"Interesting. That fits with what Dave learned from the Escobar family in Red Hook."

"They confirmed Emmanuel Guzman?"

"Close enough. Ramon Escobar's wife said his fishing buddy was named Manny."

"Bingo."

"Dave is tracking down medical records to help the ME identify Escobar. He had a badly broken leg. Had to be pinned together."

"Oh yeah, the Social Security Disability thing. That should show up on x-rays."

"Yes."

Grimaldi pushed his notebook aside and leaned back in his chair.

"So, now what?"

Brennan looked at her watch. She had two minutes before she had to report to the commissioner. Roth often kept her waiting, but God help her if she made him wait.

She talked fast.

"We're doing good. We've identified the two murder victims and the missing third person who could be a victim or a suspect. We're way ahead of the local precinct detectives. Plus, we now have a person of interest, James Beck. But I'm going to have to tread lightly until I know more about what went down four years ago and how it was handled. I'll find out what Roth wants to tell me about that. Problem is, we don't have any proof what happened four years ago has anything to do with today's murders."

"Granted. But you can say we have definite lines of investigation."

Brennan nodded. "Yes. Guzman and Beck. Beck is at the top of the list. So, you get out there and find him. Get with Dave. He should be finished with tracking down Escobar's x-rays by now. Find James Beck and bring him in."

"As a material witness? Or do you want to arrest him on the fake ID, on obstruction, something else?"

"I don't know. Let me talk to Roth first. For now, find him."

Brennan stood up to leave.

Grimaldi said, "Where do you want me to bring him? The Seven-Six?"

Brennan was quick with her answer. "No. Here."

"Okay, what about Phil and Jerome?"

"Phil is checking on the burning MO. Jerome stays in Fort Greene. Gotta go."

Grimaldi sat back in his chair. He rubbed his face. He took a long breath. Suddenly, he felt tired. And hungry. And tense from rushing through his report to Brennan. Now it was on him. And Dave Metuchen. The pressure would ratchet up until he found Beck. Fine. He wanted to find the son of a bitch, too. He didn't like being bullshitted with that phony ID and story about being in construction. He wanted to see James Beck's face when he told him he was full of shit.

He didn't know what Brennan's next move might be. She wouldn't wipe her nose unless the commissioner told her to. But he knew what his gut and logic told him.

For sure, James Beck had enemies.

Manny Guzman was fisherman number three.

Manny Guzman did not kill Ramon Escobar or Eduardo Ramirez.

The likely scenario was that whoever killed them abducted Guzman to get leverage on Beck.

Grimaldi knew that Brennan would come to the same conclusions. But that didn't mean she knew what she was getting into. She was about to open one hell of a can of ugly worms.

Warren Roth had been the police commissioner four years ago. Whatever happened in Red Hook that night wasn't some vague memory for him. Eight men dead, four wounded, four cops shot. No fucking way did that get past Warren Roth. No way did it get covered up without his involvement. And if opening that can of worms was going to cause scrutiny or embarrassment to the NYPD, there was no way Warren Roth would let that happen.

Grimaldi pitched forward in his chair.

Meanwhile, as usual, the next move was on him. And Dave Metuchen. Find someone who had killed a cop and got away with it, engineered a blood bath that used the NYPD to take out eight guys and injure four cops, ran a nasty crew of ex-cons, and somehow managed to keep the entire NYPD at bay.

Great. Just fucking great.

21

Ciro had tapped out his leads, so ran out with Beck to check out the fire. Alex and Demarco agreed to keep working their contacts to find out who was behind the murders and Manny's abduction. All of them remembered how their enemies had tried to burn them out of Conover Street four years ago, but nobody said anything about that.

Ciro and Beck remained silent as Ciro raced his Chrysler 300 through the Brooklyn streets into Red Hook. Both ends of Beck's street were blocked off. Ciro parked on Coffey Street; didn't bother to check that the spot was legal or lock the car.

Both men hurried down Conover toward Beck's building. A fire engine, two rescue trucks, a ladder truck, a pumper truck, and other fire department vehicles filled the street. As they got closer, Beck could see swollen fire hoses running into his building through the smashed open front door. He and Ciro made their way to the empty lot on the other side of the street. The iron fence that closed off the lot kept people from the neighborhood who had come out to view the fire from getting too close.

Ciro spotted the Bolo brothers standing near the fence, watching the firemen. Beck hadn't seen them. He'd been intent on looking at what the fire had done to his building. The front seemed undamaged. He couldn't see very much inside because dark smoke filled every floor. Oily, black water flowed out of his door, down the two front steps, and into the street. Dark smoke rose behind the building. Beck was about to head over to Reed Street to get a view of the back when Ricky Bolo gently took his arm.

"James."

Beck turned.

"Ricky, what do you know?"

"I slipped a Benjamin to one of the firemen. The fire started in the back. On the ground floor. Definitely arson. Somebody pumped flammable liquid through the back window – that's what the fireman called it, flammable liquid. I asked him what he meant. Said he thought it was gasoline. Gallons of it."

Beck pictured it. The ground floor in the back was a storage room, mostly empty except for rarely used standing shelving units. He hadn't done much to the room during his renovation except clean it out. Everything in the storage area was original. The old wood plank floors, the plaster and lathe walls, the tin ceiling. The only thing he'd done was extend the sprinkler system into the area because of the wood floors. There was an empty walk-in cooler that hadn't been used for decades. Beck had left the cooler and its heavy wooden doors intact.

"The thing is," said Ricky, "whoever did it, didn't light the shit right away. Fireman said a lot of it leaked through the old floor into the basement."

Beck nodded.

He knew what Ricky had told him was most likely good news. He'd built a shooting range in the basement that was virtually fireproof. The floor was concrete. All the walls were covered in double layers of five-eighths inch acoustic drywall, as was the ceiling using special hangers to hold the weight. Stacked in front of the north wall from floor to ceiling were two layers of polypropylene bags filled with forty pounds of heavy-bodied sand to stop bullets. There was also a ventilation system to dispel the gun smoke and vaporized lead.

Beck and Demarco used the shooting range more than the other members of the crew. They trained two or three times a week, shooting from various positions at various targets; moving, stopping, turning, drawing. It was the only way to build the skill and confidence to hit a moving target with a handgun, particularly if that target was shooting back.

Beck hoped that most of the flammable liquid had ended up in the shooting range where it wouldn't do too much damage.

He said, "Let's get out of here."

As the four turned back toward where Ciro had parked, Beck pulled out his phone and called his lawyer Phineas Dunleavy. He knew the fire department would inspect the building. If they discovered the basement firing range, it would be a major problem, and he wanted Phineas to have a cover story. As he waited for the phone to answer, he quickly decided the fire had probably burned up the pulley system and targets they used. They could say the sandbags were there in case of flooding from another hurricane like Sandy. The fire probably melted the first layer of bags, and maybe the lead bullets. Beck didn't think anybody would bother to rake through a ton of sand.

The conversation with Phineas was short. Beck didn't speculate about the damage the fire had done to the rest of his building. He found himself detached from the Conover Street headquarters despite the endless hours and nearly a million dollars he'd spent renovating the building. Now it had been desecrated. Violated by an unseen enemy. An enemy who had started with his closest friend and ally and had escalated the attack in another intensely personal way. He had taken away Beck's home. Not just his home, the haven he had created for other damaged men society had designated unworthy of having any home other than a five-by-eight prison cell.

As he walked away with Ciro and the Bolo brothers, Phineas told Beck not to worry. He would contact Beck's insurance broker and assign a young lawyer in his office to deal with everything. Phineas Dunleavy knew Beck well enough to know that Beck didn't want to talk about the disaster. Beck said, "There's more to deal with, Phin, but I can't talk about it now. You'll be around, I presume."

"Absolutely."

"I'll be in touch."

Beck ended the call, unsure of when or if he would reach out to his trusted lawyer. He felt a diffuse feeling of rage taking hold of him, spreading through him like a physical sensation, like an illness. It went far beyond wanting to kill whoever had done this. Destroy was a better word. Rid the earth of this enemy. And all traces of him. And anyone connected to him.

With each step, Beck became more detached from his beloved private bar and home. He felt his time in Red Hook was ending. The neighborhood had become too popular. Too many people were encroaching on his privacy. Now, more cops and fire department personnel would know about his place. Time to move on. Where, he didn't know. And right now, he didn't give a shit.

As soon as he finished his call, Beck turned to Ricky Bolo, "Did you figure out how they're watching us?"

The fire had subdued Ricky, overshadowing his success in finding the surveillance camera.

"Yeah. It took like ten minutes to find the fucking thing. A little longer to figure out how it was transmitting."

"Where was it?"

Jonas said, "Not was. Is." He pointed to the long string of warehouses on the pier between Beard and Barnell Streets, just north of Beck's building. "The camera is still mounted on the top of the warehouse at the end of the pier. We stayed clear of it, but I got a good look at it through my monocular. It's a high-end camera. Zoom lens. Swivels three-sixty. It's easy to mistake it for just another security camera. But it's not."

Ricky said, "Turn it about ninety degrees, and it's pointed right at your building. Swivel it back, and it's looking at the pier where Manny goes fishing."

Beck asked, "How does it send the images?"

"They tapped into the closest Wi-Fi signal coming from the warehouse where the camera is mounted. The company is called

Brooklyn Events. They rent out the space for weddings, conferences, parties, shit like that. We went on the other side of the pier and identified the network. It's called 'BrooklynEvents Guest.' Not exactly hard to identify."

"Can you get the password?"

Ricky said, "Already got the one for customers. We walked in and asked about renting space for a wedding. I told them Jonas was getting married to his boyfriend."

Jonas ignored Ricky's joke. He said, "I asked for the password to their Wi-Fi. It's not exactly a strong password. Brooklyn events guest one, two, three. Bad guys probably got it the same way."

Beck said, "Christ, I thought you'd have to run some superfast program to find the password."

"Why waste time? The weakest part of internet security is always the people."

"And you're sure they're transmitting the camera feed on that internet connection?"

Ricky said, "We already hacked into their router webpage. Something is using a shit load of bandwidth. It's gotta be that camera."

"Can you find out where it's sending the images?"

Jonas said, "Most likely to a webpage hidden somewhere in cyberspace."

Ricky said, "On a server hidden in fucking Korea that sends it to a site in Romania that sends it to another site that your enemy accesses online."

"Is there any way you can find out where that signal ends up?"

"Yeah, well, that's where the super high-tech hacking shit comes in. We'll probably work with Alex and a couple of geeks he knows. It's going to take some work."

Beck, Ciro, and the Bolo brothers approached an old model 2000 Freightliner step van painted to look like a commercial vehicle. The signage on the van identified it as belonging to "ABC EQUIPMENT RENTAL."

Ricky said, "Step into our office."

They entered the step van through double doors in the back. The interior had enough room for a long bench on one wall, a worktable filled with surveillance equipment, computers, and transmitters along the other wall. There were shelves bolted to the inside walls of the truck holding bins of wires, cables, tools, and assorted electronic equipment. Beck, Ricky, and Ciro sat on the bench. Jonas stood opposite them, half-sitting on the worktable.

Jonas said, "What I said about tracking down the transmission assumes whoever is behind this has taken the trouble to hide who they are. It all depends on how much trouble. We'll go back into their router and follow the transmission. See where it goes until it terminates somewhere."

Ricky said, "But, James, even once we do all that, we'll have only identified the bad guy's ISP and IP address. Finding the exact location of the computer will require digging deep into the last service provider files, which would be a lot of work and time."

"How much time?"

"Days."

Beck said, "How long will it take to give me a general idea of the location?"

"Depends on how many servers are between that camera and whoever is controlling it. If we're lucky, maybe a day. Maybe sooner."

"Do the signals to swivel or focus the camera go through all those servers?"

"Yes."

"How long to find out when the camera started transmitting?"

"Not long. When we go into the router homepage, we'll figure out when it started."

"Okay, get to work. Call me."

Ciro said, "Hey, are we concerned they can track James through his phone number?"

Jonas said, "I seriously doubt whoever is behind this can track you through your phone. You need triangulating equipment, manpower, and connections. If you have someone who can do that..."

Beck said, "I don't care. They're going to find me, or I'm going to find them."

Ricky said, "Is your phone off now?"

Beck was in the habit of keeping his phone off. "Yeah." He turned on the phone and unlocked it. Four seconds later, they heard the ping of another text coming in.

22

Monster-Boy and the Worm arrived at his safehouse in Staten Island in time to watch the fire start in Beck's Conover Street building. Monster-Boy's computer was set up on the dining room table. Monster-Boy used his mouse to zoom in on the image of Beck's building. He checked his watch. The timer should have gone off two minutes ago. At first, there was no sign of anything. Monster-Boy stared at the screen. The image made him feel near Red Hook, but his house stood near the end of a dead-end street in the northwest corner of Staten Island. It was a rundown, two-story bungalow hidden behind an eight-foot tangle of hedges and bushes that hadn't leafed out yet but were dense enough to hide the house from the few residents who lived on the one-way street. The house had been built in 1953. The first floor consisted of a kitchen, small dining room, and living room. Upstairs were two bedrooms and a bathroom. Stairs in the kitchen led down to an unfinished cellar.

The house had been well maintained and unchanged since the fifties. The proportions didn't accommodate someone as large as Monster-Boy. The Worm was comfortable skulking around under the low ceilings and small rooms.

Outside stood a one-car garage from the same era. In the garage, Manny Guzman sat blindfolded on a wooden armchair, his right arm attached to a handcuff welded to a five-foot chain attached to a steel eyebolt cemented into the garage floor. The walls of the garage were covered in soundboard. Inch-and-a-quarter plywood blocked the small window on the wall behind Manny.

A bare sixty-watt bulb hung from a cord attached to an old junction box in the middle of the ceiling. The light switch next to the access door had been turned off. A bit of late afternoon light leaked in under an old, one-piece, wooden garage door unopened for months. The garage was empty except for a small workbench set against one wall and an assortment of old tools, shovels, rakes, and a derelict bicycle leaning against the opposite wall.

In the house, Monster-Boy smiled when he finally saw the black smoke billowing up behind Beck's building. He tried to imagine the roaring inferno erupting on the ground floor in the back. He wondered how long it would be before the flames ate their way to the upper floors and penetrated the roof.

The black, oily smoke became thicker, nearly obscuring the sky behind the building. There was no sound on his picture, but with all that smoke, Monster-Boy assumed multiple calls had gone into 911. He knew there were two firehouses near Beck's address, almost equidistant, although the one on Lorraine Street had a more direct route. He willed the firetrucks to stay away until all the floors in the building caught fire. He wanted Beck to see his home burned to the ground. To feel the loss. To suffer.

He watched the crowd gather on Conover Street. It looked like the first wisps of black smoke were coming out of the front windows on the second floor. Monster-Boy nodded to himself. Good. Good.

Worm sat in a chair opposite Monster-Boy, keeping his distance, absentmindedly picking a scab on the back of his neck. Worm had bad skin. His sketchy hygiene didn't help. He stank of urine, and his jaw ached from what Monster-Boy had done to him behind Beck's building.

Worm knew bothering his master at the wrong time could bring more pain and humiliation. Despite his craving for attention, he feared that one of these times, maybe the next time, Monster-Boy would go too far and hurt him permanently. But that was part of the thrill for Worm. That, and knowing he had the power to make Monster-Boy pay attention to him whenever he wanted.

At the moment, Monster-Boy had no interest in the Worm. He stared at the flashing red lights that announced the approaching fire trucks. He zoomed back the camera lens to get a wider view. Here they come. He smiled again. The firemen with their hoses and axes would inflict even more damage to the building.

Fuck you, Beck.

Monster-Boy thought, time for his next move.

He told Worm, "Go in the garage and empty the spic's piss bucket. Then take a shower and change clothes. I've had enough of your perfume, sweetheart."

The Worm smiled. Monster-Boy had called him sweetheart.

23

It took Metuchen thirty-five minutes to finish gathering and sending Ramon Escobar's medical information to the ME's office. He met Grimaldi in the lobby of One PP. On the walk to Grimaldi's unmarked Ford Fusion, he filled Metuchen in on what he had been doing and what he'd discovered.

Grimaldi ended by saying, "So bottom line, we gotta find this guy Beck."

Metuchen nodded at his partner. Even though Metuchen had not commented, Grimaldi knew he had taken in everything and was thinking it through.

They climbed into the Ford. Grimaldi took the driver's seat and handed Metuchen a manila folder he'd been carrying.

"The first page is a summary of what I learned from that detective at the Seven-Six about Beck and the shootout near his place four years ago."

Metuchen opened the folder, glancing at the contents without comment.

Grimaldi said, "Under the summary are all the records Nina could find on the rest of Beck's crew. She got a lot done while I was waiting for you."

Metuchen flipped through the material on Beck's partners.

"She's worth her weight."

"No question."

Metuchen began reading the paperwork. He was too experienced and methodical to ask questions before he absorbed the material. He read quickly with full concentration, culling out the important facts, skimming past background information and repetitions, a technique that helped him both absorb the information and remember it.

When he finished, Metuchen asked, "Got anything about that shootout other than your summary?"

"Not yet. I asked Esposito to pull together a copy of everything he's got and send it to One PP."

Metuchen spoke slowly. "Interesting. The department downplayed the whole thing. Bad guys killed, cops injured, Beck rides off into the sunset."

"Until now," said Grimaldi.

"And just so I understand what you told me; your view is there were three guys on the pier."

"Yes. Three victims."

Metuchen summarized, "Eduardo Ramirez stabbed and sliced. Ramon Escobar burned up in the grain terminal. And Emmanuel Guzman, part of Beck's crew, missing, presumed alive. The crimes committed as payback by enemies Beck created four years ago."

Grimaldi said, "I'm solid on the first part. Not as solid on Beck's enemies from four years ago as the doers. But that's the working theory."

Metuchen stared out the windshield mulling everything over as Grimaldi headed off the Brooklyn Bridge and toward the ramp that would take them onto the BQE.

"I guess it's not surprising the bosses decided not to go after him."

"Beck?"

"Beck, Guzman, all of 'em."

Grimaldi tipped his head back and forth a bit.

"Maybe the path of least resistance. Beck was slick. He wasn't even at the scene. None of them were."

"And Esposito is convinced Beck set it up."

"Yes. He told me an ex-cop came to the precinct that night to warn him."

"Is that what you meant by this note on the summary page? Pearce Warning with the question mark?"

"Yeah?"

"Sent by Beck?"

"That's what Esposito said."

"What's his proof?"

"Didn't get to that part."

"What was the warning?"

"I don't know exactly. Something about Esposito should watch out when he tries to serve the arrest warrant on Beck."

"And he's convinced Beck sent the guy to warn him?"

"Yeah."

Metuchen shook his head. "So Beck knew Esposito was coming."

"Maybe not Esposito in particular, but he knew the cops were coming to arrest him."

"How?"

"We'd have to sit down with Esposito for a couple of hours and go through the whole thing."

Metuchen waved a hand. "Too much we don't know. It's a rat's nest, Alphonse. A four-year-old rat's nest of bullshit. No doubt Brennan will play all this up and try to make this something bigger than it is."

"Two gruesome murders and an abduction, that's kinda big."

"She'll make it bigger. Guarantee it. Brennan is going to run out ahead of this thing, trying to prove she has value. Then Roth will take what she has and give it to the big boys to run down. She'll gladly step left, take whatever credit she can, and avoid any blowback."

Grimaldi said, "I don't want to argue about Brennan. It is what it is. And I have no intention of following Esposito off the deep end. I tracked him down to get background on Beck. If what happened four years ago has anything to do with what's happening now, it might lead us to who's slicing, dicing, and killing people. If not, I don't give a shit."

Metuchen said, "Well, even a quick look at the files shows that Beck and his crew have had a lot of opportunities to create enemies. Emmanuel Guzman is a straight-up Hispanic OG gang leader, shot caller who did a lot of crime and spent a lot of time in prison."

Grimaldi said, "No surprise there."

Metuchen tapped the top of his folder but didn't open it. "Guzman is a wily sonofabitch. This background Nina pulled together shows he insulated himself from a lot of the crimes he was behind. His last bit, he ended up convicted on only two counts of a Class C conspiracy."

"State?"

"Yeah. No charges from the feds."

Grimaldi said, "Did he go to trial?"

"Plea-bargained. He worked it pretty good. Each of those conspiracy counts is a fifteen-year bit. He took the max but served the two sentences concurrently. Got out on parole after a little under eleven years. He could have easily burned a lot of guys to get that deal."

Grimaldi made a noise that said he agreed.

"What else did Nina get on Beck's crew? I didn't have time to read the files."

Metuchen spoke from memory.

"She got info on two other guys. Demarco Jones and Ciro Baldassare. Jones is black, a product of the Bronx. Arrests for assault, dealing in stolen goods, extortion, but no convictions until his claim to fame."

Grimaldi asked, "Which is?"

"Took on a local Bronx street gang single-handed. Apparently, the morons assaulted his mother during a mugging. That didn't sit well with Mr. Jones. There was a trail of ten bodies attributed to his actions."

"Ten?"

"Three of the ten dead. By the list of injuries, the seven survivors might have wished they were dead. Took him three months."

"Sounds like a careful guy."

"And patient. That's why he got away with most of the assaults. They only nailed him on charges against the last three."

"How'd he get caught?"

"On a security camera he didn't know was in the area where he ran down the three gangbangers. The camera barely caught his image. But he's a big guy apparently, so I guess the jury figured it was him. He went to trial. He'd used a baseball bat and a knife. They all had guns. The jury gave him a break. Convicted on a lesser charge. Sentenced to seven years. Served a little over four in Sing Sing. Paroled."

Metuchen continued without looking at Nina Solowitz's files.

"Ciro Baldassare is a long-time mob guy affiliated with the Bonanno family. Came up when the Fibbies were coming down hard on the New York families. Wouldn't rat out the bosses for a lesser sentence. Ended up doing almost twelve years. Most of it in Federal penitentiaries but finished up with two years at Clinton on an old assault charge. All the aforementioned villains presumably met James Beck in prison."

Grimaldi said, "That's a heavy crew."

"It is. And Beck is no slouch, either. I don't know how an unaffiliated white guy who'd never been incarcerated survived eight years in maximum-security prisons."

"He must've gone through a hell of a transformation."

Metuchen said, "Alphonse, all these guys could have a long list of enemies. We are so far from solving this, it's nuts. Does Brennan have any idea of what we're up against?"

"Why should she? We're just finding out now. But I'll tell you one thing."

"What?"

"I don't think she's stepping left of anything on this deal. This is the kind of shit that makes careers."

"You may be right. God forbid. She's probably trying to play Roth like a fiddle as we speak. I hate this kind of crap, Alphonse."

Metuchen shook his head. "My opinion, this is not the kind of situation that makes careers. This is the crap that ruins them."

Both men fell silent as Grimaldi took the Atlantic Avenue exit off the BQE and turned right on Columbia heading into Red Hook.

After a while, Metuchen let out a short laugh and said, "The more I think about it, the worse this looks. Brennan is delivering a goddamn mess to Warren Roth. And right in the middle of this pile of crap is someone who killed a cop, got away with it, and if that wasn't enough, screwed the department by using cops to take out his enemies."

Grimaldi didn't try to counter Metuchen.

After more silence, Metuchen said, "So what's the brilliant plan to find this asshole James Beck?"

"Drive to his address and see what we see."

Grimaldi turned onto Dikeman Street, heading toward Conover. That's when he saw the black smoke rising in the sky ahead of him.

Metuchen leaned forward to see more out the windshield. "What the hell is that?"

Esposito's description of how the Russians tried to burn down Beck's building four years ago flashed through Grimaldi's head. He muttered a curse, hit the lights and sirens, and stepped on the gas.

24

Ciro and the Bolo brothers huddled around Beck's cell phone in the back of the cramped step van waiting for Beck to start the video attached to the latest text message. Beck hit the play icon. There was no sound. The first frame was a shot of Manny Guzman's left arm from just below the elbow to the hand. His wrist was duct-taped to the arm of a wooden chair. Everyone looking at the video knew it was Manny's forearm. The blue twill shirt he usually wore had been rolled up, revealing Manny's skin tone and prison tattoos.

The camera shifted to the right, revealing a pig's hoof and part of the foreshank. The raw pink skin and shape of the pig's limb had an eerie resemblance to a human forearm and hand. The foreshank and hoof were laid parallel to Manny's arm duct-taped to the arm of the adjoining chair, grotesquely mimicking the human limb next to it.

Into the frame came a hand holding a sixteen-ounce glass half-filled with gray viscous liquid – gasoline thickened with dissolved Styrofoam. The hand turned the glass and slowly poured a syrupy stream of gelatinous fluid onto the pig shank and hoof. The liquid was thick enough to remain in a line on top of the pork. The glass went out of the frame, and a long-reach butane lighter came into the picture, a flame burning at the tip of the lighter. The lighter slowly lowered toward the flammable liquid on the pig shank. Everyone in the step van watching the video knew what was about to happen. The flame touched the fluid, and it ignited into a searing, flickering line of fire.

The video showed the smoky fire burning and blackening the pork. Then, if the viewers weren't already cringing, a kitchen towel came into frame, slapping and hitting the burning liquid. Not only did it fail to tamp down the flames, the thickened gasoline stuck to the towel and set it on fire.

Finally, the angle of view shifted to Manny's arm straining against the duct tape.

Now, the glass came into the frame again, this time hovering over Manny's bare left arm. The glass began to slowly tip. Just before the flammable fluid spilled over the rim of the glass, the video went black.

Beck shut off his phone and stood.

"Ricky, Jonas, we have to find where that signal is going. Fast as you can."

Beck moved toward the doors of the step van.

Ricky asked, "Where you going?"

"To find out who was holding that fucking glass."

Ciro hurried after Beck.

25

Manny Guzman sat waiting for the flammable gel to hit the bare skin on his arm. The freakishly built-up man tipped the glass half-filled with a grayish liquid that smelled like gasoline and chemicals, holding the glass in place just before the liquid spilled out. He leered at Manny, revealing a mouthful of ruined and distorted teeth. Meth-mouth, thought Manny. And that face. What the fuck was with this freak? A near giant with a face like a child, as if that part of him had never grown up.

A much smaller man who had been recording the burning of the pork shank came out from behind the smartphone set on a tripod, nodding and smiling with a creepy obsequious leer.

Manny recognized the skinny punk skel with the neck tattoos from the fishing pier. How had he let that piece of shit get close enough to shank Eduardo? Close enough to set up the monster's attack on him and Ramon? An attack Manny was sure had ended with Ramon dead.

Manny grimaced. The worst part, the part that tormented him beyond everything else, was that Manny knew there was a time when he would have never let that happen. During his days in prison, never. When he first got out, never. The thought that he had become soft and old and slow ate at him like the goddamn stinking flames burning the fucking pork next to him.

How had he become so weak? Getting comfortable with life. Hiding out in Beck's place like he was afraid of the world. Losing his edge. Part of Manny felt like he deserved what he was getting. Like he deserved to die. He spat on the garage floor, forcing himself to expel the weakness that had seeped into him.

He'd seen the punk, but not the huge, built-up, steroid-fed, prison iron-pile freak, who looked like he could pick Manny up by the neck, and the chair he was taped to, and smash him against the garage wall. No, he'd never seen this guy with the shaved head, pale white skin, and that weird childish face.

Manny pegged him as a depraved, ex-meth addict, ex-con except for the fact that he had zero prison tats. He should have been covered with Aryan brotherhood Nazi insignia and wearing one of those long fucking goatees those pricks favored. No tats or goatee, but like all those other perverts, he had clearly groomed the skinny punk as his bitch. The bastard had done time, no question. But where? Manny was sure he had never seen him in any prison he'd been in. Or the punk.

Manny blinked at the smoke from the burning meat, breathed in the smell, letting it penetrate, using it to drive the weakness out of him and strengthen his resolve to kill both of these freaks. Manny could almost taste the death in his mouth, feeling himself coming awake with hate and resolve.

The freak holding the glass taunted Manny. He dripped a little of the syrupy gas onto his bare skin, then stopped.

"Ooops. Oh gee, sorry about that. OG, get it? You stupid, fucking miserable spic."

The voice fit the body, but again, not the childish face.

Monster-Boy let a bit more of the liquid drip onto Manny's arm. Ironically, the flammable solution felt cold.

Monster-Boy clicked on the butane lighter and waved the flame over the doctored gasoline. Manny felt the heat, gritted his teeth, waited for the pain, but suddenly Monster-Boy clicked off the lighter and stepped back.

"Not yet, fucko. We got more to do first. And I'm thinking if things don't go the way I want, I'll light up your cock and balls instead."

Manny ignored everything, going cold inside, staring at the hulk, imagining how he would try to kill him. He'd never been so close to someone that big. The freak wore a collared shirt unbuttoned at the neck and loose-fitting pants. The shirt stretched over his enormous pectoral muscles. Manny could see where the striated muscles bulged at the collar of the unbuttoned shirt, merging with the thick muscles of his neck and trapezius. If he could get a blade, a sharp blade, he'd puncture and slice the carotid arteries. Fast. Fast and hard before the monster could get his hands on him. Christ, there would be nothing he could do if this beast got his hands on him.

Monster-Boy stepped back from Manny and nodded for Worm to turn off the two quartz halogen work lights illuminating the back end of the garage. The interior went dark except for the light from the flickering flame still burning and smoking and cooking the pork. It seemed like the fire would burn forever. Good, thought Manny. Let it burn. Let it stink.

Manny's tormentors walked out a side door behind him.

Manny sat in the dim garage, averting his eyes from the flame burning near his left arm, feeling the heat, allowing the stench to seep into him. He'd been in the garage for nearly seven hours. It was a small, old, wooden structure, big enough for only one car, although there was nothing in the garage now except random junk and old tools piled near the walls. And the two chairs set up for Manny and the pig limb.

There was also a forged steel eyebolt cemented into the middle of the concrete floor. A five-foot chain had been attached to the eyebolt and a single handcuff welded to the end of the chain. The handcuff enclosed Manny's right wrist.

Manny had no idea where he was. His head throbbed with a fierce ache from being hit in the head with a blackjack or small bat. It had to have only been a tap. If the big motherfucker had hit him full force, his skull would have shattered.

He'd awakened in the back of a van with a dark pillowcase over his head, his torso wrapped in duct tape, pinning his arms to his sides, and his legs taped from his ankles to his knees. He rolled around helplessly as the van rumbled and swerved on what Manny figured was one of the highways surrounding New York.

He remembered seeing the skinny bastard come out onto the pier with a fishing pole. He'd joined Manny's group shortly after they had arrived, poles baited, and lines cast into the water. It must have been sometime between six-thirty and seven, the dawn light coming on. Ramon and Eduardo stood together with Manny left of Ramon. The bait buckets and Ramon's ice chest were near the corner of the pier.

The skinny guy with the neck tats had taken a spot on the pier next to Eduardo on his right side, slinging bullshit, trying to be friendly. Manny made him for a con and a punk immediately. He'd shown up with a brand-new Penn spinning rod and reel combo, about the right size, but he had no live bait. He'd rigged his fishing line with rubber bait on the wrong type of hook.

Manny had just cast his rig in the water, so he figured he'd reel it in and set the pole down, then go tell the punk to get lost. He thought about how vulnerable Eduardo was with the punk standing next to him, both hands on his fishing pole. But there were three of them to the one stranger. Eduardo was a big guy. He had a bum leg, but he had enough weight, so no one was going to push him around. Manny had his Charter Arms revolver in his pants pocket if it came to that. And Ramon had been around, seen his share of scrapes.

The punk kept talking, laughing, and clowning around about his wiggly rubber fish bait.

Manny almost had his line reeled in. Just then, he heard the engine of a John Deere gator approaching. He turned to see one of the park maintenance guys coming toward them at the end of the pier. Maybe to empty the wastebasket. Maybe to check on what was going on. The driver didn't look as big as he'd turned out to be, sitting in the gator. He had a ball cap pulled lower, covering most of his face. Maybe somewhere his size registered, but Manny's attention was on the punk.

And then everything happened fast. Too fast.

Manny got his bait out of the water. Propped his pole on the railing.

The maintenance guy stopped the gator about ten feet from them and got out. Manny saw his size then, but he still hadn't thought much about it, thinking maybe the guy was into body-building. Not so unusual for a maintenance worker. And then Manny heard the first wet whack as the skinny guy went to work on Eduardo with his shiv, and Manny knew this was wrong, all wrong.

Eduardo's hands and arms were up, trying to fend off the attack. But the skinny little punk was in a frenzy. Hitting, non-stop, moving, cutting, stabbing, aiming high and low, neck, kidney, groin, liver, neck. Blow after blow, blood flying, Eduardo yelling, screaming. Ramon turned to help. Manny went for the revolver in his pants pocket. And then a big body in a green maintenance worker's shirt blocked everything on his right. Then it registered. The guy was huge. So fucking big. Manny took the first hit, hard and fast on his right temple. Everything went black. He didn't hear or see the blow that put Ramon down, delivered full force, caving in the entire left side of Ramon Escobar's skull.

26

Beck and Ciro Baldassare jumped out of the Bolo brother's step van. Beck rushed down Conover Street in a half-run, Ciro hustling after him. Beck cut over on Van Dyke Street and turned onto Barnell, heading along the north side of Liberty Pier so the surveillance camera on the south side couldn't spot them.

Ciro followed Beck, saying nothing. James was usually the one who kept calm and focused, but the shit they'd seen on Beck's phone had set them both off. Ciro felt like kicking down doors and beating on whoever stood in their way until they found Manny. If Beck exploded, Ciro knew he would go right over the edge with him.

They rushed past a stretch of connected warehouse buildings. All the doors and loading docks on the north side were closed. A few warehouses displayed business names, but nothing seemed to be open except a winery near the end of the pier that Beck ignored.

They arrived at a double set of glass doors that belonged to the company occupying the far end of the warehouse, Brooklyn Events LLC. Beck pulled on the door handle. Locked. Beck pulled and shook the doors so violently that Ciro thought he might break the glass. Beck pounded on the frame. Anybody inside hearing the noise would have thought there was an emergency.

Beck abruptly turned away from the doors.

"Fuck this. Let's go around to the other side. Keep close to the wall so the camera doesn't pick us up."

By the time they came around on the south side of the pier, Beck seemed to have calmed a bit and regained his focus. They arrived at another set of glass doors, also locked. Beck shaded his eyes and peered into the warehouse. Ciro looked over his shoulder. Inside they could see a finished foyer and reception counter. Past the foyer, they saw the lights on in a small office.

Beck knocked on the door, trying not to pound. Ciro stepped up next to Beck. He had dressed for a dinner date with a woman he'd been seeing. He wore Bally Scribe Novo shoes, light wool charcoal gray slacks, a starched white shirt with French cuffs, and a dark blue cashmere Milano jacket. He figured his clothes might offset Beck's black jeans, red-plaid, flannel shirt, brogans, messy hair, and two-day-old stubble.

Then again, Ciro thought Beck's appearance did fit with the rapidly gentrifying neighborhood. Except for looking like he wanted to rip somebody's head off.

Beck knocked again. Louder this time.

An older woman appeared at the doorway of the office. She was tall and trim. Her white hair cut stylishly short. She wore shades of gray, from her rubber-soled leather shoes to her slacks, top, shawl, and scarf…all knit from cashmere. The clothes complimented her white hair, which was artfully colored to bring out the silver highlights. She took off an oversized pair of Morganthal Frederics reading glasses and stared at the two large men outside her door. She did not look happy. James Beck did not give a shit. He waved her toward him but stood back so he didn't look like he would shove open her doors and storm in when she unlocked them.

The woman came to the door, brows furrowed. Perhaps she had heard the pounding on the other side of the warehouse. She stood at the glass doors but didn't unlock or open them.

Beck shouted through the doors. "My name is James. I'm a neighbor. I live over on Conover." He pointed first to his right and then behind him toward the fishing pier. "I wanted to talk to you about the murder that took place on the pier this morning."

The woman's brows furrowed more deeply. Even worried, she looked like a model who had reached a graceful mid-sixties. Beck motioned toward the door.

"Sorry, could you open the door, so I don't have to shout? We don't need to come in."

Reluctantly, the woman unlocked the door and opened it halfway.

"Did you say murder?"

Beck stopped shouting.

"Yes. Two murders, actually. And a kidnapping."

She went from looking worried to confused. Murders? Kidnapping?

"What's this all about?" She glanced at Ciro, who tried to put her at ease by smiling and thinking about what it would be like to have sex with this older broad. He decided it might be great. It didn't help to put the woman at ease.

Beck kept his distance. He didn't try to charm or cajole her. He came straight at it, concentrating on keeping his tone of voice neutral.

"Yes. I said murders, plural. Two men killed, and another man abducted. I assume the police will come to talk to you about it, but the person kidnapped was my friend…"

"Wait, wait. I'm not following you. What murders? When?"

Beck forced himself to slow down. He turned toward the pier and pointed near the end. He spoke slowly.

"Early this morning, three men were on that pier. One of them was a friend of mine. His name is Manny. Early sixties. Hispanic. You may have seen him around the neighborhood. The two others were his friends. Also Hispanic. Longtime residents of the neighborhood." Beck didn't say *unlike you* but hoped the woman would pick up on it.

"One of the men was found stabbed to death. Multiple wounds. Very brutal. If you go out there, you'll see the bloodstains."

"Stabbed to death?"

"Yes."

"Why? What happened?"

"I don't know. Nor do I know who did it. The second man was found burned to death in the abandoned grain terminal on the other side of the inlet." The woman's confusion turned to fear. Beck continued. "The third man, my friend, was kidnapped. I'm sorry to barge in on you, but I need to ask you a couple of brief questions. Okay?"

The woman straightened up, a resolve coming over here. She opened the door wide and stepped out, wrapping her shawl tighter against the crisp March evening air. A breeze off the bay whipped through her chic white hair.

"I can't see how I would know anything that would help you but go ahead."

"Thank you. Are you the person who runs this office most of the time?"

"The owners are also often on-site, but I do most of the sales and booking."

Beck nodded, speaking slowly and carefully. "Okay. Can you think back over let's say the last month and tell me if anybody you dealt with, anybody inquiring about your space or booking an event, made you feel uneasy? Was unusual in any way?"

The woman's expression changed. Beck waited. She remembered something. Picturing someone.

She said, "You think someone who came here might have had something to do with these…"

"Yes."

"Why?"

"I'm sorry. I don't have time to explain. Do you remember someone? Can you tell me about him? I assume it was a man."

"Yes."

"Did he make you feel uneasy?"

"Uneasy is a good word to describe it."

Beck asked, "Did he provide any information about himself?"

"Yes, and as soon as he left, I threw it away."

Beck nodded. The fact that she had thrown away the information showed how disturbed she had been. It didn't matter. Beck assumed the information was fake.

"Okay. Can you pin down a date? When he showed up here?"

"I'd have to look at my appointment calendar."

"Could you do that please?"

The woman hesitated, then said, "Yes."

She ushered them into the warehouse and asked them to wait in the reception area. When she went into her office, Beck took in the surroundings. Off to his right, he saw an open space facing the water. It was at least 12,000 square feet with new wooden floors, finished walls, and nearly floor-to-ceiling windows. The new construction contrasted with heavy original wood columns and beams that supported the roof.

The woman returned. She had a date written on a yellow Post-It note stuck on the end of her forefinger. She held out her finger as if she really didn't want anything to do with the note. Beck took it from her and looked at the date. January 23. They had been under observation for over a month, assuming the camera had been installed shortly after the encounter.

"Tell me about him. What did he look like?"

She adjusted the knit scarf around her throat and stood a bit straighter. Her eyes narrowed as she concentrated. "He was big. Taller than either of you. Much taller."

Beck knew Ciro was six-three. That meant the woman was talking about someone at least six-five, probably six-six.

She widened her arms and opened her hands. "Not just big, grotesquely large. You know, like a bodybuilder or something."

Beck thought of an ex-con. Someone with a body built up on a prison iron pile and fed with steroids.

"White?"

"Yes."

"How old?"

"Early thirties, but I'm not sure."

"Why?"

She shook her head slightly.

"His face. He had a very boyish face. Almost childlike. It didn't fit on that huge, muscular body."

Beck tried to picture it but didn't push the woman.

"Anything distinguishing about him otherwise? Tattoos, scars? Glasses?"

"Yes. He was bald."

"Anything else?"

The woman focused on Beck.

"His teeth."

Beck said, "What about his teeth?"

"He was trying to be charming, smiling, but with his mouth closed. And then he laughed. Opened his mouth. Just for a second. His teeth were crooked. Deformed. I'd never quite seen anything like it."

Beck nodded and remained silent, looking encouragingly at his witness, but the woman pulled back into herself as if to banish the memory. She said, "Do you think that person had something to do with…"

Beck wanted to reach out and hold the woman's hand and try to reassure her. Instead, he quietly said, "Excuse me, what's your name?"

"Oh, Catherine. Catherine Hodge. And you are?"

"James. James Beck. This is my friend, Ciro. Catherine, I don't know the answer to your question. But I don't think you have to worry about that person."

"Why not?"

Beck wanted to say – because I'm going to find him and kill him. Instead, he said, "Well, the police are involved. This is obviously serious. I'm sure they're going to take the appropriate action."

The woman nodded.

"Is there anything else you can tell me about him, Catherine?"

She thought back.

"Just that he asked a lot of questions and tried to look like he was taking notes on his cell phone or checking something. It all seemed, I don't know, too much."

"Did he ask to connect to your Wi-Fi?"

She thought about it for a moment, then said, "Yes. While he was talking to me. Like he had to check something. We make that easy. I gave him the password." She recited it for Beck.

Beck nodded. "Okay, thank you. We'll be going now, Catherine."

Catherine Hodge suddenly reached out and took hold of Beck's arm.

"If you find out anything about that person, will you come back and tell me?"

"Of course."

"Good."

Beck and Ciro headed for the front door. The woman followed them, and as soon as they were out, Catherine Hodge pulled the glass doors shut and turned every lock.

27

Grimaldi shoved the gear shift on his unmarked Ford into park. He looked at his watch. 5:15 p.m. Sunset was approaching on a long day that Grimaldi knew was far from ending.

FDNY equipment and police cars filled the street in front of Beck's burning building, so Grimaldi had parked almost two blocks north. He pulled down his visor and dropped a laminated placard on the dash identifying the vehicle as belonging to the NYPD.

Metuchen asked, "I assume that's Beck's house burning."

"Looks like it. Esposito said something about the Russians trying to burn out Beck four years ago."

"You really think they're trying again four years later?"

"Well, somebody is."

Metuchen asked, "So, what's the plan?"

"Let's go look at his place. Who knows, maybe he is standing in front of it watching it burn down."

As they approached the burning building, Grimaldi and Metuchen split up. They looked for Beck without much hope of finding him. Asking firefighters if they'd seen him, others if they knew him and had seen him, describing Beck to people who didn't know him and asking if they'd seen him.

After thirty minutes, they met near Beck's broken front door to compare results.

Grimaldi raised an eyebrow at Metuchen. "Anything?"

"Couple of people who know Beck lives there but haven't seen him. You?"

"I talked to a woman who said she thought she saw Beck earlier."

"And?"

Grimaldi said, "And nothing. He's not around here now."

"Firemen said the cause of the fire was definitely arson."

Grimaldi pinched and scratched his prominent nose. "So now what?"

Metuchen made a face to communicate his answer wasn't very satisfying. "The usual? Check known associates. Hangouts. Girlfriends. Ex-wives. Relatives."

Grimaldi said, "None of which we know anything about, except for known associates. And even that isn't much. Guzman is out of the picture." Grimaldi pointed a thumb over his shoulder at Beck's building. "Demarco Jones is based here. So he's in the wind."

"That leaves Ciro Baldassare. File says he's based in Staten Island."

"We could reach out to the organized crime guys covering that territory. Odds are Baldassare is known to them. Depending on what they tell us, we'd probably have to haul ass out to Staten Island to find him."

Metuchen said, "Not with all this going down. He's probably with Beck if he's anywhere."

"Shit, let's get the hell out here. It stinks around here."

Grimaldi and Metuchen fell into silence and headed back to their unmarked car.

Grimaldi said, "If Beck is anywhere, he's out trying to find out who set his building on fire."

"And took his partner Guzman." Metuchen lapsed into silence and then said, "Brennan doesn't want us to arrest him, right?"

"She said just bring him in for now."

"And we're supposed to convince this cop-killer ex-con to come with us how?"

Grimaldi responded, "I don't know. Say please? I don't even know why Brennan thinks he'll cooperate with her."

"She believes she'll charm him into it."

Grimaldi said, "Fat chance. But maybe Beck is smart enough to know the department has a hell of a lot of resources that could help him."

"Guys like Beck don't work with cops. And the NYPD won't work with a cop killer."

"Brennan will. She makes her own rules."

"Not without Roth letting her."

Grimaldi said, "I suppose. But Brennan knows Beck has a better idea of who's behind the murders and kidnapping than we do."

"That's not saying much." Metuchen slowed his pace, lost in thought. "You know, there may be a shot here."

"What?"

"Beck might think he's smart enough to play Brennan. Work with her. Find out what she knows, then take matters into his own hands. He's still got Jones and Baldassare with him. Plus, connections to who knows how many hard guys."

Grimaldi nodded. "Interesting. He's sure as hell played the department before. But we still have to find him."

"I know. What was that you said?"

"What?"

"About his connections."

"Yeah?"

"That might be a way to find him. He's been out here for years. Guarantee you he's not clean. He's connected to a lot of felons. We need to find who they are. Track him down that way."

Grimaldi said, "Our best shot at that is Jeffrey Esposito. He's got a file on Beck that's ten inches thick. He's obsessed with the guy. Beck is his white whale."

Metuchen picked up his pace.

"Good. Let's go swing by the Seven-Six and talk to Esposito."

Grimaldi said, "Done."

28

As Beck and Ciro headed back to their car after talking to Catherine Hodge, Ciro said, "That description fit anybody you know, James?"

"No. And trust me, somebody who looks like that I'd goddamn remember."

"It fits somebody who was inside."

"An iron pile, juicer, meth addict. Yeah. Definitely."

Ciro nodded. "Maybe he's someone Manny ran into. Made an enemy of."

"We already considered that. I don't think so. The main thing is, now we have a description. Anybody who knows this freak isn't going to forget him."

Just then, Beck's phone rang. He checked the caller ID. ABC Equipment.

"Ricky, what've you got?"

"Looks like Staten Island. The routing wasn't all that complicated. We think the feed ends in Staten Island."

"Good. Good. How close can you get?"

"We got a ways to go. The provider is Verizon. That can make it complicated. They cover a lot of territory. Have to verify the location is Staten Island. Then get it down to a small section of the island. Then match the ISP to a physical address. That'll take more time."

"Okay, understood. You don't need to explain. I won't understand it anyhow. Put that aside for now. We have another lead."

"What?"

"We might have a description of the bastard. We talked to a woman at that events company. Guy showed up on January twenty-third who creeped her out. Bullshitted her about renting the space. Asked about her Wi-Fi connection. She gave him the password."

"Sounds like a possibility."

"She said he's a white male. Thirties. Big. Huge big. Body-builder-juicer big. Six-six, maybe taller. Bald. Teeth that marks him as a possible ex-meth addict."

"Shit. If he was anywhere near your security cameras, he'll be easy to spot."

Beck said, "Exactly. Tell Alex to check our footage starting on January twenty-third. Maybe a week or so earlier. Our witness said he was wearing a white shirt."

"You have a camera on the storage place next door, too, right?"

"Yes, and maybe you can tap into the security cameras for the garden supply place on the corner. I think there are also some CCTVs in the lot across the street keeping tabs on construction equipment in there."

Ricky said, "Got it. Don't worry. We'll get into every camera feed in the area. We have administrator codes and access to all the companies that run security setups in the city. There's not a lot to sort through in that area. If he's been around, we'll find him."

"Okay. Good. If you pick him up, maybe we'll get lucky, and you can identify a vehicle, too."

"Definitely. As a matter of fact, I'll also check today and yesterday, see if we can pick up anybody who matches that description who might have set the fire."

"Good idea, Ricky. You got Alex, who can help. If you need more people, reach out. Whatever it costs. Stay in touch."

Beck cut the call. Ciro could see that Beck was pumped up. As they headed back to the car, Beck told Ciro everything that Ricky Bolo had told him.

Beck stopped and turned to Ciro.

"Hey, I don't want to wait for Ricky to come up with an image. We need to start now."

"Agreed."

"The way that woman described him, he's gotta be a juicer. If Ricky is right, and he's based in Staten Island, maybe we can find this asshole if we find out who's supplying him with steroids or growth hormones, or whatever shit juicers take. Who would know the suppliers? Joey B?"

Beck and Ciro had cut over to Barnell to stay out of view of the surveillance camera. They took Van Dyke and were halfway to where Ciro had parked.

Ciro said, "Yeah, sure. Joey knows who's peddling that shit. I'll call him. If he's around, I'll hook up with him and get on the trail. If he ain't around, he can put me in the right direction."

"Good."

"What are you going to do?"

"I don't know. Check in with Phineas about the fire. Get back to Alex's place and the Bolos. It might be time to respond to the sick fuck's videos. See what he wants before he lights Manny's arm on fire."

Ciro said, "Jeezus Christ, we gotta find this guy."

Beck and Ciro were so involved in their conversation that when they reached Conover Street, they didn't notice anybody until they heard a voice say, "Well, well, Thomas Eaton. I'm glad I ran into you, pal."

Grimaldi and Metuchen were crossing the street in their direction.

Beck looked up. He said nothing. Shit. Bad mistake. He should have realized that the detective in the cheap suit with the big nose might come back to the neighborhood looking for him with his building on fire.

At first, the two detectives were smug and cocky about finding Beck, but that quickly turned to tension and fear when they realized they hadn't prepared for the chance meeting. They were up against hardened criminals who were almost certainly armed.

The older Italian detective stopped three feet in front of Beck. Ciro stood on Beck's left. The smaller Dave Metuchen moved about six feet in front of Ciro. The detectives had grown accustomed to always having the upper hand. The authority of their badges and guns on their side ensured that. But not this time. This time they were facing two men who did not fear them, and they had no backup.

Metuchen, to his credit, stood his ground, covering Ciro. Slight, dressed in his conservative suit, Metuchen looked like a civilian, like a John Q not even close to being able to handle Ciro Baldassare.

Beck looked at both detectives. He knew what they were thinking – how to take down these two if it goes bad.

Both cops were armed, but their suit jackets were covering their weapons. It would not be easy getting to their guns. Beck could close the distance between him and the older Italian cop and knock him down or out before he pulled his gun. But Ciro was too far away from the smaller detective to stop him from drawing his weapon. If the other detective moved an inch, Beck knew Ciro would not hesitate to use the Smith & Wesson .45 concealed under his jacket.

If it came to a draw, Ciro would win, and an NYPD detective would die.

He and Ciro would walk away, but they would have to flee. For years. Maybe forever. Better than returning to prison, but saving Manny would be impossible if they were on the run.

Despite the pressure to find Manny, despite the fact that someone had tried to burn down his home, Beck calculated everything in less time than it took to draw a single breath. He had to get Ciro out of this. Fast. He had to end this right now.

Beck said to Grimaldi, "Hey, I'm glad I ran into you, Detective. I need to talk to your boss." Beck quickly turned to Ciro and put out his hand. Ciro hesitated just a bit before he took Beck's hand and shook it.

Beck spoke quietly so the cops couldn't hear him. "Call Phineas, get him on standby. If they don't arrest me, I'll need D to pick me up. Tell him to wait for my text. Get with Joey B." Then, loud enough for the cops to hear, Beck said, "Thanks, I'll see you later."

Ciro hesitated for just a second. He wasn't the type to leave a partner holding the bag, but the look in Beck's eyes convinced him to turn and walk away.

Beck turned back to Grimaldi, "Is now convenient?"

Beck had caught both cops off guard.

Grimaldi looked at Ciro's back. Now it was his turn to make the calculation. Try to stop the Mafioso and take both in or let him go and settle for Beck. He looked over at Dave Metuchen, who gave a quick shake of his head. Metuchen had already made his decision. It wasn't worth the risk of getting into a shootout. Beck had made a smart move. So be it. They had what Brennan wanted. And without shooting anybody or getting into a brawl with two guys who looked like they could easily beat them down.

The big guy was already approaching the driver's side door of a white Chrysler.

Grimaldi came to the same conclusion. He smiled back at Beck, playing along, pretending that Beck really wanted to cooperate.

"Sure, Mr. Easton. It's a little late in the day, but the deputy inspector works long hours. I expect she's available."

Beck smiled back. "The name is Eaton."

Grimaldi nodded. "Oh, yeah, right. Eaton." He gestured toward his unmarked Ford. Beck felt a wave of revulsion at the thought of getting into the vehicle.

"Did you say, deputy inspector?"

"Yes. We work on a special detail."

Beck looked at his watch as he allowed Metuchen and Grimaldi to flank him on both sides and move him toward the car.

"You said – she?"

"Yes. Deputy Inspector Dianne Brennan."

"Where does she work?"

"One Police Plaza."

Metuchen opened the back door.

Grimaldi put a hand on Beck's shoulder and stopped him. He began patting Beck down, checking for weapons, as he said, "You have anything on you for protection, Mr. Eaton?"

"No. I rely on law enforcement for that."

Grimaldi gave Beck an insincere smile.

"Good to hear. Okay, step in."

Just before he got into the car, Beck said, "Are there any decent restaurants around police headquarters? Maybe I could take you all out to dinner."

Grimaldi resisted the urge to shove Beck in the car and tell him to shut the fuck up.

Beck said, "Assuming it's not against regulations."

29

Once they had Beck settled in the back of the Ford, Grimaldi told Metuchen to take the wheel. He climbed into the front passenger seat and sent a text to Brennan's private phone.

> Have Beck. Went down w/o hassle. We're heading to 1PP. BTW, asshole says he wants to take us all out to dinner.

Three minutes later, Grimaldi got Brennan's text.

> Bring him to my conference room. I'm not hungry.

Grimaldi looked at his watch.

> ETA 6:15

Metuchen looked at Grimaldi. Beck watched from the backseat through the cross-hatched metal barrier bolted to the frame of the car. Grimaldi held up his cell phone so Metuchen could read the texts. Metuchen showed no reaction.

Beck sat back, thankful they hadn't handcuffed him but feeling like he was in a cage. He discreetly sent a quick text to Demarco:

> Bring car to 1PP and wait for me. Might take some time.

Then he slipped his phone into his pocket and tried to fight down the tension and anger riding in a police car caused. It brought back too many horrible memories. He looked out the grimy passenger window long enough to make sure they were heading toward Manhattan, then closed his eyes. He tried to clear his mind. To think calmly, although every part of him wanted to be out there looking for Manny, figuring out the next move, heading for Staten Island with Ciro to find Joey B.

He had to play this very carefully. Maybe he wasn't under arrest, but right now the NYPD had control of him. Beck figured the chances of him ending up under arrest were at least fifty-fifty. If that happened, it could be disastrous. He'd go through a process that could easily take thirty-six hours. More if the NYPD wanted to fuck with him. By the time he was arraigned on some bullshit charge and Phineas got him out on bail, Manny would almost certainly be dead. And his enemy would still be out there. Beck wondered if he had made a huge mistake. No. There had been no choice. He realized if Ciro had killed the smaller detective, he wouldn't have been able to stop him from killing the other one. Ciro Baldassare wouldn't leave a witness.

They parked the car in an underground space at police head-quarters and led Beck to an elevator. A key card called the elevator and unlocked access to the upper floors. Grimaldi stood next to Beck while Metuchen dealt with the elevator. They exited on the seventh floor and led Beck along a cheerless institutional hallway until they reached a small conference room. Frosted glass panels separated it from the hallway. The door that gave access to the room stood open.

Grimaldi motioned for Beck to enter and have a seat. The rectangular conference table had room for six chairs, but there were only four. Of the four, only three matched. There were no windows, but the fluorescent ceiling fixtures made the room bright. At one end, there was a whiteboard with a tray holding markers. Metuchen followed Beck into the conference room.

Beck took a seat facing the door so he could see whoever entered. Metuchen sat across from him. Grimaldi disappeared without saying a word. Metuchen pulled out a small notebook from the inside pocket of his suit jacket, dropped it on the table, and began writing in the book, his head down, ignoring Beck.

Beck looked at his watch. 6:27 p.m. He sat back and crossed his arms. There was nothing to say or do but wait. He wondered how long before their female deputy inspector boss appeared. He tried to picture her. He imagined she would be a no-nonsense, heavy-set, African American woman. Someone who had made her way gradually up through the civil service ranks with a lot of perseverance and attitude.

Every minute he waited felt like five. Beck decided not to look at his watch.

Down the hall, Grimaldi knocked on Brennan's office door frame. She looked up.

Grimaldi said, "He's here."

"Is Dave with him?"

"Yeah. Where we at?"

Brennan said, "His excellency is not happy. Reporters were all over the stabbing scene, and somehow they found out about the body burned up in the grain terminal."

"Not surprising."

Brennan gave Grimaldi a disgusted look and said, "It was already on the six o'clock news."

"Nobody got pictures, did they?"

"No, thank god. We have to close this thing, Alphonse. Roth called an all hands-on meeting for eight."

"Tonight?"

"Yes, tonight. You think he's going to wait until morning?" Grimaldi didn't respond to Brennan's comment. "What's Beck know? How can he help us? Where did you find him?"

"Did you hear someone set his building on fire?"

"Yes. That's on the news, too."

"We found him not far from his place. We figured he might be there checking the damage from the fire. He was with one of his crew. By the look of him, it was his mobster buddy, Ciro Baldassare."

"You let him go?"

"Strategic choice. It would have meant a brawl. Maybe a shoot-out. We figured Beck was the prize. Why make it complicated."

Brennan knew she had been harsh with Grimaldi. She tried to make up for it by saying, "I agree. You made the right move. What were they doing when you found them?"

"It looked like they might be coming from the pier opposite where the stabbing took place."

"Not his building?"

"No."

"Why were they on that pier?"

Grimaldi frowned.

"I suppose they were trying to find somebody who might have seen something. Which is what we should be doing, or the homicide detectives from the Seven-Six. That big pier is right across from where those guys were fishing."

"It looked like a bunch of empty warehouses to me."

"No, not all of them."

"You think Beck found out anything?"

Grimaldi thought about it and nodded. "Yeah. I do. The two of 'em were talking about something when they ran into us. They were so involved with it, they didn't spot us until it was too late. We got lucky."

Brennan looked at a pile of pages on her desk held together by a large red rubber band.

Grimaldi asked, "What's that?"

"A copy of Jeffrey Esposito's file on Beck."

"Get anything more out of it?"

"I've skimmed through a lot of it. Beck might be the smart-est ex-convict either one of us has ever run into. And the most dangerous." She pointed to the stack and said, "Eight bad guys dead, four wounded, four cops shot, and nobody laid a finger on Beck. Or anyone associated with him. Not the Eastern European gangs, not us. Plus, a bunch of other suppositions and serious accusations that Esposito puts together that implicate Beck on other fronts."

"So how is Beck out there running free?"

"Because it's all too sketchy and outside an official investigation. No ADA that I know of would touch it unless someone from above forced it."

"And nobody ever wanted to."

"Nope."

Grimaldi nodded but said nothing even though it confirmed Esposito's complaints about a cover-up.

Brennan asked, "What's my leverage on this guy? I need to know what he knows. I need to find out what's going on with him. I need a way in."

"Threaten to lock him up."

Brennan shook her head. "It's an empty threat."

"Only if you look at it in the long term. You've got nothing that will stick, but if you arrest him, he'll lose a day or so looking for his friend, fisherman number three. I don't think he wants to waste a minute."

"Then why did he come in without a hassle like you said in your text?"

"He made a choice. He and that goddamn mobster with him could have put up a fight. And they would've won. But it most likely would've meant shooting Dave. He was in a position to draw. I wasn't. I was too close to Beck. He figured it out. Going against us would have meant disappearing. For a long time. And Beck wants to find his friend. He made a calculated decision. He turned himself in so the mobster could go free. Now he's got to figure out a way to avoid getting arrested. You've got leverage."

Brennan nodded, her eyes darting, thinking. Suddenly, she stood.

"All right. Let's go see what we've got. You sit down next to Dave. Don't say anything unless I ask you."

Brennan stood and smoothed her suit pants, tucked in her shirt blouse, squared her shoulders. Her breasts thrust out for a moment and were further emphasized as she put on her suit jacket. Grimaldi didn't stare, but he saw what he saw. He had always admired Brennan's figure. Who wouldn't? He'd thought about what she would look like naked. What man around her hadn't? But right now, he was more interested in watching Brennan ready herself to face James Beck. She knew what she wanted. But Grimaldi knew that right now, Brennan didn't know how to get it.

This was going to be interesting.

30

Monster-Boy sat on a wooden chair with his pants off, his feet propped against the edge of the old wooden kitchen table, his knees bent back, and his legs spread wide.

The chair was pushed back far enough so that the Worm could fit between the chair and the table while kneeling on the floor.

When the Worm had come out of the shower, Monster-Boy took the opportunity to dirty him again. He'd told the Worm to leave his clothes off, get down on his knees, and clean him using his tongue.

While both of them enjoyed the humiliation, Monster-Boy turned on his cell phone to check his text messages. He only turned on his phone and computer when he needed them so that there wouldn't be any signals going out to the internet or the cellular network. But now, he had to check.

He'd sent his last text to Beck over two hours ago. He checked the time to make sure. 4:21 p.m. He looked at his watch — 6:54 p.m. Over two hours had passed. There'd better be a goddamn text from James Beck coming in.

Monster-Boy held the cell phone. Looking at the screen, he moved his hand up and down slightly, waiting for a signal to come through. Waiting, waiting, feeling the rage build. Nothing. He waited. Still nothing.

Clearly, Mr. Beck did not understand. No problem. No problem at all. Let Beck think he could play this game. It would make what was coming all the more satisfying.

Monster-Boy dropped his feet to the floor and stood up so quickly he knocked the chair back. He squeezed the phone's off button hard enough to nearly break the case. Worm froze. This wasn't good. This was dangerous.

Monster-Boy tossed the phone onto the kitchen table and pulled up his pants, snarling, his face twisted. As he zipped and buttoned his pants, he spoke softly but with an intensity that made the Worm move away from him.

"I'm going to burn off that goddamn spic's arm. I'll burn it off. I'll burn it and chop it off and keep burning pieces of him until Beck gets it. Until Beck understands."

And then he turned, moving fast out the back door, heading for the garage. He yelled over his shoulder, "Come on, shit-boy. You're going to like this."

But the Worm knew he wouldn't like it. He didn't even like thinking about it.

31

Brennan entered the small conference room with Alphonse Grimaldi trailing behind. Metuchen rose from his chair and moved over so Brennan could sit directly across from Beck. Grimaldi walked around the end of the conference table, pulled the last empty chair from Beck's side, and rolled it next to Metuchen. Brennan dropped her folder on the table and sat. There it was. Three against one.

Beck ignored the two detectives and focused on Brennan, even as he saw the disheveled Italian say something quietly to his partner. The one who looked like he should be working in a bank.

Beck hadn't intended to stand up when Brennan entered, but he did. Not to be polite. He wanted to get a better look at her. His assumption about her couldn't have been more wrong. Dianne Brennan looked like she might have been a college athlete at a Big Ten school. Volleyball? Not quite tall enough. Track? Maybe track. A long-legged, middle-distance runner.

Brennan hadn't had the time or inclination to play sports, but she did work out every other day, running on a treadmill and working a full circuit of conditioning machines. She had the kind of body that made clothes look good. Even the middle-of-the-road business attire. Well-designed but cheaply made clothes that she could afford on her cop's salary.

Beck was most surprised by her red hair. Actually, a little more complicated than red. Strawberry blonde? Beck couldn't quite describe it but thought if that color was natural, she was a lucky woman.

The only thing that saved Beck from getting completely caught up in Brennan's physicality was the expression on her face. What was it? Anger? Annoyance? Or maybe pressure from her boss. Whatever was putting that look on her face could make her impatient. And that could make his situation more dangerous.

Beck hadn't put his hand out, and neither had Brennan. It would be a goddamn cold day in hell when James Beck shook a cop's hand. Or Dianne Brennan the hand of a cop-killer.

Beck pulled into himself, mentally putting a wall between him and the woman. Right now, she had a great deal of power over him, and Beck found himself resenting it. He couldn't let her pick up on his mood. He couldn't give her any advantage. For sure, he wasn't going to be the first one to speak.

Beck sat down just before Brennan. She sat straight up on the edge of her chair. Beck sat back in his. Was she trying to raise herself up so she could look down at him? Beck didn't mind. He wanted to keep his distance, and he was still tall enough to be nearly on the same level as Brennan. He returned her gaze, looking into her interesting green eyes, noticing the slight dusting of freckles across her nose and along her cheekbones.

Brennan said, "I'm Deputy Inspector Dianne Brennan. I work directly with Police Commissioner Roth on high profile cases. Is it James Beck…" Brennan looked down at a legal pad she'd dropped on the conference table, "or Thomas Eaton?"

Beck ignored the point she was trying to make.

"Beck."

"Mr. Beck, my detective tells me you wanted to speak to me."

"I didn't see a way to avoid it."

Beck's answer gave her a moment of pause. Before she had a chance to respond, Beck sat up, leaned forward, and said, "How would you like to work this?"

Beck had taken her by surprise. He was trying to take charge. Brennan responded quickly, "Let's start with some questions."

Beck said, "Sure. Assuming you'd be willing to answer one or two questions from me."

Shit. He'd maneuvered her into agreeing to something before she'd asked him anything. Something you never allow a witness to do. Too late. She had to make the best of it.

"Fine. Why were you on the pier in Red Hook this morning?"

"I was looking for my friend."

"Emmanuel Guzman?"

Beck didn't show any surprise that Brennan was able to identify Manny.

"Yes. He'd left around dawn to meet his fishing buddies on the pier. It was after twelve, and I realized he hadn't returned, so I went looking for him."

"He lives with you?"

"Yes."

"What's the situation with that, Mr. Beck? If you don't mind my asking."

"I do mind. But I'll tell you anyway. Manny Guzman lives in my building because he needed a place to reside so he could make parole. Look, rather than you carefully asking questions, building up to what you really want to know, how about I just tell you everything I know, and then you let me know what's happening on your end?"

Brennan tried to hide her annoyance. Again, Beck set the terms, but she decided the main thing was to get him talking and go from there. She said, "Fine," noticing Grimaldi shift uncomfortably in his seat.

Beck nodded. Maybe Brennan was different from the typical hard-ass police official. Maybe she didn't give a shit about dominating a situation if it got her what she wanted. Maybe that was the reason she had ascended to a high rank despite the fact she was a woman in a male-dominated organization.

Beck spoke without breaking eye contact, without hesitation, and without guile. He started with a question that further set the context.

"What do I know? I know one man was brutally murdered with a knife."

Brennan interrupted immediately.

"How do you know that?"

Beck answered quickly. "From the amount of blood I saw on the rocks near the pier." He continued without hesitating. "Another victim was incapacitated, taken into the Red Hook grain terminal, and burned alive."

"We haven't confirmed he was burned alive."

"He was." Before Brennan could ask how he knew, Beck said, "I'll explain how I know in a minute."

Brennan bristled. This guy was telling her to wait. To keep quiet.

Beck watched her carefully. She gave him a tight nod. He told himself to be careful. The redhead had a temper.

"Okay, two dead. One missing. Manny Guzman. And lastly, an attempt to burn down my building using gasoline. Perhaps the same thing he used to kill the man at the grain terminal. I don't know his name other than Ramon. The man on the pier knifed to death was Eduardo. Don't know his last name, either."

Brennan interrupted, taking the opportunity to let Beck know she knew something he didn't.

"His last name is Escobar. Ramon Escobar. We've identified the other victim. Eduardo Ramirez. Both lived in Red Hook."

"Okay, thanks. What else do I know? I know Manny Guzman was abducted. I believe he is still alive."

"Why?"

"I'll explain that in a minute, too. A couple more things first. Escobar was burned alive. I haven't seen the body of Ramirez, but my gut tells me that murder fits the pattern of the kind of knife attack you see in prison."

"Why?"

"Like I said, by the amount of blood I saw on the rocks. And I could also see blood at the end of the pier from twenty yards away. That tells me there were multiple wounds. And the victim moved around, fighting back, bleeding over a large area. That's the pattern you see in prison — a sudden attack inflicting as many wounds possible in the shortest amount of time. Non-stop stabbing until the COs stop it.

"The burning in the grain terminal also feels like a prison-style method – throwing flammable substances on enemies and lighting them up. Granted, immolating an entire body is extreme, but it fits a pattern."

"So, you're saying what?"

"I believe there were probably two men involved in the murders. Both ex-convicts."

"Based on the methods used."

"And the amount of damage inflicted."

"And you're familiar with those methods because?"

"Of my time in prison." Beck didn't give Brennan time to pursue that fact he'd admitted being in prison. He quickly said, "And one other thing."

"What?"

"Manny Guzman is getting a bit older, early sixties, and maybe a bit slower. But one man couldn't have done all that damage, taken out three guys, transported two bodies before Manny would have killed or at least wounded one of his attackers."

"How?"

"Take my word for it."

"And how do you know Ramon Escobar was burned alive, and Emmanuel Guzman is still alive?"

Beck said, "Let me ask you one question before I explain."

"Which is?"

"Do you have any leads, any suspects, any idea who is behind the murders, the kidnapping of Manny Guzman, and setting my property on fire?"

Brennan shifted in her chair. Beck had maneuvered her into a corner. She wanted to know how he knew what he knew. He claimed to have evidence but hadn't yet provided it. If she refused to tell him the true status of their case, that they had no leads, it might eliminate any incentive to share his evidence with her. Assuming he really had evidence. Her gut told her he did.

She thought about avoiding answering Beck with some bullshit about not being at liberty to divulge anything to a civilian but rejected the idea. The result would be the same. Beck would shut down. Then what? Arrest him until he revealed what he knew? He'd lawyer up and refuse to say a word. She also realized that what Grimaldi had told her about Beck also applied to her. She, too, had no time to waste. She couldn't wait for any information that might help her investigation.

James Beck was clearly different from typical ex-cons who would lie and make promises they never intended to keep because they couldn't help themselves. She didn't think Beck had lied. And she didn't believe he was dumb enough to promise evidence he didn't have. But she had to take back control of this meeting. Now.

Brennan leaned across the table toward Beck.

"In terms of where we are with this case, Mr. Beck, let me make it clear to you that there is no other law enforcement entity on this planet with more resources and capabilities than the NYPD. Don't underestimate us, or me.

"As far as your question, you already know the answer. We don't have a suspect. We would have to be incredibly lucky to have a suspect at this point. And frankly, unless you explain to me how it is that you know so much about how the victims died, *you* are emerging as a logical suspect."

Beck's opinion of Brennan diminished. She had started out being honest and then resorted to the usual – threaten him with arrest on a bullshit charge. He hid his anger and disappointment. He remained silent and unmoving.

Brennan said, "And let me be clear. If we did have a better suspect, we would be out there pursuing that suspect instead of talking to you. If you are wise, Mr. Beck, you will help us unleash our resources. If you have anything material to tell me that would help us find the perpetrator, now is the time."

Interesting, thought Beck. She lightened up on the threat and pivoted to the practical. He knew Brennan was right about the resources she had. Maybe he could make something of this. But how to protect himself and his men? Working with a cop was dangerous for anybody, guilty or innocent. Particularly the innocent who were too inexperienced to know that being not guilty had shit to do with anything. Just the process of defending yourself was incredibly dangerous and expensive. For Beck and his crew, an arrest was exponentially worse. An arrest meant a world of trouble and pain, incarceration, and the possibility of injury and death for men with their records.

Beck looked carefully at Brennan, calculating where her loyalties lay. Young. Good looking. A woman. Her first loyalty had to be to herself. Otherwise, she'd never have gotten this far in such a large and competitive organization dominated by men. After that, her loyalty would be to her boss. The top guy. Warren Roth was her ticket to where she wanted to go. And after Roth, maybe her detectives. She needed them. Everybody else could go fuck themselves. Beck had no illusions that she would have any loyalty to him or even interest in him beyond his usefulness.

Beck made his decision. He reached for his cell phone. Grimaldi and Metuchen both sat up.

Beck said. "I need my cell phone to show the inspector something."

He pulled out his phone from his front pants pocket and placed it on the table. Beck looked at Metuchen and Grimaldi and then back at Brennan.

Beck said, "In terms of knowing Ramon Escobar was burned alive, this will explain that."

Beck cued up the video and slid the phone over to Brennan. Grimaldi and Metuchen moved closer to her. She positioned it on the table so they could see the phone's screen and set the video in motion. Beck ignored the detectives and watched Brennan. Her expression grew darker with each second she watched a man burning to death.

She pushed the phone back to Beck without comment.

"I presume you don't know who sent you that."

"I have no idea."

"I'd like to turn that over to our tech people."

"Hold on. In terms of knowing that Manny Guzman was abducted and believing he's still alive, as of three hours ago – I have another video."

Brennan's eyes narrowed.

He cued up the video of Manny's arm next to the pig shank and hoof.

"I got this at four twenty-two this afternoon. I can verify the arm belongs to Manny Guzman by the tattoos." He hesitated and then said, "Just, well, prepare yourself."

Again, Brennan watched the video on Beck's phone. This time, her brows furrowed, and she squinted at the images. Again, Beck closely observed her reaction.

"That's horrifying. I'm sorry about your friend. Why were these videos sent to you? What do they want?"

"I don't know. I haven't taken the bait. But I'm thinking I have to respond to whoever sent this, even if it means giving them the upper hand."

Brennan said, "I agree."

Beck took his phone back from Brennan. Without any discussion, before Brennan could stop him, he typed a short text and sent it.

"What did you say?"

Beck held the screen to Brennan. The text said:

What do you want?

Brennan said, "I hope he answers. And I'll need that phone."

Beck sent the text. He glanced at her detectives and then back to Brennan. Now for his next move. He said, "Maybe we should talk about this privately."

Beck knew if she agreed, this might work.

Brennan hesitated. Agreeing would insult her detectives. But Beck probably had a reason for excluding them. She decided to agree now and smooth it over later.

She nodded to Grimaldi and Metuchen that they should leave. As soon as the door closed, she said to Beck, "What do you want to tell me that you can't tell them?"

"Nothing. You're going to tell them anyhow. Or not. I just wanted to make it simpler."

"What do you mean by simpler?"

Beck said, "I don't like cops. Cops have never done anything for me but cause me pain and suffering. Cops have lied to send me to prison. Withheld evidence. Made sure I suffered eight years of hell. The fewer cops, the better, okay?"

"Does that dislike include me?"

"Why shouldn't it? I don't want to be here. Every fucking second I spend talking to you means I can't be out there looking for my friend. Now, can we finish this? And when I tell you what I know, will you let me out of here? Yes or no. If we can't agree to that, you might as well arrest me now."

"You trust me to keep my word if I say I won't arrest you?"

"I'll take the chance. If I tell you the rest of it, will you let me go?"

Brennan hesitated. She'd never felt this controlled by a criminal suspect. But so far, Beck had been forthcoming and provided her with valuable evidence.

"On two conditions. I get the phone, and you understand that letting you go doesn't mean I will condone or overlook any vigilante bullshit on your part. You find this monster; you promise to call me and turn him over to me."

139

Brennan wrote down her personal cell phone number and email on her business card and slid it across the table to Beck.

Beck left it on the conference table.

"First, I'm not giving you my phone. I guess you could call your two detectives back and try to take it from me, but I suggest you get more than those two. I need the phone in case this fucking maniac contacts me. He wants something. I'm his target. I need to be able to hear from him. You want the videos, tell me how to get on your Wi-Fi and I'll send them to you, or somewhere you can download them. I'll forward you all the texts, too."

Brennan thought for a moment. "We can get you another phone with the same number. Our tech guys might be able to find the source of that number."

"Having the phone won't get them anything that isn't on the videos and texts. Trust me. And I can't waste time waiting for another phone. I'm a minute from getting up and leaving right now, Inspector."

"All right. Send me the videos and texts. You can keep the phone if you agree that you won't try to kill whoever is behind this."

"Agreed," said Beck. "But if I have to defend myself, I will. And I'll take the consequences."

"Fair enough."

Brennan felt that the deal she made with Beck had compromised her. But so what. She needed what he had. She took back Beck's phone and logged him in on the One PP public Wi-Fi. Then she logged into her personal Dropbox account, waited for the code to confirm Beck's phone was allowed access, and started uploading Beck's video files.

Once the videos transferred, she handed Beck his phone, slid her business card to him, and said, "Send me the text files. I presume you don't want me scrolling through all your texts."

"Thanks."

As soon as Beck finished forwarding the texts, he pocketed his phone, sat back, and thought over what he wanted to do next. He knew Brennan was right about the NYPD resources. And he knew he wanted them working to find Manny. He thought carefully about his next move.

He hadn't yet picked up Brennan's card with her cell number written on it.

Brennan said, "Now what?"

Before Beck could respond, his phone vibrated and pinged. Another text had come in.

32

Ciro Baldassare drove over the Verrazano Bridge as fast as the traffic would allow. He'd already gotten in touch with Joey B, one of the few mob-affiliated men he trusted. Joey B's loyalty to Ciro was unwavering. He was Ciro's youngest cousin. Ciro had vouched for him and made it possible for Joey B to be part of a Bonanno crew. Once Ciro had decided to trust him, Joey did nothing to lose that trust.

Like many of his generation, Joey B seemed to be able to simultaneously text, talk, watch a ball game, and cruise the internet. But put him in a situation that involved violence, his attention narrowed down to a singular focus, and he became a formidable force. Joey B's surname was Baldassare. But the B in Joey B didn't stand for Baldassare. It stood for Big.

Joey had been addicted to weightlifting and the performance-enhancing drugs that went along with it since high school. Joey stood only five-six, but he was almost as wide as he was tall, and pound for pound stronger than any man Ciro knew.

Ciro had set up the meet at a pub on Hyatt Street near the St. George Terminal. He picked the location because he knew Beck wanted to meet him in Staten Island. If Beck took the ferry over or drove over on the Verrazano, Hyatt Street was close.

As Ciro turned the corner onto Hyatt, a red Honda pulled out of a parking spot. He quickly grabbed the space, didn't bother to pay the parking meter, and headed into the bar.

The bar room was long and narrow, with dark wood and brick walls painted a color that reminded Ciro of dried blood.

A handful of regulars sat at the bar. Joey B stood at the far end, talking on his cell phone, and watching a well-endowed bartender wearing jeans and a low-cut black t-shirt pour Black Sambuca into a brandy snifter placed next to his cup of expresso. Joey wore a white t-shirt, Puma tracksuit, high-top Nike basketball shoes, and a moderate amount of bling – one gold chain around his twenty-inch neck, a gold bracelet on one wrist, and a gold Versace Sport Tech watch on the other. His 4XL black Italian Metisse suede shirt hung on the barstool next to him.

Ciro nodded to the barmaid and pointed to the Sambuca and expresso, indicating he wanted the same.

Joey B ended his call as Ciro approached. The look on Ciro's face made Joey tip his head back and stare at his cousin.

Ciro responded with pursed lips and a tight shake of his head. "We got trouble, J. Some stronzo maniac snatched Manny."

"What? No."

"Yeah." Ciro sat on the barstool next to his cousin so they would be at the same height. "Lemme fill you in."

He leaned toward Joey B and spoke in low tones. The barmaid, Milly, served him and made herself scarce. She didn't want to be anywhere near their conversation.

33

Beck sat, staring at his phone.

Brennan said, "What? What does it say?"

Beck held the phone up and leaned across the conference table so Brennan could see the text. She stood and leaned toward him. An unexpected feeling of intimacy passed as the distance between them closed. Confusion clouded Brennan's expression. Beck had texted:

What do you want?

Brennan read the answer to Beck's text. "Everything." She stood back, "What the hell does that mean?"

"It means he's crazy.

"What are you going to text back?"

"Nothing. There's nothing to say to that."

"So, what are you going to do?"

Beck stood. "I'm going to find him. What are you going to do?"

Beck began to make his way around the conference table.

"Stop."

"Why?"

Brennan said, "Don't play me for a fool, Beck. You're not just going to try to find him. You're going to find him and kill him."

Beck tried to keep his voice low, but he failed.

"Then you find him first, so I don't have to." Beck immediately lowered his voice. "Listen, keeping me here or locking me up won't do either of us any good. I've found out more in the last few hours than your entire fucking police force."

"Then it sounds like you haven't told me everything."

Beck sat down.

"All right, this is the rest of what I have."

He quickly related what he had learned from Catherine Hodge. And then he said, "You should have gotten that information before I did. You should already have a sketch of him and a hundred cops on the street trying to find if anyone has seen him."

Brennan held up a hand and forced herself to be calm.

"Please. Calm down. You're right. We should have done all that, and we should have people checking prison records with the DOC to identify him. And more. Which we will, I promise you. But understand, I'm not in charge of this investigation. The commissioner is personally taking charge of this case. He's calling together the entire command staff in less than two hours."

"And until then?"

"I keep doing what I'm doing. And when the commissioner takes charge, this case will be the number one priority for everybody in this department."

Beck said, "So what's your part in all this?"

"To move fast. Without the inertia that's inevitable with a massive organization like the NYPD holding me back. To be the eyes and ears of the commissioner so he can direct the resources of this department."

"And that means coming after me?"

"What do you think? You're the key to this, Mr. Beck." Brennan leaned forward. "Let's drop the bluster and bullshit. The only reason you're out ahead of us is because you're the intended victim. And based on what I know about you at this point, there's a good chance you did something to someone to cause this attack on you and your friend." Brennan leaned back. "I'm not stupid, Mr. Beck. If I let you go, I know damn well you're going to look for whoever is behind this and try to put a bullet in him. If you do, that makes me responsible."

Beck said, "Perhaps. But if you don't let me go, you reduce your chances to find someone who's already committed multiple murders and who's going to commit more horrible crimes until he's stopped, and you'll be responsible for that."

Brennan nodded. "So what do I do?"

Beck looked at Brennan, trying to see past her defensiveness and find the character in her. Finally, he said, "You have two choices. First choice – lock me up. In forty-eight hours max, my lawyer gets me out. Maybe by then, the NYPD will have found the maniac who's stabbing and burning human beings. But I doubt it. Then I'll be out there, and you'll have zero control over what I do.

"Is arresting me now the safe move? Probably. I presume you'll get credit for bringing what I told you to the commissioner. Will that be enough to keep your job? Maybe. But for how long? Manny Guzman will almost certainly be dead. Who knows how many others? What happens if it all goes to shit? What happens if you never get the guy?"

"And choice number two?"

"We work together. There are things I can do that you can't. Connections I have that you don't. And, I agree, your side can do things I can't."

Brennan didn't respond. Beck watched her intriguing green eyes shift as she thought it through. He forced himself to keep quiet until she spoke.

"Letting you go, Beck, guarantees I'm on a shit list. Even if you agree to share everything you find with me. Even if you agree not to kill whoever is behind all this."

"Why?"

"You killed a cop, Beck. You know how many people in the NYPD want you to go down? There's no getting around that."

Beck leaned forward. "I'm not going to even bother trying to convince you of anything about me killing that cop. Go read the trial record. And the appeal. Or don't. I don't give a shit. Just don't bullshit me that what other cops think about me is going to stop you. There's only one person you have to worry about, Brennan. Your boss. The commissioner of police. You go in and tell him you made a decision. Tell him you let me go so that I could be the bait for this bastard. Tell Roth he can't fucking lose. If the bad guy kills me, then the cop-killer gets what's coming to him. If I kill the bad guy, you arrest me, and the NYPD gets another chance to send the cop-killer to prison. Either way, Roth wins. If Roth wins, you win. Decide now, Brennan, or call in your detectives and lock me up. I'll still do what I have to do."

34

The prospect of seeing the spic's arm on fire sent a quiver of antic-ipation through Monster-Boy. He carefully poured his mixture of gasoline and Styrofoam on Manny Guzman's bare left arm from the crook of Manny's elbow down to his wrist, at times using his forefinger to spread the viscous liquid. He glanced back at the Worm to check that he had the camera set up to begin shooting.

Manny Guzman shifted slightly, readying himself in his chair. While he had been alone, he had managed to free his handcuffed right arm, which had also been duct-taped to the right arm of the chair. He'd turned his arm clockwise and counterclockwise, back and forth, weakening and stretching the duct tape, then he leveraged his forearm up and down, up and down, clock-wise, counterclockwise. It had caused him considerable pain, but Manny enjoyed the feeling. He'd kept at it until the tape split, and he was able to free his right arm from the chair. His wrist was still handcuffed to the chain bolted to the garage floor, but he was confident the chain was long enough so he could execute his plan.

Then he had used the thumbnail and fingers on his right hand to tear at the duct tape binding his left arm to the arm of the chair. His goal was not to escape. He couldn't see any way to do that. But he knew the monster intended to set his arm on fire. Manny's goal was to use his burning left arm as a weapon. He'd grab the freak around the neck with his flaming left arm, lock it into a chokehold with his right arm, and hold onto him no matter what, hold on until he had burned through the freak's throat or strangled him to death. He was confident he'd have enough slack in the chain to get his right arm behind the monster's head. It would mean holding on to his right biceps with a burning left hand, but so be it.

After Manny split the duct tape binding his left arm, he pressed the tape back onto the arm of the chair, trying to make sure it looked as if the tape was still intact. Then he did the same to the tape on his right wrist, using his mouth and chin. He knew the torn tape wouldn't pass close inspection, but he didn't expect there to be one. He expected the monster to be too busy torturing him.

Keep pouring it on. That's right, more. Go on, more, as much as you want, you sick fuck. The more you pour on, the more you'll burn.

Monster-Boy finished covering Manny's arm and looked around for his long-neck lighter. Just as he picked up the lighter, his phone signaled that a text had come in.

No, Manny thought. *No, no. Don't stop. Not now!*

35

Ciro stood outside the pub on Hyatt Street, leaning against his all-white Chrysler 300. Demarco Jones had called him forty-five minutes earlier, telling him that he and James were on the way to meet him. Demarco had picked up Beck two blocks from One Police Plaza seven minutes after Dianne Brennan had decided to let him go.

Ciro was about to check on their whereabouts when Beck's Mercury Marauder slid to a stop in front of him. He climbed into the back seat of the Mercury.

"Hello, boys. Nice to see you, D. And you, James. Can't believe you got bailed out already."

"I used my Get Out of Jail Free card."

"No shit. What's happened?"

"Tweedledum and Tweedledee took me to their boss at One Police Plaza. She's a deputy inspector. They're on some sort of special squad. We went around and around until she saw it my way."

"You said she?"

"Yeah. A surprisingly young and attractive woman. Irish redhead, if you can believe it. Name is Brennan. We're working together."

"Fuck no."

"Fuck yes. No way around it. It was either that or sit in a holding cell waiting a couple of days to get arraigned. Assuming they'd let me post bail."

"Arraigned for what?"

"For killing Manny's fishing buddies. I'm their prime suspect."

"What kinda bullshit is that?"

"The usual kind. What happened with you? Did you meet with Joey B?"

"Yeah. He left to make a collection. He's available if we need him. He put me on track with the right guy. I got a meet set up. We can head over there now."

"Good. Where's there?"

"Todt Hill."

Beck said, "Let's leave your car here. Give Demarco the address. I'll fill you in on what happened with Ms. Deputy Inspector while we drive."

Demarco entered the address in his GPS.

Ciro said, "Bad luck with those two cops."

"No shit. You think that dapper little detective would've pulled on you?"

"If he had, I'd have shot him dead. My days of serving time are over, partner."

Beck nodded, saying nothing. There was nothing to say. He knew Ciro Baldassare had long ago determined he'd shoot it out with the cops before he'd go back to prison.

Demarco put the Mercury into drive and headed for Todt Hill.

Ciro said, "So what happened?"

Beck had already told Demarco on the drive over from Manhattan about his meeting with Dianne Brennan. He summarized it for Ciro. He ended by saying, "I know both of you aren't in favor of me making a deal with her. If you want to step left of this, I understand."

Ciro said, "I ain't stepping anywhere. Not until we find the son of a bitch who's got Manny and empty our fucking guns into him and make sure what's left of him disappears. I don't give a shit what deal you had to make, James. You did what you had to do. The cops get in our way, we'll deal with it and cover our tracks. There's no way this back-stabbing, burning, kidnapping cocksucker lives."

Beck didn't try to calm Ciro down. He knew it was useless. The big man had stepped over whatever boundaries usually kept him in check.

"Agreed. Last thing, I got another text."

Demarco asked, "Another video?"

"No. It was an answer to a text I sent when I left police headquarters. I decided I'd better respond to the asshole before he lit Manny's arm on fire. I texted him and asked what he wanted."

"And?"

"He texted back – everything."

Ciro said, "Everything. Fuck does that mean?"

"Means he's crazy."

"Did you text him back?"

"No."

"Good. Fuck him."

Beck said, "And whoever else is working with him. One guy didn't pull all this. We have to find Manny and everybody behind this mess. So who are we meeting with?"

"Woman named Marie Rizzo."

"And she is?"

"Widow of an old-timer. The grandmother of the person we want to talk to."

"Grandmother?"

"Yeah. Her grandson is Lyle Rizzo. According to Joey B, Lyle is the guy who supplies the guys who supply the drugs to the juicers in the area. We got no doubt this guy is a juicer. So, if the Bolos are right about the computer feed ending up on the island, it's a good possibility this shitbag is buying his drugs here. Rizzo ought to be able to lead us to him."

Beck asked, "Good. Just curious, why is this drug dealer living with his grandmother?"

"Family problems."

Demarco asked, "Like what?"

Ciro made a face. "You know. Things that happen."

"Things like somebody went missing?"

"Yeah. The father. He went missing. Like forever. The mother is in Florida or something. The family house got sold to pay off various people, so our boy is bunking with grandma. Anyhow, Joey reached out to him. He left a message. If he ain't home when we get there, we'll have Nonna Marie call her little polpetto and tell him to get his ass home."

Demarco said, "So I'll come in, too, right?" He watched Ciro in the rearview mirror and got an exasperated look from him.

Ciro said, "You gotta make a thing of it?"

"I'm just asking."

"No you ain't. You're making a point."

Demarco said, "What's that?"

"That a fucking old lady mob widow don't want no black guys in her house."

Demarco said, "Really? You sure?" Ciro gave Demarco the finger. "Okay. Guess I'll stay in the car and keep an eye out."

Ciro said, "For what?"

"Make sure no black folks are sneaking around the neighborhood where the white mobsters live."

"Ha, ha."

Beck said, "While you're on the lookout, check in with Ricky and Alex. See if they came up with anything new. By the way, you hear anything more from the Bronx?"

"Nothing that might explain who's after us. I'll keep on top of Alex and the Bolos."

"Good."

Ten minutes later, Demarco pulled up in front of a 4,000 square-foot English Tudor on Keune Avenue. The neighborhood was heavily wooded, dark, and quiet. Lights were shining both upstairs and downstairs in Marie Rizzo's house. Before Demarco turned off the car engine, they heard a dog barking inside. A big dog.

Demarco said, "If she sics the dog on me, I'm gonna shoot it."

Ciro said, "Take it easy. All the old Italian ladies have dogs. It's probably a decrepit mutt with one of those wheelie things attached to its ass."

"I'll still shoot it."

Beck and Ciro exited the Mercury and approached the front door. The temperature had dropped. Beck wished he had a coat. Anxious to get inside, he hurried to the front door imagining a squat, annoyed Italian grandmother in a floral print housecoat and slippers. The door opened, revealing a tall woman doing her best to look desirable. She wore a pink, Juicy Couture velour tracksuit with a zip front hoodie and matching drawstring pants. Underneath the jacket, she wore a tight-fitting t-shirt that emphasized her generous bust. She was heavily made-up with platinum blonde hair cascading around her shoulders that Beck figured had to be a wig. Her long fingernails looked like she'd just stepped out of a Korean nail salon.

She yelled at the barking German shepherd standing next to her with the phlegmy voice of a life-long smoker.

"Buddy, quiet! Sit!"

The ferocious dog didn't look like it was anybody's buddy. To Beck's surprise, the dog responded immediately.

Marie Rizzo was commanding, sexual, and working hard to be intimidating.

She looked at Ciro and Beck. Beck saw that his dark jeans, black brogans, and flannel shirt didn't pass muster. He didn't care.

"Take off your shoes, gentlemen."

She turned and gave them space to enter. The dog stayed by her side, standing this time, ears swiveling, eyes boring into Beck and Ciro. The dog emitted a low growl.

"You didn't bring guns into my house, did you?"

Ciro said, "No."

Beck figured Marie Rizzo knew Ciro was lying, but Ciro Baldassare wasn't going to let the woman make all the rules. Taking his shoes off was his limit.

She led them past a living room and a dining area to a den filled with heavy furniture upholstered in leather surrounding a fireplace made of fieldstones. She motioned for them to sit on the couch. She took a chair near the fireplace. The dog dropped down next to her, his eyes and ears trained on Beck.

Beck resented the dog's attention. Ciro was the one with the gun. Maybe the dog sensed he wasn't a mob guy.

"So, what's this all about? People come into my house middle of the night; I'm thinking somebody died."

Beck answered quickly, "Somebody did."

Marie ignored Beck and looked at Ciro. "You, I know. Him, I don't."

"This is a good friend of mine."

Marie glanced at Beck briefly.

"You know, if it wasn't Sally-Boy Lenzo who called me, you two wouldn't have gotten past the front door."

Like hell we wouldn't, thought Beck.

Ciro didn't comment.

Beck recognized the name. Salvatore Lenzo had been the head of a crew that Ciro had come up in when he first became an active member of the Bonanno crime family. As far as Beck knew, Lenzo was retired, but apparently he'd intervened for them with Marie Rizzo.

Marie turned toward Beck, eyeing him. She blamed him for the intrusion. Beck didn't care about that either.

"What's this about somebody dying?"

"More than one somebody. So far two people and a third person abducted. A close friend of mine and Ciro's."

"Why do you think my grandson can help you?"

Beck shifted in his seat. He hadn't come to be grilled by Marie Rizzo. His movement made the dog emit a low warning growl.

Beck looked at the dog and then at Marie Rizzo. She touched the dog on the head and shushed him.

"We think your grandson might know people who have dealings with the person responsible for the problems."

Marie Rizzo shook her head. Her smoker's voice hardened. "I don't want my grandson getting involved in anything that will cause trouble for him."

Ciro said, "That won't happen. We have to talk to Lyle. We need to find this murderer before he hurts our friend. It's better for everyone if we do."

Marie said, "What the hell is that supposed to mean?"

Marie Rizzo's tough-gangster-moll aggravated Beck. It was bad enough the grandson wasn't here when they'd arrived. He was about to respond to her when his phone signaled that he'd received a text. It was from Alex Liebowitz.

R & J grabbed an image of our guy. Sending it to you now.

Marie Rizzo repeated her question. Louder this time.

Whatever patience Beck had left evaporated. Beck raised his voice, which set the dog to growling again.

"It's better for everyone means exactly what it sounds like, particularly you and your grandson. And if that fucking dog keeps growling at me, I'm going to kill it." Beck saw the instant fury his threat caused in Marie Rizzo, but it didn't stop him for even a second. "We're not here to answer your questions. We're here to see your drug-dealing grandson. The one who sells illegal prescription drugs – steroids, growth hormones, whatever garbage juicers shoot into themselves. Your grandson wants to make a business out of that, I don't give a shit. Unfortunately, his business might have connected him to a violent murderer whose crimes have the entire NYPD looking for him. You don't want your grandson, or you, or anybody you know, or anybody who has any connection to you getting involved in that. Not for any reason.

"We are going to find this murderer. And if we're lucky, and you're lucky, we will eliminate every trace of him from the face of the earth before anybody else finds him. You and your grandson will be better off if we do that. We don't have time for your questions. It's stupid, and it's rude. Get your grandson here now, and let us solve this problem for you."

Marie Rizzo glared at Beck. She turned to Ciro. "Your friend has some mouth on him."

Ciro Baldassare returned her look and said, "You want us to go find Lyle?"

Beck's speech and Ciro's cryptic question took the bluff out of Marie Rizzo. She knew what it meant if Ciro Baldassare had to find her grandson. It meant her grandson might not survive the meeting, and, despite her connections to a few of the old-timers, there wouldn't be a damn thing Marie Rizzo could do about it.

The toughness and cheap glamour drained out of Marie Rizzo. She reached into the pocket of her velour jacket and pulled out her cell phone. She made the call, poking in the phone number with the tip of a garish fingernail. She didn't look at Beck or Ciro as she spoke. She didn't want to see them hearing the desperation in her voice as she told her grandson to get home – now.

When she finished the call, Beck said, "When?"

"He's at his girlfriend's house. Ten, fifteen minutes."

Beck looked at his watch for what seemed like the hundredth time that night. Fifteen minutes was an eternity when there was a maniac out there intending to set fire to his friend.

36

At 7:45 p.m. Dianne Brennan entered the office of NYPD Commissioner Warren Roth. She'd been summoned.

Roth sat behind the same sturdy desk Teddy Roosevelt had sat behind 125 years earlier when he was president of the board of the New York City Police Commissioners. The rest of the furniture in the office – breakfront, cadenza, bookshelves – was also ornate and imposing. And there was still room in the office for a place where guests could be photographed with the commissioner in front of floor-to-ceiling drapes flanked by eight-foot-high flags on poles – the American flag on one side, the State of New York flag on the other.

Roth looked like he belonged in the office. He had been a large man all his adult life. In his college days, he had played offensive guard for U Penn. He was a bit smaller than most of the linemen he faced, but Roth was sturdy and strong. Now in his early sixties, he fought every day to keep his weight below 235. The commissioner had just wolfed down a too-rich meal of Garganelli from an Italian restaurant on Ann Street, and most of a torta di ciocccolata for dessert. He knew the meal would add two pounds when he weighed himself in the morning. Two pounds it would take him a week to lose.

The meal, working late, and the two unsolved brutal murders in Brooklyn made Roth's already bad mood worse. Not that you could see it. Warren Roth kept his emotions in check. He spoke quietly and made sure to look decisive even when he wasn't. Warren Roth believed image was the key to running an organization as large and complex as the NYPD.

The commissioner motioned for Brennan to sit in the chair placed next to his desk on his right. Brennan had been around Roth enough to notice the edge of impatience coloring his manner. She glanced at the files on Roth's desk. One manila folder was labeled "James Beck." The other, thicker folder had a numbered code on the cover and a blue seal bearing the words "The Police Department of the City of New York." Brennan knew very few people other than the commissioner would read that file. Brennan decided that whatever was in the thick folder, it included Jeffrey Esposito's case file on Beck.

She sat down and waited for Roth to speak, glad that she had time after her meeting with Beck to prepare for this meeting. She had a legal pad on her lap, a pen in her hand, and a thumb drive in her suit jacket pocket.

Roth got right to the point.

"What did you find out from Beck?"

She pulled a single sheet of paper from between the pages of her legal pad.

"These are bullet points I wrote up after he left."

She handed the sheet to Roth, knowing he disliked being read to or talked at. She waited while he read each point. Roth took his time. When he looked up, Brennan anticipated his first question. She pulled the flash drive from her jacket pocket and handed it to Roth.

"I downloaded the videos Beck showed me. There's nothing else on that drive. I labeled them video one and video two."

Brennan waited to see if Roth was going to view them. He looked at his watch. He had seven minutes before his eight o'clock meeting with various division chiefs and command staff, but Brennan knew Roth wouldn't worry about keeping them waiting.

Roth swiveled to the desktop computer on the credenza behind him and slipped the flash drive into a USB port, clicked his mouse to wake the computer and twenty-seven-inch monitor.

159

He was adept enough to locate the file folder and click on the WMV files.

While Roth waited for the first video to appear onscreen, he asked Brennan, "So your guy Beck is in communication with the person responsible for the murders and abduction."

Brennan chafed at the description of Beck as "your guy" but ignored it.

"We haven't confirmed that whoever texted him those videos is responsible for the murders, but he's our prime suspect, and yes, he's in communication with Beck."

Roth waived off Brennan's overly cautious statement.

"Why'd you let Beck go?"

"Because the alternative didn't gain me anything. If I'd made up some bullshit charge to hold him, it wouldn't have stuck. He would've almost certainly made bail and be out there anyway. This way, I have a chance to keep him as a source of information. I made it clear to him he shouldn't take any action…"

Roth cut her off. "Don't even say it. Any warnings you gave Beck mean nothing. He's going to do what he's going to do. And I don't want it to blow back on the department. And do you really think he'll keep giving you information?"

The first video of Eduardo Ramirez being burned alive in the dungeon-like grain terminal came on-screen before Brennan had to answer. The horror of seeing a human being writhing and dying an unimaginably painful death quickly changed the mood in the commissioner's office. The image blown up on a larger screen made it even more shocking than it was on Beck's cell phone. Brennan doubted that death and depravity had ever entered the NYPD commissioner's office with such a horrible impact.

Roth remained silent as the second, longer video played, showing the grotesque pig's hoof and shank set on fire next to a human hand and forearm. The repulsive silent threat conveyed by the grisly video made Roth turn off the computer screen as soon as the video ended.

He turned back to his desk, exhaled, grimaced. He muttered, "What the hell are we dealing with here?" Brennan had no answer. "So, your conclusion is that the sick bastard behind this is after Beck, using Beck's friend as leverage, the arson attack, whatever other threats he can come up with."

"Yes."

"Why, we don't know."

"No, sir."

"And it's not clear what he wants."

"Agreed. Basically, I guess he wants to destroy James Beck."

"You think Beck knows why this is happening?"

"No. And he claims he doesn't know anybody who matches the description he got from his witness."

"Or so he says."

"I believe him."

Roth asked, "Why?"

Brennan shrugged. "My gut. He didn't look like he was lying."

"Ex-cons are good liars."

Brennan said, "If Beck was lying, he's extremely good at it."

Roth leaned back in his executive chair. "So, what are you doing now?"

Brennan sat up straighter.

"I've got Grimaldi and Metuchen back in Beck's neighborhood trying to find the woman at the event's business to confirm Beck's story. And if she does, I told them to get her in front of a sketch artist."

"Those drawings can be hit and miss."

"I know. I'll try to get Stein on it if it comes to that."

Roth nodded. "So you've got Grimaldi and Metuchen interviewing Beck's witness. What else?"

"I told Grimaldi and Metuchen to see if there are any CCTV images from security cameras in the area that would help our investigation. I presume you'll want to get TARU on that, too. Although, from the short time I was in there, I didn't see too many businesses around those crime scenes. Particularly near that grain terminal."

Roth nodded.

Brennan didn't know if Roth's nod meant he would deploy the forces she suggested or not. She had no command authority beyond her small crew of detectives. And even that authority was limited. Ultimately, all detectives were under the supervision of the Chief of Detectives. Anything she wanted in terms of NYPD resources like the Technical Assistance Response Unit (TARU) or manpower to canvas the neighborhood with sketches of the suspect had to come through Roth.

Brennan continued. "I've got Nina and William Jablonsky running through DOC files to find anybody paroled or released in the last six months from state prisons. Phil Harris is helping them."

"Anything else?"

"I talked to the tech guys downstairs about analyzing Beck's videos and texts to see if they can use the information to find who sent the texts."

"Don't they need his phone for that?"

"No. The tech guy told me he didn't need Beck's phone. Whatever they need is embedded in the files. They said even if they had the phone, it wouldn't matter. They didn't sound confident they could find the sender. I let Beck keep his phone so he can stay in touch with whoever is texting him."

Roth was looking at Brennan, but she could tell he wasn't listening carefully.

"You honestly think you'll ever hear from Beck again?"

Brennan knew Roth would come back to this issue. She measured her words carefully, anticipating where her answers would lead.

"I think that it depends on two things."

Roth nodded as if saying – go ahead.

"If I feed him information that helps him."

Roth nodded again.

"Or, if he gets into a situation where he needs our resources."

"To do what?"

"For now, to rescue his friend."

Roth said, "And you think that's all he wants to do?"

"No. I think Beck wants to find out what the hell is going on and kill whoever is doing this to him."

"So how are you going to stop him? How are we going to stop this goddamn cop killer, who already set this department up once to do his dirty work?"

There it was. A rare flash of Roth's anger that showed his true position on James Beck.

Brennan leaned toward Roth. This was the moment of truth.

"I'm not going to stop him."

"What do you mean?"

"Beck is most likely always going to be ahead of us. He's the one the killer wants. He's the target. The videos prove that. I want to be able to use that to our advantage. I'll be able to keep track of Beck because he'll want to know what I'm doing and maybe even ask for my help."

Roth said, "I don't want that bastard setting up the department to do his dirty work again."

Brennan realized Roth had already read the Esposito file.

"That won't happen. One of two things will. The suspect will kill Beck. That could let us find the murderer and solve this case. And Beck's death will eliminate a thorn in the department's side. Or, Beck will find the doer and kill him. That closes the case for us, and the department will have another chance to send Beck back to prison for murder. I agree that working with Beck creates risk. But it seems to me, it's worth the risk."

Brennan paused. She watched Roth take in what she had said. She wasn't sure she had convinced him. She decided to play one more card.

"Your mandate to me is clear, Commissioner. You want me out there getting the information you need to do your job. That means I bring you everything I find out, however I find it. That's what I've done. My guys managed to find Beck and bring him in. The fact is, the information he's already provided has advanced this case. We have a description of a prime suspect and a line of investigation." Brennan paused. She knew she had to be careful with what she said next. "So far, Beck has provided us more than anybody else on the force has come up with. I don't think we should lose that resource." Brennan sat back. She had made her pitch. "So, now you know everything I know, sir. Whatever you want me to do from this point on is obviously your call."

Roth nodded and checked his watch.

"I'm late for my meeting."

Brennan knew the answer to her first and only question would show Roth's hand.

She said, "Do you want me to be in the meeting?"

Brennan knew most of the personnel who would be in the meeting. Roth would call in his old-line palace guard: First Deputy Commissioner Michael Stone and Deputy Commissioner of Operations Kevin Cavanaugh. Once he'd invited those two, all the chiefs who feared they might be missing something significant would try to get into the meeting.

She figured the executive officer of the Patrol Services Bureau would be there, looking annoyed because he had no idea what was going on. Also, the executive officer of the detective bureau would attend to cover for the chief of detectives, who wouldn't participate in the gangbang unless Roth specifically asked him but would want his man there to make sure nothing got by him. And, of course, Fernandez from the Seven-Six would be there. Beyond that, Brennan would eventually find out from her assistant Nina Solowitz who attended the meeting. Nina was helping prepare for it right now.

This was the moment of truth. If Roth told her to attend, she was done. He'd tell her to present her findings to the big boys, and that would be that. Part of her wanted that to happen. She would have done her job to add value and then slipped out of harm's way. That would be the safest course for her.

But part of her wanted to run with what she had. To prove herself. And show every one of those sanctimonious old boys she could produce as well as any of them.

But there was another reason Brennan wanted to stay the course. She had made the decision to release Beck without first asking Roth. She had done a good job of justifying her decision. But if things went bad with James Beck, her justification would be worthless. She knew the old white men running the department would jump at the chance to blame her. Use it as a reason to advocate for getting rid of her. The only way to prevent that would be to stay in the investigation and ride herd on James Beck.

And, frankly, James Beck intrigued her. She did believe that he did not know the identity of his enemy. But she also believed that Beck hadn't told her everything. There was more to get out of James Beck. More that could help her.

The decision was up to Warren Roth. She saw the wheels turning in his head. She figured he'd seen the wheels turning in hers, too.

Finally, Roth said, "No. You don't need to be in that scrum. Follow up on what you've started." He pointed a large finger at her. "But Dianne, you keep a tight rein on Beck. This kind of thing can go south very easily. Beck has got all kinds of baggage. Whether it was self-defense or an accident or intentional, he killed a cop. And he's also connected to a bloodbath in Brooklyn that injured cops. So let's be clear, Inspector. You've got a good thing here. You deserve it. And you're doing good work for this office. But if this goes down, you go with it. That's not a threat. That's just the way it is. Are we clear?"

Roth hadn't told her anything she didn't already know. She also knew she was taking an enormous risk. It didn't matter. There was no turning back.

Dianne Brennan looked directly at Warren Roth and said, "Yes, sir. It's clear."

37

Lyle Rizzo walked into his grandmother's den, car and house keys in hand, with an attitude and two wannabee tough guys. His crew.

He glanced at Beck and Ciro as if they didn't matter and asked his grandmother, "What's going on?"

Marie Rizzo had sense enough not to answer or add to her grandson's mistakes.

Ciro watched Lyle Rizzo and his friends, waiting to see if they were stupid enough to say something to him. Beck knew that one word, any word, would unleash a violent reaction none of them were prepared to face. For a moment, Beck hoped the assholes would mouth off. He needed a release for his anger and frustration.

Nobody spoke.

Ciro said to Lyle Rizzo, "Tell them to leave."

To save face, Lyle Rizzo remained silent. Before it ignited Ciro Baldassare, Marie Rizzo intervened. "You two, leave. Now."

The two didn't hesitate or ask Lyle if he wanted them to stay. The most one of his friends could do was say, "I'll talk to you later, L," as he hurried out of the room in his stockinged feet.

Ciro and Beck waited until they heard the front door close.

Ciro held back from slapping Lyle Rizzo and nodded toward the living room. Now that he didn't need to look tough in front of his friends, Lyle kept his mouth shut and led the way.

Lyle Rizzo looked much like Beck had expected. Except for the glass eye. His left eye was almost an exact color match to the right, but it didn't move in the socket. Lyle was five-feet-six, overcompensating for his short stature with about thirty pounds of extra muscle, mostly in his chest and arms. He wore tight, dark jeans and an untucked, fitted maroon shirt unbuttoned enough to reveal a massive gold chain on a hairless bronze chest.

They followed Lyle into an oddly furnished living room. There were four large ornate wooden chairs upholstered in a dense red fabric around a glass coffee table. Nothing else.

Ciro pointed to one of the chairs.

Rizzo sat.

Ciro and Beck remained standing.

Ciro said, "You know who I am?"

"Not really."

"Good. You'll want to keep it that way. I'll say it once. Do not fuck with me." Ciro nodded toward Beck. "Or him. Definitely not him. Listen carefully to what he has to say."

Beck didn't bother to introduce himself. He waited for a moment until he had Lyle Rizzo's full attention.

"Every word you hear from us doesn't leave this room. Understood?"

Lyle looked up at Ciro and back to Beck.

"All right."

Beck continued, "We're looking for someone who killed two people in a way that has attracted too much attention from the NYPD. He's holding a friend of ours hostage."

"What's it got to do with me?"

Ciro said, "Say another word, and I'll knock your other eye out of your fucking skull. Shut up and listen."

Beck pulled out his cell phone and showed Lyle the image from Ricky Bolo. The picture was grainy, taken from a distance, showing their enemy from above, his face slightly turned away from the camera. The image matched the description given by Catherine Hodge. Big, bald, white shirt. A juicer.

"We're looking for this man. We believe he's the killer. We need to find him before the police do."

Lyle leaned forward to look at the picture. Beck watched him carefully for any signs of recognition. He didn't see them.

"We've tracked him to Staten Island. Clearly, he uses what you sell." Rizzo shifted in his chair. He wanted to say something but didn't.

Beck said, "Make sure you understand that if you sold some shit to a guy who sold it to another guy who sold it to this motherfucker, you..."

Ciro cut in. "Are dead. Any connection to this guy, any connection, is a death sentence. Our people won't put up with it."

Beck said, "Unless you help us take care of this problem."

Rizzo said, "Can I talk now?"

Ciro nodded.

Lyle reached out for Beck's phone.

"Lemme look at that again for a second."

The picture was a full shot from head to toe. Beck watched Lyle expand the photo so he could see the face and chest. He looked back at Beck and Ciro once more.

"Okay. First off, this photo is shit. But even so, he's gotta be using to get that big."

Beck asked, "Assume he's buying on Staten Island. How do we find him?"

"Listen, I don't have any contact with the buyers. And I don't deal with a lot of sellers. Three guys total, mostly two guys. Between my two main dealers, we got sixty, seventy percent of the market on the island covered. My third guy takes care of, say, another ten percent. He actually has a cousin who helps him, but I don't even know his name."

Beck interrupted. "I don't give a shit about any of that. How do we find this guy?"

"I know, but you gotta understand, we don't supply everybody. We sell to basically three kinds of users. One of my dealers supplies the dudes I put in the category of guys who need to get strong..."

Beck interrupted again. He held up his phone. "Which one of your guys supplies freaks like this?"

"I can't guarantee it. Like I said, we don't cover the whole market. That guy could be buying his shit from other people."

Ciro said, "Give us a name."

"All right, all right. From that picture, even though it's crap, that dude looks like he's on a complicated regimen. If he's buying from my people, he's dealing with my guy who covers the hardcore juicers. That would be Brian Bozek. Nickname is Genghis Khan."

Ciro said, "Genghis Khan?"

"Yeah. He has a look. It's good for business."

Beck said, "What look is that?"

"He's big, bulked up, bald except for a pigtail in the back. Fu Manchu mustache in front."

Beck shook his head. "So this idiot has a Fu Manchu mustache but calls himself Genghis Khan?"

Lyle shrugged. "He likes that name better."

"Where do we find him?"

Lyle looked at his watch.

"This time of day, I assume he's home. It's as good a place to start as any."

"Address," said Ciro.

Lyle recited an address.

"A house?"

"Yeah."

Beck asked, "He live alone?"

"Nah. He's got a girlfriend. If he's not home, she'd know better than me where to find him."

Ciro said, "Don't call Genghis whatever the fuck and tell him we're coming. Don't call anybody. Don't tell anybody anything. Not even grandma."

"She don't want to know."

"What's your phone number?"

170

Lyle made a face but recited the number. Beck entered it into his contacts.

Ciro said, "Don't leave town. Stay home with grandma. If I need to find you, I don't want to have to look for you."

Rizzo said, "You fucking serious? How long?"

"Until I tell you. And don't ever bring two stronzos like that to a fucking meet with me. It don't work that way. Do I have to worry about those two assholes getting into my business?"

"No. They're cool."

"Do I have to worry about you fucking skipping off and being somewhere I can't find you?"

"No."

Ciro said, "I hope not. I don't need the goddamn aggravation of burying bodies right now. Stay here. If we don't find this Fu Manchu asshole, we'll be back."

38

Monster-Boy turned away from Manny and read the text. It wasn't from James Beck. He told Worm, "Turn all that shit off and bring it into the basement. He took his lighter and glass of thickened gasoline and hurried out of the garage.

While the Worm cleared out the garage, Monster-Boy sat at his computer, shutting down the surveillance camera and erased any links to it. He destroyed the smartphone he'd used to text videos to James Beck via a burner phone number.

Now Monster-Boy and Worm sat in the kitchen waiting. Not for a response from Beck. He didn't expect one. Monster-Boy was waiting to execute the next step in his plan to destroy James Beck and everyone connected to him.

Nothing had been done to the kitchen since Monster-Boy's mother, Ruth, had lived there as a child in 1967. Ruth had been a nervous child, prone to sullenness. She had grown to just under six feet tall, a full-figured woman but trim, even though she drank at least half a bottle of inexpensive white wine every night during much of her adult life to settle her *nerves*. Ruth kept her weight in check because she couldn't afford to eat between meals and spent eight hours a day on her feet working in a one-room beauty shop that catered mostly to elderly women who had their hair washed and blow-dried once a week.

Ruth had inherited the house from her parents, Monster-Boy's grandparents, when they died within a year of each other in 1989. Her father from a heart attack, and her mother from a burst femoral artery aneurysm. Inheriting the house turned out to be as much of a burden as a boon. The property taxes and expenses sucked up most of her income. Which was why Ruth grabbed the opportunity to marry as much for a financial lifeline as for love. She was twenty-three. Her husband, Ronald, was ten years her senior. She gave birth to her only child a little over a year later. Her husband died from a heart attack when Monster-Boy was four years old. During those four years, Monster-Boy's father had barely noticed him. Not out of selfishness. Ronald lived somewhere on a spectrum that didn't include the ability to be affectionate or attentive to a child. Ronald did well at his bookkeeper's job but not at much else. His death ended the dark, brooding presence in Monster-Boy's house and made life less difficult for Ruth except financially. Ruth had doted on Monster-Boy while her first husband was alive, and even more so after his death.

Ruth remarried two years later to a man who had a secure job and shared her attachment to alcohol. Ten years later, Monster-Boy's stepfather, Charles Lawrence, died in a work-related accident. The sixteen-year-old boy never had feelings toward his biological father beyond an ever-present sense of unease. Charles Lawrence was more outgoing and generally friendly toward the six-year-old, and, as a result, Monster-Boy became attached to him. Four years after Charles's death, when Monster-Boy was nineteen, Ruth died from complications involving alcoholism, diabetes, and depression. That's when Monster-Boy inherited the small bungalow on a dead-end street in the northwest quadrant of Staten Island. He had not set foot in the house for ten years.

Monster-Boy's mother hadn't had enough time or money to update the house's furnishings, appliances, or fixtures during either marriage. So Monster-Boy sat on the same sturdy wooden chair with his feet on the worn, scarred wooden table he remembered from his youth.

The Worm, of course, had no memory of Monster-Boy's house. The closest he'd ever come to living in a house was a near-derelict, poor-white Alabama sharecropper's shack his mother and grandmother lived in. He'd never known his father. Or his grandfather. He'd only known women in his life, mostly his gaunt mother ravaged by methamphetamines with deep creases, perpetual scabs on her face, and ruined teeth. She'd managed to finally kill the meth habit with addictions to alcohol, heroin, opioids, and the last stop – fentanyl. Her mother, Worm's grandmother, had become her drug supplier after grandma become addicted to the opioids she needed to kill the pain from a car accident that broke both her legs and a hip.

Unsurprisingly, Worm felt uncomfortable in Monster-Boy's house. He'd spent most of his life in squalor or correctional facilities. The house was old but spotless. Monster-Boy insisted on that.

Worm absentmindedly picked at a scab on his jaw and asked, "So, when is he coming?"

Monster-Boy glanced at the ornate kitchen clock.

"Ten. He's got seven minutes before he's late."

"You think he'll come?"

"The amount of shit I'm buying, he'll come."

Or thinks you're buying, thought Worm, but he didn't say anything. He was worried about an outsider coming to the house with their hostage in the garage. He figured Monster-Boy was planning to get rid of the spic, but he hadn't yet. Worm wished he would, but he knew Monster-Boy wanted to torture him as long as possible before he killed him.

Suddenly, there was a light rapping on the back door. The sound startled Worm. Monster-Boy smiled.

"Couple of minutes early. I told him to come around back."

Monster-Boy moved with his usual quickness. It always surprised Worm that someone as large and bulked up as Monster-Boy could move so fast.

Monster-Boy opened the back door of the house without asking who was there. Monster-Boy always did shit like that. Worm wondered if maybe he should make himself scarce. Before he had time to decide, Monster-Boy's drug dealer stepped into the kitchen. Worm hadn't seen many men as big as Monster-Boy; this guy was close. As tall as Monster-Boy and only about fifteen, twenty pounds lighter. He wore a tight spandex t-shirt ironically branded with the word Monsta. It did a nice job of revealing his grotesquely large neck, thick trapezius muscles and shoulders, massive chest, and huge arms with veins that looked like small snakes trapped under the skin. Like Monster-Boy, this guy was bald except for a weird, foot-long pigtail growing out of the back of his head. Along with the pigtail, he had a bushy Fu Manchu mustache that extended past his jaw. Worm couldn't tell how big his legs were because he wore loose-fitting jeans.

Acting the gracious host, Monster-Boy made a sweeping gesture toward the kitchen table and said, "Have a seat, brother." He gestured toward Worm and said, "This is Anthony. Anthony, Brian."

The Worm smiled, but not by way of being friendly. He smiled at how easily Monster-Boy had come up with a name for him. He'd never thought of himself as an Anthony.

Brian Bozek nodded to the Worm but didn't reach out to shake his hand. It hadn't taken more than a second for him to realize the skinny skel with the dirty hair and neck tattoos was an ex-con. Which meant this juicer he'd met at the Xtreme gym on Victory Boulevard was a criminal, too. Well, fuck it. So am I, Bozek told himself. But he did wish he'd brought his gun with him – a .357 Taurus. He had a Kershaw Cryo II combat knife in his backpack. It had a flipper tab that let him open the 3.25-inch razor-sharp blade in a fraction of a second. He could do a lot of damage with it quickly. He should've clipped the knife to his jeans pocket instead of dropping it in his backpack but fuck it. This one sale was big enough to make his whole month. He told himself, an opportunity like this comes along, you damn well take it.

Monster-Boy clapped a big hand on Genghis Khan's muscular shoulder and said, "Have a seat, brother. Did you bring everything?"

Brian dropped his backpack on the kitchen table and said, "Everything you ordered. We're talking a little over five K, and that's with every discount I offer."

Bozek wasn't opening his backpack until he saw the money.

Monster-Boy had already pulled out a wad of cash from his back pocket. He slapped the bills on the table and said, "That's the price. Let's get 'er done. We got places to go and things to do."

Brian sat down at the kitchen table; the skanky asshole Anthony sat across from him with a stupid, feral grin on his face. Monster-Boy, that's what they called him at the gym, stood looming over him on his right.

Genghis was uncomfortable with the juicer freak hovering over him. He said to Monster-Boy, "Have a seat, big guy."

He moved the cash to his left as if moving it out of the way so he would have room to lay out the drugs, but the move was meant to place the cash closer to him and farther from Monster-Boy. Bozek didn't count it or put it in his pocket. He wouldn't have come to a strange house except for the fact that the place was near the gym where he'd met the bald fucker, whose name he didn't even know. The guy had told him his name was Eugene. A name that had popped into Monster-Boy's head at the moment. Like the name Anthony he had given to Worm. He'd told the dealer he was taking a trip and needed a full supply of drugs for his four-month-plus regimen.

Genghis Khan waited for Monster-Boy to sit, and then he reached into the backpack and began taking out his cache of drugs.

"Okay, so on the menu tonight, my friends, we start with a ten-week supply of T-Enathate, four hundred. Tren E, eight hundred. D-Bol, enough for a hundred per day."

Bozek pulled out boxes and packets, each one sealed and loaded with various steroids.

"Then you got six weeks' worth of Testosterone prop EOD, Trenbolone Acetate, EOD, Masteron…all in hundred-milligram doses."

"A hundred?"

"Yep, as ordered. Next, you said eight to twelve weeks of 50 migs Winstrol or Anavar. You said you take both most days, so I got you enough for the whole twelve weeks. You want to make that eight instead of twelve, we can do that if you prefer."

Monster-Boy smiled a close-mouthed smile and said, "Twelve, dude. I'll take the whole twelve weeks."

"Good enough. Then I got you Halotestin to start about the third month out, your call. And your anti-estrogens. The full-boat, Nolvadex, Arimidex, Proviron. You can taper up as you go, however you want."

Monster-Boy said, "What about the GH?"

Bozek's drugs covered most of the table. He made room for four more sealed packets, taking them out two by two.

"This is as much as I could get on short notice. I'm throwing it in at half-price. It should do you." Bozek sat back in his chair. "This is a hell of a regimen, my man."

Monster-Boy said, "Gotta stay big, brother."

Brian pointed at the table loaded with steroids and hormones. "Add weight and workouts, and you got it covered, dude. By the way, just checking, I know I asked you, but do you want any insulin?"

"No. I don't do no shows, so the Winstrol and other stuff cuts me up enough."

Bozek tried to appear relaxed, but he found himself nervous and on edge. He was accustomed to making others uneasy. He was getting sloppy. Or greedy. Should've brought a wingman. But who the hell would've wanted to get involved in this shit? And what the fuck was that whiff of rotting burnt meat he smelled every once in a while?

39

Manny had heard the throaty sound of a car with a glasspack muffler. He pictured a high-performance Mustang or American muscle car. It had stopped near the front of the house and parked, shutting down quickly. Manny assumed the text that had stopped the freak from lighting up his arm had something to do with the car's arrival.

Manny estimated he had been in the garage for about ten hours. They'd brought him in with a pillowcase over his head. That made him think they might not kill him. But Manny gave up that idea when they started making their fucking videos.

While the skinny bastard cleared out the work lights and his camera, Manny was able to get a better look at the size of the garage and the walls around him. The garage was only big enough to hold one car. In front of him, he could see an old wooden garage door, one piece. The kind with two big springs attached to the sides and opened by lifting at the bottom. Behind him was a wall with one window covered with plywood. There was a workbench on one wall and tools propped against the other wall, but it didn't matter since the chain kept him far away from the surrounding walls. There was a side door on his left that gave access to the garage. Next to his chair was a bucket for a toilet.

Manny Guzman knew there were three ways this could go. James and the crew would find him and kill those two bastards. Not likely any time soon. If Manny had no idea who that freak was, he couldn't see how James would. He'd be starting the search with no information. But then again, if anybody was going to find these assholes, it would be James.

The second possibility – he might be able to kill the freak. He'd freed his arms from the duct tape attaching them to the chair. He was still handcuffed to the chain embedded in the concrete floor, but between the chain and his outstretched arm, he had about six feet. And his left hand was free. He might be able to surprise the big guy and get his arms around the freak's throat and choke him out. It wouldn't be easy to hang on to someone that big and strong.

And then there was the second guy to worry about. A typical prison skel, a sneaky piece of shit, the kind who would creep up behind you and shank you while his partner distracted you. Taking both of them out would be next to impossible unless he found a weapon in this fucking garage stinking of burnt pig's meat, and that didn't seem likely.

The third and most likely possibility – they would kill him. But they hadn't killed him yet. They had wanted to make their fucking videos. Obviously, to extort something from James. Or maybe just to fuck with him. Maybe they would make more videos. Light the gasoline on his arm or whatever that shit was. Fuck 'em. Until they did, it gave Manny time to figure out a way to hurt them. Maybe even kill them.

Time to start looking for a weapon. In the dark. Unable to move beyond a diameter of the length of his chain and one arm's length. Without making enough noise to alert the assholes.

40

Monster-Boy stretched, leaned back in his chair so far it looked like he might break the back, and told Bozek, "Count the dough, pal. Make sure it's all there so we can wrap this up."

As Bozek began counting the money, Monster-Boy stacked the drugs into a more compact pile and then stood up. He headed toward the stove behind Bozek.

"You want coffee, man? I gotta get some caffeine in me. We're driving tonight."

Monster-Boy's question made Bozek lose his count. But he sure as hell wasn't going to start over. He turned back to the pile of bills. There'd been two thousand in hundreds, but the rest of the bills were fifties and twenties. This was going to take time. He decided the hell with it. It looked close enough. He shoved the bills into his backpack and palmed the combat knife.

He turned to answer Monster-Boy, who had his arm back, fully extended, ready to hit Bozek with a ten-pound cast iron skillet aimed at Genghis Khan's head. Fuck! Should've kept my mouth shut while the asshole was counting. He'd had his head down. It was perfect.

Monster-Boy followed through on his swing, trying to adjust for Bozek's moving head.

Bozek reacted quickly, lifting his left arm to fend off the iron skillet.

The cast-iron frying pan cracked into Bozek's forearm, breaking the ulna bone, then hit Bozek's forehead, and tore off a flap of skin above his left eye. The horrendous blow knocked Bozek off the kitchen chair. He landed on his right hand, the hand holding his combat knife.

Bozek was stunned but conscious.

Monster-Boy howled and swung the skillet at Bozek's head with a vicious backhand as if the iron pan were a tennis racket. But reversing the momentum of his swing had taken too long. Bozek rolled to his feet and turned away by the time the skillet came at him. He took most of the blow on the side of his right arm and shoulder. The pain was intense, but Bozek's thick muscles absorbed most of the impact.

Monster-Boy reacted instantly. He reversed his swing again, but not before Bozek flipped open the blade of the Kershaw knife. He swung at Monster-Boy's arm as he fell away from the skillet and sliced Monster-Boy's forearm, sending blood spattering against the kitchen wall.

The cut made Monster-Boy smile. Still holding the skillet, he circled away from Bozek and yelled at Worm, "Get to work, bitch."

Bozek tried to regain his balance as Worm launched himself at the wounded bodybuilder. He attached himself to Bozek's back, grabbing him around his thick neck, stabbing the big man over and over in his chest and head, puncturing and tearing at any body part he could reach.

The rage and terror in Bozek increased. He backpedaled, smashing Worm into the wall behind him, striking backward with his own knife. Worm tried to use Bozek's head and neck for cover, but Bozek stabbed over his shoulder and slashed at Worm, catching the side of Worm's head, his neck, and shoulder. He reared back and slammed Worm into the wall again, this time with enough force to dent the old plaster and lathe. He knocked the air out of Worm, weakening his grip. Bozek ripped Worm's arm off his neck, bent over, and threw the skinny ex-con off. Worm landed hard, hitting a leg of the kitchen table and the floor.

Monster-Boy had watched with a leering grin, utterly confident, positioning himself for the coup de gras.

Bozek's left arm was almost useless. His vision blurred by the blood streaming into his eyes from the head wound, but he stayed on his feet, trying to get his knife into a defensive position. Monster-Boy's concentration narrowed. He stood motionless, like a wild animal poised for the kill, waiting for his moment, ignoring Worm, ignoring everything but his target. He gripped the iron skillet in his left hand, holding out his bleeding right forearm to defend against Genghis Khan's knife. He weaved back and forth just a bit, getting his feet positioned, a sadistic grin twisting his face, and then, with sudden speed and deadly accuracy, he exploded, swinging full force at Bozek's temple.

The side of the iron skillet shattered all four temporal bones in Bozek's head and ruptured the meningeal artery. The brain compressed, and a flood of arterial blood burst into the skull cavity.

The blow spun Bozek around. If he hadn't been such a big man, the impact would have knocked him off his feet. He staggered in place for a moment, lost consciousness, then crashed to the floor like a felled tree. It shook the house. Monster-Boy stepped forward and, with a roar, added a crushing overhand blow to Bozek's head, shattering the front of Genghis Khan's skull.

Out in the dark garage, Manny Guzman heard the huge body drop, Monster-Boy's bellow, and the final cracking sound of the cast iron skillet hitting a human skull. Still on his hands and knees, Manny stopped for a second, and then with even more urgency renewed his search for something, anything that he might use as a weapon. But the grimy floor in the one-car garage offered nothing for Manny except dirty hands.

41

As Demarco drove toward the address for Brian Bozek's house, from the backseat, Ciro said, "If Fu Manchu is home, how do you want to play this? I recommend with guns in hand."

Beck said, "Not Fu Manchu. Genghis Khan."

"Whatever the fuck."

"Let's skip the guns-in-hand thing. Let's start with hands-on persuasion if it comes to that. We need this joker alive."

Demarco said, "I recommend you save your hands, James." He reached under the driver's seat and pulled out a steel baton. "Try this."

Ciro said, "Is there a tire iron in the trunk? Better than that thing."

Beck said, "Let's just see if the guy is home first."

Demarco parked in front of a modest ranch-style house made of red brick with a green-shingled roof. There was a carport on the left side. A dark red Nissan 370Z Coupe sat parked in the driveway.

Beck said, "Pull in tight behind that car."

Ciro said, "If he gets through us, you shoot him."

Demarco said, "The guy you described ain't going to fit in that car."

As Beck and Ciro stepped out of the Mercury, Beck knew Demarco was right. So where was the drug dealer's car?

They heard the front door open. A Korean woman, early twenties, wearing flip-flops, sweatpants, and a tight sky-blue tank top came out onto the landing. She left the front door open and closed the storm door. She stood under the glare of a light fixture mounted over the front door. Her straight black hair fell past her shoulders. She had a tight figure and a Taurus snub-nose .357 Magnum five-shot revolver in her right hand.

Beck looked at the Nissan. The car fit her. The gun didn't.

Ciro hung back about ten feet behind Beck and slipped his Smith & Wesson .45 out from underneath his jacket. He held the gun behind his right leg. He knew the .357 revolver was going to be difficult for the small woman to shoot, but if she hit Beck in any part of his body, at the very least, Beck would lose a limb.

The young woman remained standing near her front door and said, "Who are you?"

Beck answered, "Friends of Lyle Rizzo. You don't need the gun."

"Lyle Rizzo is a fucking one-eyed snake. Why are you here?"

"We're looking for Brian. He may need our help."

"For what?"

"Is Brian home?"

She didn't answer.

Beck said, "He's not here, which is why you're holding that gun. You're worried about him."

"Should I be?"

"Yes. You want to know what's going on?" She ignored Beck and looked past him to Ciro. Beck said, "Yes, he has a gun in his hand, too. Trust me, you raise that revolver a quarter of an inch, he'll shoot you. Even though your chances of hitting anything with that cannon are slim."

Ciro smiled at her and took the Smith & Wesson out from behind his leg.

Beck said, "Hey, we're not here to shoot anybody. We just want to make sure Brian is okay."

"What does that mean?"

"We think he's selling to someone he shouldn't have anything to do with. Where is he?"

Her face tightened. Beck thought it might be anger. But then the girl looked like she might cry. She suppressed it with a tight shake of her head and shoved the gun in her back pocket. The weight of the weapon pulled down on her sweatpants, revealing the strap of her thong panties running along her hip.

Beck had no jacket on. He held his arms up, then patted himself around his waist. He said, "I'm unarmed. Come on, it's cold. You must be freezing out here. Let's go inside and talk."

She pointed at Beck, "Just you. I ain't letting more than one of you into my house. Yeah, I see the other guy in the car. Both of 'em stay out here. And you keep your hands where I can see them."

Beck held his hands open and visible. He turned to Ciro and nodded. Ciro nodded back but didn't move otherwise.

Beck followed the girl into her house. Once inside, she walked up three steps that led to the living room. A large couch upholstered in black velvet and a sixty-five-inch flat-screen television took up most of the room. There was a kitchen off to the right. Beck assumed the bedrooms and bathrooms were down a hallway that led past the kitchen area. The rest of the furnishings were sparse, as if the people living in the house were there temporarily. Even so, there was plenty of clutter. Clothes hanging off chairs., CDs, magazines, and a bong on a coffee table. Dishes in the kitchen sink.

"So, Brian isn't here."

"No."

"Anybody else in the house?"

"No."

The girl dropped onto the couch and curled her legs underneath, settling into the soft cushions, appearing even smaller than she had standing outside.

Beck sat opposite her in the only chair in the room – a large, brown leather recliner.

"When was the last time you saw Brian?"

"A few hours ago. He had an appointment."

"With who?"

"He never tells me that."

"Did he tell you when he'd be back?"

Instead of answering, she pulled into herself more and frowned, looking petulant.

Beck tried to muster the patience to deal with her. He looked at his watch. Nearly eleven. Beck leaned forward. His voice hardened. "Call Brian. Tell him he has to come home right away. Friends of Lyle Rizzo need to talk to him. Right now. It's important."

Annoyance replaced the petulance.

"He hates if I call him when he's doing business."

Beck grimaced. He knew if he pushed her too hard, this could get worse. And there was still the gun in her back pocket.

He softened his tone.

"What's your name, by the way?"

"Lee."

"Lee, what?"

She hesitated then answered, "Lee Yung."

"Lee, why don't you send him a text. It really is important. It's for his own good."

The annoyance turned to anger, but not at Beck. Her voice raised to nearly a shout.

"I already did. Twice."

Suddenly a tiny black and white kitten appeared out of nowhere, jumped onto the couch, and settled in the girl's lap. She scratched its head and stroked the kitten as much to comfort herself as the animal. Everything looked sweet and cuddly, except for the revolver in her back pocket.

"Lee, if you know where he went, you should tell me."

"I don't."

Beck's frustration kicked up another notch. Lee kept petting the kitten, trying to act as if Beck wasn't there.

"Are you sure it was business?"

"Yes."

"And you know about Brian's business."

"Enough."

"So, you know that he went to deliver drugs."

The kitten started to bat a tiny paw at Lee's hand.

"Yes. Before he went out, Brian opened the safe in our bedroom and loaded up a backpack."

They were talking now. Beck tried to sound concerned for her. He wanted to keep the conversation going.

"Do you know any of his customers?"

"Some."

"Do you know a guy around six-six, maybe taller, white, bald or shaved head, built-up, big? Someone you'd figure uses a lot of steroids or whatever bodybuilders use."

"No. Not really."

"What does that mean, not really?"

"Brian talked about a guy like that, but I've never seen him."

"Is that the guy he went to see tonight?"

"Maybe. Could be, but I don't know. He didn't tell me."

"I understand. But why do you say it could be?"

"Because he took a lot of stuff. I could tell because the backpack was full." She finally looked up at Beck, ignoring the kitten. "Who is this guy you're looking for?"

"He's bad news. He's committed two murders. There is a lot of heat on him. A ton of cops looking for him. Anybody who has anything to do with him is going to have problems. And that includes Brian. The police aren't going to be as patient or polite as I am, Lee. They'll come in here and grab you up and put you in an interrogation room until you tell them whatever you know. About everything. And if you lawyer up or refuse to talk to them, they will charge you with a list of crimes that will ruin your life."

She yelled at Beck, "I already told you what I know."

Beck spoke softly. "No, Lee, you haven't told me everything. Tell me how Brian came to supply him. Tell me his name. Tell me where I might find him. Tell me whatever you know. And please do it now."

She hesitated, looked at Beck. He looked back, waiting for Lee to realize that he wasn't leaving until she told him everything. And to understand that the gun in her back pocket would be useless against him and the men waiting outside.

She still tried to act put out. Mostly from force of habit. That was her way. But she talked.

"Brian calls him asshole Eugene. Or Monster-Boy. That's what they call him at the gym. Brian says he's really big. Bigger even than Brian."

"Is Eugene his real name?"

"I don't know. Brian met him about a month ago. Brian says he gives him the creeps, but he decided to sell to him anyway. I guess because Eugene buys a lot from Brian."

"You know where we can find Eugene?"

"No. Brian keeps addresses and phone numbers in his head. Some notes scribbled in a little notebook about orders. But he always has that notebook with him. Not that you could read it. It's all scribbles and stuff."

Lee started petting the kitten again.

"You said Brian met him a month ago?"

"Three weeks, a month. Something like that."

"At the gym?"

"Yeah. Xtreme. Over on Victory Boulevard. A lot of hardcore lifters and guys into performance-enhancing stuff go there."

"Is that where he met him tonight?"

"I don't know. I don't think so."

"Why?"

"He didn't take his gym bag. If he was going to the gym, he would work out."

"Anything else you can tell me?"

Lee shrugged. "No."

"Do you know anybody who can tell me where Eugene lives?"

"No. Maybe somebody at the gym knows."

"Extreme on Victory Boulevard?"

"Yes."

Beck looked at his watch again. Lee saw Beck frown at the time.

"They're open twenty-four hours on weekdays."

Beck said, "Okay. Thanks."

The kitten jumped off Lee's lap.

Beck stood up to leave.

"Lee, is this Brian's house or yours?"

"Brian's."

"Is there any place you can go? I don't think you should be here alone."

"Why?"

Beck wasn't going to explain anything. He begrudged taking the time to warn her.

"Do you have family or friends you can go to?"

Lee shrugged. "My mother."

"Where is she? Is she close?"

"Yes. Over in Bull's Head."

Beck wanted to tell her, get dressed, get out of this house, stop living with a drug dealer, get rid of that ridiculous gun that's going to kick back and hit you in the face if you ever shoot it. Wake up and realize how close you are to ending up in jail.

Instead, he said, "Go stay with your mother. Tonight."

James Beck turned and left. He didn't look back at the small woman and her kitten, both of whom watched him quietly close the door behind him.

Just then, Beck's cell phone made a pinging sound. Another text message. From Monster-Boy Eugene? He opened the text. It wasn't from the bad guy. It was from Brennan.

Shit.

42

Brennan wolfed down most of a ham and provolone sandwich and then got back to work. In four hours, she and her detectives and her assistant Nina had made good progress.

Phil Harris, Nina Solowitz, and William Jablonsky had camped out in the Real Time Crime Center at One P.P. – the central repository for multiple databases on crime and criminals. The team of three worked well together.

Phil Harris was the ladies' man on Brennan's team. Divorced, African American, always well-turned-out, usually in a stylish sport coat and slacks outfits matched with a robust assortment of fashionable shoes. Harris was the one on Brennan's squad who seemed to be three degrees away from every detective in the NYPD.

Although it didn't fit with Harris's image, he happened to be the most technically proficient on Brennan's squad. And although he was a charmer and a talker, when it came to crunch time, Phil Harris knew what it meant to be a First-Grade NYPD detective. He'd earned his rank with top-notch detective work and felt completely entitled to the status his gold shield conferred on him. Harris never pulled rank. He just operated as if things should be done his way, but always with affability and interest in the people around him. Not surprisingly, when he walked into the RTCC, he found that he knew two people on duty that night.

Solowitz knew which databases they needed to search. Harris cleared the way to access them. And Jablonsky worked the terminals to identify the person of interest described by James Beck's witness, Catherine Hodge.

As Jablonsky pulled up suspects, Nina and Phil Harris culled out any photos that didn't fit Catherine Hodge's description. They eliminated over a third of the possible because of visible tattoos on necks, hands, and faces. They rejected eighty-five percent of the remaining because of their height and weight. They got it down to thirty-eight possible suspects. Nevertheless, the advantage of a target with an unusual description didn't change the fact that Catherine Hodge could not match any of the mugshots with the man who had visited her.

Metuchen and Grimaldi had tracked down Hodge at her home in Brooklyn Heights, where she lived in a small apartment in a co-op townhouse on Pierrepont Street. Grimaldi sat with Hodge and patiently showed her the images. By eleven o'clock, they had shown Catherine Hodge photos covering everyone released from the New York State Prison system in the last fifty-one weeks.

Grimaldi called Brennan and reported their results. He ended by saying, "I think we should call it a night. This woman is burned out. Losing her patience. And effectiveness."

"Okay, I hear you. Let's not overdo it in case we need her help later on. I'll tell Nina and Phil to stop. I'm going with the assumption that our suspect was not in the New York State system. We can't waste any more time on this."

"Agreed. Have you heard anything from Beck?"

"No. I'm going to text him as soon as I hang up."

"Okay. Let me know if there's anything useful."

"I will. You and Dave come back here and bunk down. I'll tell Phil and William to do the same. I'm heading home to clean up and grab some sleep, too. Let's figure we'll reassemble at six tomorrow, my office. Unless something comes up, and I have to roust everybody."

"Got it."

Brennan ended the call, stood up at her desk, and stretched.

She shoved the hard copies of the case files on her desk into a desk drawer. The files included everything Esposito's files, plus information on Beck's trial and incarceration. Brennan had read enough of Esposito's file to know there were portions she wanted to check more carefully. All the hard copies had been scanned to a flash drive by her assistant, Nina. She pocketed the flash drive, slipped her notebook computer into its case, and left everything else in her office so she could pick up where she left off in the morning.

As she headed for the elevator, she sent a text to Beck. The walk home to her apartment on Pine Street would take twelve minutes. She hoped to hell she'd hear from James Beck before she got there.

43

Monster-Boy stood in the kitchen holding onto Genghis Khan's ankles.

"Jeezus, Worm, you're leaking all over the fucking place. Go get a towel and hold it against your head until the bleeding stops."

Even with his strength, Monster-Boy knew it was going to be a bitch hauling the dead, mutilated body of Brian Bozek up to the second floor of the small house. He had a deep cut on his arm and goddamn Genghis Khan weighing 257 pounds. Dead weight. Totally fucking dead weight. The Worm wasn't going to be much help. He'd suffered half a dozen knife wounds, two of them severe. And there wasn't enough space on the stairwell for him anyway. He couldn't get next to Monster-Boy and grab one of Bozek's legs.

Fucker was pretty slick the way he got that knife out. Shouldn't have happened. Shouldn't have distracted him while he was counting the money.

Most of Worm's cuts weren't too deep, but the one on the side of his head was long and bleeding a good deal. And the puncture on his trapezius is gonna fucking hurt, thought Monster-Boy.

Monster-Boy shifted his grip so that he had one of Genghis Khan's thick calves under each of his huge arms. He walked backward, dragging the dead body out of the kitchen, leaving a long smear of blood on the floor. He had to strain to get the inert corpse up onto the stairs, and then Bozek's head caught on the nose of the bottom step. Monster-Boy exerted a massive effort to pull the head up onto the tread. The sound of the head banging against the stairs annoyed him. Then he had to do it again. And again.

"Shit!"

Monster-Boy pictured cutting the goddamn head off, but the guy's neck was so thick he'd need an axe, or a chainsaw. He didn't have either one. He would have left the body where it was, but he needed it upstairs. He didn't care about the mess he was making. He was just about done with the fucking house now. And soon he'd be done with the broke-down slave he'd cultivated. Even though things had gotten messy, his plan was on track. The Worm had tried to do his job, but he'd fucked up getting cut like that. And Monster-Boy was getting annoyed with him in general. It was becoming tedious trying to figure out new ways to degrade and humiliate him. What a piece of human garbage that guy was.

Christ, another body I'll have to deal with, thought Monster-Boy.

Halfway up the stairs, a burner phone in Monster-Boy's pocket rang.

"Fuck!"

He transferred Genghis Khan's heavy right leg under his left arm, holding both massive legs with one arm so the corpse wouldn't slide down the stairs as he answered a burner phone in his pants pocket with his right hand.

"Yeah?"

"It's me."

"I know it's you. You're the only one who has this number."

"Might know something any time."

"All right. Call when you do. Thanks."

Monster-Boy cut the call. Everything was on track. All that moron Beck had to do was follow the crumbs he'd laid. Monster-Boy smiled his crooked-toothed grimace of a smile. He got Bozek's legs back under each of his over-developed arms. He yelled down the steps, "Worm! Get up here and pick up his fucking

194

head." He waited for the Worm to get into position. "Just hold it up so it doesn't catch on the edge of the stairs."

The phone call had energized Monster-Boy. With Worm pressing a towel to the side of his bleeding head with one hand and holding up Genghis Khan's head with the other, Monster-Boy dragged the corpse up the stairs so quickly the Worm could barely keep up.

44

Beck stood on the steps in front of Brian Bozek's house, staring at Brennan's text while Demarco and Ciro watched from the car.

Where are you? Any progress? Call me. Brennan.

Beck felt a rush of anger and antagonism. The fucking presumptuousness of it. Brennan thought she had the right to tell him to stop whatever he was doing and report in while his friend was facing torture or death, or both. He shoved the phone in his pocket.

Demarco said, "What was that?"

"A text from the cop."

Demarco pursed his lips and shook his head.

Beck said, "I know."

"I know you do, James. You know damn well we can't have that. Not with the shit we're looking at dealing with."

Ciro answered. "Jeezus, what'd she want?"

"Where are you? What are you doing? Call me."

"What is she? Your wife or something?"

Demarco said, "A wife who can arrest you if she don't like the answer."

"Or shoot you," said Ciro.

Beck said, "Let me worry about her. In the meantime, the drug dealer's girl gave us a lead on Genghis whatever. It looks like he could be supplying our guy. He might be there now."

Ciro said, "Where's there? I can't believe we're lucky enough she told you where to find the son of a bitch."

"No, not that lucky, but she gave me a lead on how we might find out."

"What lead?"

"The gym he hangs out in. It's on Victory Boulevard. The place is called Extreme. It's where the hardcore juicers and bodybuilders work out. The drug dealer and the bald bastard both work out there. The girl said they call him Monster-Boy."

Demarco said, "Monster-Boy sounds about right."

From the back seat, Ciro said, "Okay, D, turn back the way we came in and take the first right while I look up the gym's address. The first right will take you to Victory. It's most likely a left on Victory, but I'll let you know."

As Demarco drove off, Beck asked, "You guys hear any more from Alex or the Bolos?"

Demarco said, "They called in. Said the closest they can figure is that the feed from the camera ends up somewhere in the northwest quadrant of Staten Island. That's as close as they can get without going into hundreds of servers and searching for what I don't know."

From the backseat, Ciro said, "That's where the gym is. Northwest section of the island. It's spelled Xtreme with an X. Take a left when you hit Victory. Says the place is open twenty-four hours."

Just then, Beck's phone pinged again. Another text.

Demarco was concentrating on driving but asked, "What are you going to do about that woman?"

"I can't have her issuing a goddamn warrant for me. I'll have to string her along."

Beck composed a text:

I'm following a lead. Did you find anything?

Brennan's phone pinged as she opened the door to her apartment building's lobby. She assumed Beck had answered her text. The

197

last fifteen hours had bored deep into her. She felt as if tension had tightened everything from her knees to her neck. Not surprising after witnessing the two gruesome deaths, the pressure from Roth, the workload, and worrying that her fate depended on a dangerous and unreliable man. She rolled her head and took a deep breath, but everything felt so tight it didn't do anything except show her how deep the stress had penetrated.

She looked at Beck's text. Eight words. He had given her virtually nothing and had the gall to ask for something in return. She resolved to keep him on a short leash. No way was she going to let James Beck ruin her career.

Brennan took the elevator to her studio apartment on the eleventh floor, 750 square feet, always on the verge of looking cluttered. The mortgage and maintenance ate up 54% of her net salary. But the apartment rose just high enough to let her see a bit of sky and bring a few hours of sunlight into her space. The apartment was within walking distance to 1 PP and provided what she needed, including a decent size shower and bathroom, and, right now, a shower was what she wanted above everything else.

Brennan knew she was done with texts. She had to talk to Beck. Her hair and clothes felt gross, but she wasn't going to waste time on a shower before she spoke to him.

She sat on her Budot sleeper sofa, the most expensive item in her apartment, and dialed Beck's number.

45

The map on Ciro's phone told them they were in front of the Xtreme gym on Victory Boulevard. But nothing in the rundown strip mall looked like a gym.

Demarco decided to turn into the narrow parking lot and make sure whether or not this was the location. Five storefront businesses were facing the boulevard, all dark, none of them a gym.

After a bit of cursing and confusion, they found out Xtreme gym wasn't located on Victory Boulevard but rather behind the mall on a dead-end street. It looked like a garage, which is what it used to be. A concrete block garage converted into a bare-bones gym. They might never have found the gym if it hadn't been for the halogen floodlights shining over the doorway.

Demarco peered out the windshield. "Good location for a murderous freak and drug dealers."

Beck said, "More cars parked out here than I expected this time of night."

Ciro said, "Tucked out of sight back here. I like the setup."

Beck reached into the compartment between the seats. There was a pair of brass knuckles near the bottom. He pulled out one of them. His hands had been damaged in too many fights. He was already looking at arthritis in his old age, assuming he reached old age.

Demarco again pulled out the expandable steel baton from under the driver's seat. The baton extended twenty-one inches with a flick of the wrist. It was one of his favorite weapons. The baton increased Demarco's already formidable reach. In his hand, one or two hits quickly disabled most attackers.

Ciro stepped out of the car and checked the .45 Smith & Wesson at the small of his back.

There was no discussion. No game plan. Beck led the way with his partners following. They entered through a single solid metal door that had no signage or address on it.

The late hour, out of the way location, harsh fluorescent lights, concrete floor and block walls, racks and racks of weightlifting plates, barbells, dumbbells, the benches and powerlifting stations – all made the Xtreme gym a strange and improbable place. Anytime a weightlifting plate hit anything, or a barbell banged onto a rack, the noise reverberated off the concrete block walls.

But it was the clientele that made the place furtive and uncomfortable. There were no women in the gym. And all the men were hardcore lifters, all of them obviously using steroids. Their grotesquely bulging muscles, tattoos, and preening created an air of debauched narcissism.

Beck quickly counted nine men in the gym. All of them turned to look at the three men who stood out in their street clothes amidst the skin and muscle show.

Beck ignored the stares. He wanted to find whoever was in charge. He spotted an old, gray, tanker-style desk in the far corner opposite the entrance. Beck headed straight for the desk, ignoring the menacing looks from the various behemoths. He wasn't menaced.

On the desk were old newspapers, muscle magazines, an ancient Gateway computer that couldn't possibly be working, and a 1985 Western Electric touch-tone phone. More weird shit.

There was nobody sitting at the desk.

Beck sat in a battered chair and opened desk drawers, pulled out folders, glanced at them, and dropped them in a pile on the desk. Ciro and Demarco turned toward the gym area. It didn't take long for a voice to yell out from the far side of the gym, "What the fuck are you assholes doing?"

The heavily muscled gym manager stormed toward his desk, followed by a small pack of lifters trying to look tough and pissed off.

The manager wore shorts and an Athlio compression shirt. The shorts revealed heavily muscled legs striated with veins, the shirt emphasized his muscled-up torso and built-up arms and chest.

The manager didn't impress Ciro or Demarco. Nor did the other muscle boys accustomed to intimidating people with their bloated muscles and strutting.

Beck ignored everything and kept searching through the pile of folders to find anything labeled "members" or "new members."

The manager kept coming, looking like he was going to shove Ciro Baldassare out of his way.

Ciro pointed at him and said, "Don't."

The manager slapped Ciro's arm aside.

The punch came in a fraction of a second. Ciro hit the manager in the middle of his face, followed by two fast right, left hooks to his ribcage. The first punch flattened the manager's nose, splintering the cartilage and breaking the nasal septum at both top and bottom. Ciro's next two punches cracked a floating rib on the right side, fractured two middle ribs on the left side, and injured the cartilage. The manager would not breathe normally for seven weeks. Three seconds and the manager was on his knees gagging.

For a moment, everything stopped. And then one of the lifters who held a forty-five-pound dumbbell raised his arm as if to throw the dumbbell at Ciro.

Demarco stepped forward and whipped his steel baton at the foolish man's wrist, cracking the radius bone. Then he reversed the swing and cracked the baton up into the underside of the man's jaw, shattering the jaw and sending him down. Demarco stomped on his sternum to make sure he stayed down.

There was no bravado, yelling, or shoving from Demarco and Ciro. Every blow was focused and intended to incapacitate. The muscled-up lifters nearby froze, but others from farther away surged towards the desk area, mostly to see what was going on.

Ciro had no interest in being rushed by a ton of muscle on the run. He drew the Smith & Wesson and fired one shot into the ceiling. The sound of the gunshot exploded and reverberated off the concrete surfaces. Everybody stopped and ducked.

Beck came around from the desk, his right hand covered with the brass knuckles. He grabbed the nearest juicer behind the neck, pounded his knuckled fist into the side of his head, and ran him as fast as he could into the nearest wall. The lifter's head banged into the concrete block. Beck rammed his shoulder into the man's back and pinned him against the wall.

"Don't fucking move."

Demarco had his Glock out now. He and Ciro pointed their guns at whoever looked defiant, then herded them against the wall where Beck had put the first lifter.

Demarco lightly smacked several of them with his baton and told them, "Noses on the wall. Nobody moves."

Ciro kicked and shoved a straggler.

In three minutes, the fight was out of every juiced-up, fake tough guy in the gym.

The manager was still on the floor in front of his desk moaning, trying to wipe away the blood that streamed from his nose all over his compression shirt and shorts.

Ciro and Demarco stepped back, guns pointed at the men standing against the wall who had become their prisoners.

Ciro announced, "The first asshole that moves, I shoot in the head."

To emphasize the point, he fired another .45 round in the concrete block wall above the men, causing them all to flinch and duck.

Demarco took up a position near the door to prevent anyone from leaving or entering.

Beck made his way to the fallen manager. He grabbed a handful of hair and pulled him up off the floor, gripped the back of his shirt, and shoved him into his desk chair.

Ciro placed the .45 in his waistband and walked down the line of men, holding the lifters against the wall with one hand as he checked pockets for cell phones and wallets. He threw the cell phones toward Demarco, extracted drivers' licenses from two wallets he'd found, and dropped them on the floor. Demarco gathered the cell phones with his foot, picked them up, and slipped them into his coat pocket.

Beck kicked the manager in the shin and said, "Sit up. Focus."

He took a hand towel off a pile of them on a file cabinet and handed it to the manager so he could use it to staunch the blood flowing from his shattered nose.

Beck slapped him gently on the side of his head to get his attention.

"I'm going to ask you this once. Concentrate." Beck held up his brass-knuckled fist. "If you lie, I'll punch you in the nose. If you lie again, I'll break your elbow. You'll have a hard time lifting a pencil."

Beck waited for a response, for a sign of defiance. There wasn't any.

He took out his cell phone and pulled up the picture the Bolos had sent him. He expanded the image so that it showed mostly the head and torso.

Beck said, "Who is this?"

The manager hesitated and said, "I don't know him."

Beck smacked the manager's ear. He considered hitting his broken nose, but he didn't want the manager to pass out.

"I didn't ask you that. I know he works out here. Who is he?"

The manager nodded, "Yeah. He's worked out here. But I don't know him."

"Since when?"

"I don't know. Maybe a month ago."

"Is he the one you call Monster-Boy?"

The manager hesitated and said, "Yes."

"What information do you get when someone joins?"

"They fill out an application."

"Show me his application."

Beck let the manager go to the standing file cabinet. He pulled out two file folders, one marked A-M, one marked N-Z. He shuffled through pages of applications until he found the page he wanted. He handed it to Beck.

One side was a pre-printed form asking for name, phone numbers, email. Height and weight. Workout goals. Questions about medical history. Nothing had been filled in except a scribbled name and address: Billy Lindberg. 39 Maple Street, SI.

On the back of the form was a copy of Lindberg's gym membership card with the same address and an illegible signature."

The manager said, "That's him. That's all I have."

Beck folded the single page and stuck it in his shirt pocket.

He asked the manager, "Where's your wallet?"

The manager hesitated, then went to the desk and opened the middle drawer. He handed his wallet to Beck.

"Your phone?"

The manager, still holding the towel to his nose, took his cell phone out of the same drawer and handed it over.

Beck put the phone in his back pocket, extracted the manager's driver's license, and checked to make sure the picture matched. He didn't bother to read the name.

Beck dropped the wallet on the desk, ripped the landline phone cord out of the wall, then smashed the handset against the desk until it cracked apart. Without another word, Beck headed for the exit. Before he left, he turned to the men still standing facing the wall.

"You dickheads keep your mouths shut, or we'll come to your houses and shoot you. And burn this drug-infested, freakshow shithole to the ground."

Ciro fell in behind Beck. Demarco let them pass while he made sure the muscle heads stayed facing the wall, then turned and followed them out.

They piled into the Mercury Marauder. Demarco started the engine and slowly pulled out of the mall, as if to make the point that nobody was going to make them rush off.

Beck asked, "Anybody get dinged seriously?"

Ciro growled and rubbed the hand that smashed the manager's nose.

"I take it you got a lead on this prick who I'm going to shoot in the face until my goddamn fucking gun is empty."

Beck pulled out the membership form.

"Maybe. Could be all bullshit, but it's more than we had when we went in there. Let's get a couple of miles away from here, pull over somewhere, and get to work."

Before they traveled half a mile, Beck's phone rang.

He stared at the screen. Brennan. Beck felt like throwing the phone out the car's window.

46

After the fourth ring, Brennan expected to hear a voicemail message. When she heard the word "Beck," Brennan hesitated, waiting for more.

She recovered quickly and said, "It's Brennan. I need to know what you're doing."

Beck wanted to say, *Need? Who gives a fuck what you need? You need to go do your goddamn job and leave me the fuck alone.* Instead, he forced himself to say, "I'm doing what I told you. I'm looking for my friend."

"Where? What are you doing?"

Beck knew this wasn't the time to answer Brennan's question after what had just happened.

"We may have a lead. Is there anything you've found at your end that might help me? Did you check to see if anyone released from the prison system matches that picture?"

Brennan was tired of having Beck turn her questions back on her, but she decided to play along. Make it clear to him the resources she had.

"We pulled up over eighteen-hundred convicts' records within four hours going back a year. We culled out thirty-eight possible matches. We showed each one to your witness. In-person, with experienced detectives watching her reaction. Your witness didn't confirm any of them. Based on that, we don't believe your suspect was in the New York State prison system. Now, I need to know where you are and what you're doing."

There it was – her *need*.

"I'm trying to find somebody who can identify the son of a bitch in that picture."

"How?"

Beck hesitated. "Using connections to people who might have supplied him with the illegal drugs he uses. People that wouldn't come within a mile of the NYPD, and if they did, would never cooperate."

"You're not giving me much, Beck."

"Inspector, don't you want plausible deniability or whatever the hell it's called?"

"Let me worry about my deniability. That's not your decision. Why are you holding out?"

"Because I don't want to waste your time on something that might amount to nothing. And because you're sitting on top of a very blunt instrument. What happens if a hundred cops descend on the wrong place at the wrong time? My friend dies."

"Don't take us for fools, Mr. Beck."

Beck's patience for debating with Brennan had run out. But not his sense of self-preservation.

"I don't take you for a fool. That doesn't mean you don't work in a foolish system. I'm not your enemy. The enemy here is time. And I need a little more of it. I promise you I will contact you as soon as I have something you can act on."

Beck cut the connection.

Brennan stared at her dead phone. She felt like throwing it across the room.

She wasn't going to control James Beck with a damn phone call. Brennan took a deep breath, looked up at the ceiling, and exhaled.

As usual, she had no leverage. No power. Feelings she detested. Feelings that made her inert, which added to the emotional pain, which she knew would cause physical pain in the form of a throbbing headache and backache if she didn't do something about it.

It was one thing to have circumstances imposed on her by the command structure of the department. It was quite another to have someone like James Beck controlling her. That, she would not tolerate.

She pulled her notebook computer out of its case and reached in her jacket pocket for the flash drive that held Esposito's file on Beck and Beck's NYPD file.

She plugged in her notebook and turned it on. While the machine booted up, Brennan went into her small kitchen and filled her coffee maker. While the coffee brewed, she undressed, folding each item of clothing, and dropped them into the laundry bag hanging in the bedroom closet.

Shower, clean clothes, coffee. And then work. Dianne Brennan always turned to work. She would outwork the arrogant, entitled men that Roth had met with earlier and would always defer to. And she would work her way out from under James Beck's control. Control belonged to her. Not to a blundering, reckless macho asshole.

47

While Beck had been on the phone with Brennan, Demarco had entered the address on Monster-Boy's gym membership into his smartphone and plotted a route to it.

Beck asked, "How far?"

"Four point two miles, twelve minutes."

"Let's go."

Ciro, sprawled out in the back seat, asked, "What do we do when we get there?"

"I don't know. Knock on the front door? See who's inside?"

Demarco said, "It's past midnight, James. Think that's a good time to go knocking on doors?"

Beck muttered, "Fuck." He pressed a button on his phone. Alex Liebowitz answered on the second ring.

"What's happening?"

"We got a lead. Might not be worth much, but I need everything you have on who owns a property in Staten Island."

"Go."

Beck recited the address and waited, knowing Alex was already typing in the address on a custom-designed interface that sent the information to multiple search engines. In nine seconds, Liebowitz started reciting information, pausing as more details came up.

"Okay, that's in Dongan Hills at the east side of the island. Mostly white, middle-class, modest homes. Lot of Italian and Irish in that area. That address belongs to a modest house. Wood frame. Wood-slat siding. Let's see, sits on a corner lot. Purchased in 1995 by a Richard and Elaine Montello. Mortgage with Santander Bank. Built in 1980 by Emile Diggs. He sold to the Montello family. Three bedrooms, one and a half baths. 1,520 square feet. The house, the transaction – all looks pretty normal."

Beck listened carefully but didn't respond. Liebowitz kept searching and commenting.

"What else we got…residents include Mr. and Mrs. Montello and his son Richard Jr. And until two years ago, a now-deceased mother-in-law. The Montellos have, let's see, six relatives in the area, mostly New Jersey. Are you lookin' at this place for the guy who's got Manny?"

"Yeah."

Beck pictured Alex's surprised expression, but Alex didn't say anything.

"Doesn't sound like it fits," said Beck.

"Not really."

"All right, spend a little more time on it and let me know if you find anything unusual. Specifically on the background of the current owners."

"Will do."

Beck ended the call, thinking about what Alex had found until Demarco asked, "What'd he say?"

"In so many words – this address is the last place we'd find a maniac juiced-up arsonist killer who burns and stabs and abducts people."

Ciro said, "Maybe it's the perfect cover."

"I doubt it. It doesn't add up unless Monster-Boy somehow disposed of an Italian-American family of three and moved in without the neighbors noticing."

Demarco said, "Not to mention it's pretty damn far from that gym."

Beck said, "True. Clearly not in the northwest corner of the island."

Ciro said, "More like the opposite. The southeast."

Beck held up the gym membership. "But this tells me there's a connection."

Ciro said, "Maybe he just pulled an address out of his ass. Just made it up. Nobody at that fucked up fag-hole, freak-house of a gym was going to check."

Beck nodded.

Demarco turned into a parking lot behind a Rite Aid pharmacy. He parked in a spot so the Mercury wouldn't be visible from the street. He and Ciro waited, knowing Beck was thinking it through, trying to come to a decision.

After about a minute, Beck said, "We can't let this go. It's all we have. Trouble is, I can't figure out how we wake up a family in the middle of the night to ask them about this gym membership without them calling the cops. Or worse."

Ciro asked, "Worse like the guy comes to the door with a gun or a baseball bat in hand?"

"Yes."

Demarco said, "Or worse like a six-seven juicer called Monster-Boy opens the door?"

Beck said, "Shit," and pulled out his cell phone, but he didn't dial a number.

"What are you thinking?" asked Demarco.

"Everything I'm thinking ends up putting Manny in danger if he's in that house."

Demarco and Ciro lapsed into silence.

After a moment, Beck said, "There's only one way. It's the last thing I want to do, but I can't come up with anything else."

"What?"

"Go in with that deputy inspector."

"Fuck that," said Ciro.

Demarco said nothing, silently shaking his head.

"You want to hear my reasons?"

Ciro said, "You want to hear mine? She's a fucking cop. Her job is to arrest people like us."

"I know. That's why I don't want you guys to be near this. But bringing her in can help us."

"How?"

"It gets her off my back. If I keep putting her off, she'll put a warrant out on me."

"For what?"

"Whatever the fuck she comes up with. But the main reason, with her on the scene, it gets me into that house. Or at least a chance to show this name and address to the people living there and find out what their connection is to Xtreme gym and someone calling himself Billy Lindberg. The other thing is, if she agrees, it gives me leverage."

Demarco asked, "How so?"

"If she agrees to go in with me, I'm betting she'll hide that from her boss as long as she can. She can still hurt me, but I can hurt her. Look, I don't want to argue about it. I've got to find out the connection between this address and the son of a bitch trying to wipe us out. There's more upside than down. You guys can make yourself scarce."

Demarco said, "No. That's not the move."

"What isn't?"

"Making ourselves scarce. First off, you're not going to tell her that address unless she agrees not to come without a bunch of cops, right?"

"Yes."

"So me and Ciro should be there if something blows up. You and the lady cop might not be enough." Beck agreed but didn't say anything. "And the more of us are involved, the more we dirty her up, James."

Beck looked at Ciro. "You agree?"

"I guess that's the move. You bring the broad over to the dark side like you said. Me and Demarco hang back but stay close by in case things get out of hand. Nothing is perfect, but fuck it. We gotta do whatever it takes to get Manny back. Deal with the consequences later."

Beck nodded once and dialed Dianne Brennan's cell phone.

48

Monster-Boy had been trying unsuccessfully to doze when his burner phone started vibrating. It wasn't because he couldn't fit on the couch in the living room or the annoying pain from the bandaged knife wound on his forearm. He couldn't sleep because of the stench permeating the small house. The dead body upstairs hadn't started to decay, but the sphincter and bladder had lost all muscle tone releasing the considerable amount of fecal matter and urine in the huge cadaver, which, in turn, mixed with the metallic rotting smell of the blood decomposing in the kitchen and on the stairs.

Monster-Boy leveraged himself off the couch and pulled out the burner phone in his front pocket.

"Yeah."

"He took the bait. Must've at your gym. The bitch is meeting him."

"When?"

"Leaving soon, or just left."

"Beautiful. Stay on it."

Monster-Boy shut the phone and yelled, "Ha!"

His impatience and fatigue disappeared.

He yelled out, "Worm!" Time to move. Everything he needed was in the van. Kevlar vest. Shotgun. Ammunition. Pistol.

"Worm! Wake the fuck up. Let's go."

As Monster-Boy tied the laces on his size fifteen cross-trainers, Worm came ambling down the steps with a gauze bandage wrapped around his head and another one taped to his trapezius muscle. The bleeding had stopped, but not the pain.

"Geez, it fucking stinks in here."

Monster-Boy was on his feet, grabbing a dark blue windbreaker to wear over his Kevlar vest.

"Yeah, I know. Time to move. Looks like they took the bait. How're you feeling?"

"Fucking hurts."

"Take a handful of Advil. Let's go."

"How 'bout some Oxy?"

"Don't be stupid. You gotta be alert."

Monster-Boy was already out the door. On the way to his truck, he told Worm, "Remember I'm saving Beck for last. Got it?"

"Yeah, yeah. I got it."

49

Brennan had been up, awake, and working when Beck called.

"We have an address that might be connected to the suspect."

"Where? How'd you get it?"

Beck said, "It's in Dongan Hills on Staten Island."

"Staten Island?"

"Yes. I'll text you the address. How about you start heading out here. We can talk more while you're on your way. Figure out where to meet. How fast do you think you can get here?"

Brennan checked her watch. Half-past midnight.

"I don't know. I should arrange for backup."

Beck said, "I don't think you need that."

"Why?"

"I doubt the bad guy is here. I'll explain when I see you. You should get moving."

"If the suspect isn't there, who is?"

"Somebody who might be connected to him."

"Listen, I can't run around blind. Tell me what's going on?"

Beck's first impulse was to hang up and do whatever he could without her. Too late for that. Brennan wouldn't relent now. But he had to make sure she didn't do something rash.

"Okay, but I have to make it brief. Then you decide if you want to come out here. I found someone who I think has been supplying drugs to the suspect. That person led me to someone more connected to the bad guy. That led me to finding out a name and address this asshole is using. I doubt he'd use his real name or address, but I still need to check it

215

out, see if the maniac just made it all up or if there's some kind of connection."

Brennan asked, "Do you know who is living there?"

"The house belongs to an Italian family of three. And the house isn't near where I think the killer is based."

"How'd you find out all this?" Before Beck could answer Brennan said, "Never mind."

"Right. I don't have enough time to explain even if I wanted to. We should move on this fast."

"What if you're wrong, Beck? What if he's in that house? You want me and my driver to go in there without backup to take down a giant who's killed two people, abducted your friend, and tried to burn down your house?"

Running full blast for twelve hours, dealing with everything, including a brawl at the gym, didn't help Beck's focus or patience. He forced himself to give this one more try.

He tried to speak calmly. "I don't believe he's there. Like I said, I don't believe a murderer would use his real name and address? And so far, the name doesn't even match the address. What's it going to look if you show up with a SWAT team for nothing? I assume you'd have a hard time explaining that to your boss."

"That's none of your concern."

Beck said, "Look, I'm trying to keep you in the loop so you don't accuse me of going off on my own. All I want to do right now is find out how this murdering son of a bitch came up with this name and address."

"What's the name?"

"Billy Lindberg."

"And the address?"

"Where are you now, Brennan?"

"My apartment. It's near One P. P."

"I'll text you an address. It's not the address of the location. It's where we can meet if you want to be in on this. It shouldn't

216

take you longer than forty-five minutes to get there. I'll give you an hour. Don't bring an army with you."

Beck hung up before Brennan could argue with him.

Ciro said, "Think she'll come without backup?"

Demarco said, "No way of knowing. We have to figure out a way to tail her when she gets onto the island. See who's with her."

Beck said, "She gets chauffeured around in a black Chevy Tahoe. No markings on it."

Ciro asked, "How do you know?"

"I saw it on the pier. It shouldn't be hard to spot this time of night. It's got tinted windows, black rims. You can see the flasher lights in the grill."

"Assuming she comes in the same vehicle."

"I'm assuming a deputy inspector working for the commissioner has a vehicle assigned to her."

"I guess we'll find out." Demarco had been scanning maps on his phone. "Text her to meet you in the Walgreens parking lot off Clove Road. We'll cruise around the house on Maple while she's on her way. See if any cops are assembling."

Beck asked, "What's the address of Walgreens?"

"Twenty-two-seventy Clove Road."

"Okay, we'll pick her up when she comes off the expressway. See if she's got other cops trailing her. If she doesn't, you let me off and I'll meet her in the Walgreens parking lot."

Ciro said, "Jimmy, maybe we should be there so you can introduce us to your new girlfriend."

Beck said, "Some other time. Before she gets here, we can figure out where you two can set up in case the bad guy is in that house. Which he isn't."

Ciro asked, "What do we do after you and your sweetheart find out what's what with that family?"

"Fuck if I know."

Demarco asked, "What do we do if she double-crosses us and shows up with reinforcements?"

Beck said, "We don't give her the fucking address, and we see what we can find out ourselves. Of course, that will mean she comes after me, but I can't worry about that now. We gotta find this guy…"

Ciro finished Beck's sentence for him. "Shoot the mother-fucker and get Manny."

50

When Beck hung up on her, Brennan suppressed an urge to yell at her phone. Instead, she hit the speed dial for William Jablonsky's phone. She wondered if he'd had a chance to fall asleep. Probably. It took five rings to get an answer.

"William."

"Yes."

"It's me. I need you and the Chevy."

"Okay. Where?"

"Pick me up at my apartment. Fast as you can. I'll be outside waiting."

"Where are we going?"

"Staten Island."

Her next call was to Dave Metuchen. He answered on the third ring, sounding completely alert.

"Boss."

"I guess you weren't sleeping?"

"Just finished cleaning up."

"Where's Alphonse?"

"I think he's bunking in the Major Case Squad office."

"Okay, find him. Something came up. I need you two to get out to Staten Island."

"What's up, something going on with Beck?"

"Yes. He says he's got a lead on our suspect. I'm going out there to meet him. If it turns out to be something, I want you guys nearby." Brennan held her phone to her ear with her shoulder as she searched Google Maps on her computer to locate the 122nd precinct in Staten Island, confirming it was the closest precinct to Dongan Hills.

"You and Alphonse go to the precinct on Hylan Boulevard."

"That's the One-Two-Two?"

"Yes. Check in with whoever is in charge there. Find out what kind of personnel might be available for an arrest. Wait to hear from me. How soon can you get there?"

"This time of night, forty-five, fifty minutes. We'll use flashers."

"Okay. Call me when you're in place and sit tight."

Metuchen said, "Got it. If Beck is on Staten Island, there's a good chance he's working something with his mob friend, Baldassare."

Brennan paused for a moment before she said, "Yes. I suppose so."

She ended the call, grabbed her gun, police ID, briefcase, computer, and flash drive. She was dressed in jeans and a gray, long-sleeve, cotton turtleneck. She slipped on a pair of Merrell waterproof trail shoes and reached into her closet for a light down jacket she'd bought on sale – just right for a cold March night.

As she came out of her building lobby, Jablonsky was just pulling up in the Chevy Tahoe.

51

Monster-Boy sat in a rusted-out Econoline van parked on a quiet street about a half mile from the address he'd put on that dumbass gym membership card. The interior of the van was completely dark. He'd already removed the interior light bulbs so there'd be no light if he opened the door. A nearby poplar tree blocked the ambient light from the few streetlights in the neighborhood. Clouds darkened the slight glow from the crescent moon.

A Remington V3 Tac-13 shotgun rested on his lap, a compact, hi-tech weapon with a short bird's head-shaped handle instead of a stock. The Worm sat in the passenger seat, picking at the scabs on his jaw, a blank look on his face. He'd put up a stoic barrier to the pain from his knife wounds.

Monster-Boy ignored him, methodically loading six Winchester PDX1 12-gauge Defender shells into the Remington. Each shell contained a heavy one-inch slug and three 12-gauge copper-plated balls of buckshot, a combination designed to kill and maim. The one-inch slugs would hit with massive impact, and from the distance Monster-Boy planned to shoot, the heavy 12-gauge shot wouldn't spread much at all.

His cell phone vibrated.

"Yeah?"

"It's Dongan Hills. That's as close as I know."

Monster-Boy already knew the address but appreciated getting confirmation.

"When?"

"Thirty, forty minutes."

Monster-Boy cut off the call. He had plenty of time to get into position. He finished loading the shotgun.

52

Demarco, Beck, and Ciro had quietly cruised the neighborhood around the address on Maple Avenue in Dongan Hills. There were no signs of police gathering anywhere within a four-block radius of the house, and the house itself looked quiet and peaceful. They came back around to the address for one more look, Demarco peering out his window, double-checking the numbers on the front door.

He slowed down the black Mercury Marauder as they peered at the modest, wood-frame house located on a corner lot. Two steps up led to a small porch, the second floor overhanging it supported by two pillars. The house sat on a corner lot. A walkway led to the backyard on the left of the house. On the right was the lawn that ran to the street corner. The place was quiet. No lights on inside. Demarco turned left at the corner and cruised by the part of the backyard that opened on the street side. Demarco made another left and slowly glided past the neighbors on the street behind the Montello house. He made a final left turn, drove a block, and pulled over, shutting down the Mercury.

Beck said, "I can't believe that maniac is in there. Or Manny."

Demarco said, "Doesn't seem likely, but when you and the cop visit, we should cover the house just in case. If he is in there, and he takes a runner, we have to nail him."

Ciro said, "Hopefully, he won't finish off Manny before he does."

Beck didn't respond to Ciro's comment. He knew Brennan wouldn't let him near the house with a gun. If Monster-Boy was in the house, maybe he could at least slow him down somehow. Maybe with the brass knuckles still in his back pocket.

"After you guys drop me off to meet the deputy inspector, Demarco, how about you take a spot in the backyard? Ciro, park somewhere out front where you won't be spotted. Put him down if he gets past me and the cop."

Demarco said, "There's no garage or shed in the back. There's above-ground half-windows in the foundation. I'll check the basement before I take a position."

Beck nodded. "Good. If you see something, Manny tied up in there, you two will have to get him out. Text me, and I'll lead the cop away from the address."

Ciro shifted restlessly in the back seat. "Maybe we should bust in there now. We go in, clear the place, ask questions later."

Demarco said, "Only if I see Manny in there. If we bust in on the homeowners now and scare the shit out of them, how many answers you think we'll get?"

"I don't know. Maybe a lot."

Beck said, "No. We made our play. Letting the cop get involved was the right choice. Gets her off my back. Gets her compromised. And she should get more cooperation from residents in there explaining the gym application. We can't trade all that for the remote possibility the bad guys and Manny are in there. They're not." Beck checked the time. Twelve minutes after midnight. "Let's head over to the expressway and see if we can pick up the inspector. Make sure she's alone. And by the way, if you guys do end up jumping in, don't wait for me. Do what you gotta do, get in the car, and get the hell out."

Demarco took Hylan to Clove. They didn't have to wait for Brennan's SUV. They drove past the Chevy Tahoe as they were heading toward the expressway.

Demarco said, "Is that it? Looks like it."

Beck said, "It is. You see those flashers in the grill and the light bar behind the windshield?"

"I did."

Demarco accelerated to Fayette Avenue, made a U-turn, and drove back toward Walgreens. He pulled over a half-block away.

Beck said, "Wait here. I'll walk to the Walgreens. If I see any other cops around, I'll come back. If not, I'll text you to get into position."

Ciro said, "When you see your new sweetheart, give her a kiss for me. That'll help keep her occupied long enough for me and big D to get set up."

Beck stepped out of the Marauder. "Sure. Right on the lips."

He strolled to the Walgreens lot, carefully checking the two other cars he spotted, one parked on the street, the other in the lot. They were both empty. The only light in the area came from fixtures mounted high up on the wall of the drugstore. Brennan's Tahoe occupied a parking space near the entrance reserved for the handicapped. Fucking cops, thought Beck. They make up their own rules.

He sent a text to Demarco with a thumbs-up emoji and walked into the parking lot hunched over against the cold March air. He still had the same clothes on when he left Conover Street. He wished he'd grabbed a jacket.

He passed in front of the SUV, taking his time. He came around on the passenger side and was about to tap on the door when the tinted window powered down.

Brennan said, "Climb in behind me."

Beck didn't say anything. He leaned over and checked out Brennan's driver. Young guy. Trim. He looked alert and out of place in his suit, a blue sweater underneath, and tie. He looked at Brennan. She really was an attractive woman. The bright yellow light from the parking lot fixtures etched her features clearly. Beck stared for a moment, then looked behind her to see if anyone else was in the back seat. There wasn't.

Beck stood for a moment where he was, listening to the sounds of the night, killing time for Demarco and Ciro to get in place. The temperature felt like it was mid-thirties, the air moist from the nearby bay. Beck thought he heard the chirps of tree peepers, the first harbingers of spring. An owl far off in Ocean Breeze Park made a weird warning screech.

Brennan said, "What are you waiting for? Get in."

Beck climbed into the rear passenger seat.

Brennan nodded toward the driver. "This is Officer Jablonsky. He's part of my team."

Jablonsky reached a hand back to Beck, who shook it, thinking, this guy looks more like a grad student than a cop. Which was close to the mark, since Jablonsky was six months out of the NYPD police academy and taking first-year law courses at night at Fordham.

Neither Beck nor Jablonsky said anything.

Beck asked, "It's just us?"

Brennan said, "That's what you asked for."

Again, not a direct answer. Beck wondered if Deputy Inspector Dianne Brennan was ever going to play it straight. Were there cops heading for that neighborhood now that she had him in the backseat?

She said, "Seems like you've had a busy night."

Beck wondered if Brennan had heard anything over the police radio about a problem at the Xtreme gym. He didn't take the bait. He kept silent.

Brennan didn't let it go.

"On the way out here, we monitored a bunch of 911 calls about people injured in a gym on Staten Island. The precinct sent a squad over to investigate."

Beck shrugged, thinking apparently they didn't get all the cell phones.

He said, "Interesting. Speaking of gyms," he held up the gym membership form for Billy Lindberg. "I found this in a gym." He handed it to Brennan. "The manager confirmed someone matching our description works out there. The address on the membership is nearby."

"I'm not comfortable with your methods, Mr. Beck."

"And I'm not comfortable with someone trying to throw a forty-five-pound dumbbell at me. If someone tries to hurt me, I'll defend myself. You want to be a law enforcement officer, call the local precinct and tell them to search that shithole for illegal prescription drugs. This isn't fucking tiddlywinks, Brennan. You want to do this or not?"

Brennan looked at Beck for a moment. He didn't try to decipher the meaning of the look.

Brennan said, "What's the address?"

Beck gave Jablonsky directions. Brennan told him to drive there. No lights, no sirens. As they arrived, Beck pointed out the house. Jablonsky pulled up quietly and parked up the street facing the house. He shut down the SUV.

Brennan said, "Looks like everyone is asleep."

Beck said, "Yes."

"Do you know who's in there?"

"I'm assuming the owners. The house belongs to a family by the name of Montello."

"Montello?"

"Yes. Richard Montello."

The name sounded familiar to Brennan, but she didn't know why so she said nothing about it. She asked Beck, "How do you know that?"

"The internet. There's no record of anyone named Lindberg owning the house, but I still want to know why the asshole picked this address. And despite the late hour, I can't wait for a better time to find out."

Brennan nodded and looked at the membership application. She handed it to Jablonsky. He looked at it and handed it back without comment.

"You sure about who lives there?"

"That's what the property records say."

"This is probably a complete waste of time."

And yet, here you are, thought Beck.

"It's a lead. It's the only one I've got. And I presume the only one you have."

Brennan said, "Okay, here's how we're going to handle this. William, you pull up and park in front of the house. Turn on your flashers. Mr. Beck, you stay in the vehicle. I'll see who's home. I'll question whoever is in there."

Beck said, "You want me to stay in the car?"

"Yes."

"Why?"

"Would you consider telling me exactly what happened at that gym and if any of your crew was involved?"

Beck didn't answer.

Brennan turned to face Beck directly. "You said let's drop the bullshit. So let's. You brought me out here because you know goddamn well you can't go waking up people in the middle of the night to interrogate them. There's a good chance the residents of that house will call the police before they open a door. I am the police. And the farther away from you I am when I knock on that door, the better for me. And the more information I'll get. Stay in the car."

Beck said, "Whatever you say," thinking – you better fucking come back with the goods.

Jablonsky eased the Chevy SUV into gear, drove forward, and turned left. He stopped in front of the Montello residence. As instructed, he turned on the light bar mounted at the top of the windshield and the flashers hidden behind the grill. The flashing white and blue lights lit up the dark street. Beck realized the lights would help if an innocent family was in the house, hurt if the killer was. He peered out from behind his tinted window. He knew he wouldn't see Demarco. He did see the dark shape of the Mercury Marauder parked about a hundred feet behind him, across the intersection and facing the house.

Jablonsky put the vehicle in park and turned off the engine.

Brennan moved to open her door and turned back to Beck. "You're not armed, are you, Mr. Beck?"

"No."

"Do I have to frisk you?"

"Be my guest."

Brennan climbed out of the SUV.

53

Monster-Boy saw the lights flashing on Brennan's SUV.

He watched a tall woman standing on the sidewalk, clipping her police ID onto her down jacket. A slim young man in a suit and tie waited next to her. Cute. He was placing a tri-fold badge wallet into the breast pocket of his suit jacket.

No James Beck.

Monster-Boy squinted, trying to see through the tinted window into the SUV. He thought he saw the shape of somebody in there. Most likely Beck. Probably told him to stay the fuck out of the way. Good. It was too soon for Beck to get what was coming to him.

Monster-Boy knew Beck's pals were here. They'd arrived about five minutes earlier. One went behind the house. Right where he'd told the Worm to hide. Monster-Boy figured Worm had about a fifty-fifty chance against Beck's nigger. He was a big buck. Moved nice and easy. But the Worm had the element of surprise. If he'd hidden like he was told, he might survive. If not, tough shit. Collateral damage. His expiration date was just about up anyhow.

That left the Italian in Beck's car. That fucking wop was already dead. He just didn't know it.

All he needed now was for that dumbass cop in the house to do his part.

54

Beck watched Brennan and Jablonsky take the two steps up to the front door of the small house. He powered down his window, thinking he might be able to hear something, although he was probably too far away.

Brennan reached out and pressed the doorbell. Beck heard the electronic ding-dong chime inside the house. Brennan stepped back to see if any lights went on upstairs. The windows remained dark.

Beck leaned out of the SUV, trying to get a better view.

Brennan stepped back to the front door. She rang the doorbell and knocked on the front door. Finally, lights went on upstairs.

She stepped back, checked to make sure her ID was visible, and motioned for Jablonsky to stand to her right.

Beck thought he saw movement in one of the windows upstairs. A light went on. He thought he heard footsteps coming down the stairs but didn't believe he could have.

A porchlight came on, illuminating Brennan and Jablonsky. Beck could see them better now. Brennan had dressed more like a fashionable suburban mom than a deputy inspector. The jeans fit well enough to reveal her long, shapely legs and. And then Brennan unzipped her jacket and pulled it back behind the Sig-Sauer in the holster at her hip.

A muffled voice sounded from behind the door.

Brennan leaned toward the door and held up her ID to the glass panel set in the door.

She raised her voice loud enough to be heard through the closed door. "It's the NYPD, sir. Are you Richard Montello? Sorry to disturb you, but we're conducting an investigation."

A man's voice shouted through the door.

"I'm a cop. I'm armed. Hold your ID up to the glass again and leave it there."

Brennan did as asked while she reached back and gripped her gun. Jablonsky pulled his suit jacket back and did the same. Beck thought, shit, this is not a good situation for a rookie.

She said, "All right, sir. My name is Dianne Brennan. I'm a deputy inspector. This is officer Jablonsky. If you're holding a weapon, place it on the floor and open the door. Now, please."

Beck had no trouble hearing the shouting voices.

From inside the house, a man's voice said, "I'm calling 911."

Brennan knew enough not to allow that. Anything could be going on inside the house.

"There's no need to do that right now. Is there anybody else in the house?"

"My wife and son."

"Officer Montello, open the door now! And show me your hands."

This is fucked, thought Beck.

Brennan pulled her Sig-Sauer out of her holster and pointed it down against her leg. Jablonsky did the same. He held a Glock.

Beck got out of the SUV. This bullshit had to stop, now. Brennan was wasting too much time. If Manny was in there, they could be killing him.

Brennan stepped to the side of the front door so she wouldn't be hit if someone fired through the door. Jablonsky did the same on the other side.

Brennan yelled, "Open this door now!"

The door didn't move. No response from the occupants.

Beck broke for the house. He ran across the lawn and up the steps in seven seconds. He never hesitated. He timed it so that all his momentum, all his weight and force, were behind the kick that landed just above the door locks. The door flew open as the frame splintered, releasing both the deadbolt lock and the handle lock. The door knocked Richard Montello back. He had a semi-automatic gun in his right hand, pointed to the ceiling. Beck's momentum carried him through the open door. He grabbed Montello's wrist with one hand, the barrel of the gun with his other hand, and twisted the weapon out of Montello's grip. Still holding Montello's wrist, Beck pulled downward and shoved Montello into a La-Z-Boy chair with his right forearm.

Montello's son was standing in front of his mother, holding a rifle. He shouldered it and pointed it at Beck.

Brennan found a light switch near the door and turned on the overhead lights in the living room. She stepped into the room, looked at the father, pointed her Sig at the young man, and yelled, "Put down the rifle now!"

The mother yelled, "Stop it, Richie! Put it down. Put it down!"

Richie listened to his mother.

Jablonsky had stepped close to Richie, his gun dangerously close to the young man's head. He reached out and took the rifle away from Richie. Beck kept the father's gun and angled around the son and mother heading upstairs. In a normal tone of voice, Beck asked, "Is there anybody else in the house?"

The mother yelled, "No!"

Brennan looked around quickly, holstered her gun, and said in a more normal voice. "Okay, everyone calm down. Let's start over." Her ID was now in her left hand. "My name is Dianne Brennan. I'm an NYPD Deputy Inspector." She looked over at Jablonsky and motioned for him to lower his gun. "Did anyone call 911?"

Nobody answered.

"I assume that means no." She pointed to the mother and son. "You two, please take a seat. Then I'll need to see some identification."

Beck reappeared, ignored everyone, and headed to the back of the house. And from there, down to the basement.

When he came back, he released the magazine from Montello's weapon, a Glock-17. Then he ejected a bullet from the chamber. The gun had been ready to shoot. He handed everything to Brennan, said, "There's no one else in the house."

In the next instant, the sound of a shotgun firing broke the silence of the night.

55

Monster-Boy shoved the Econoline's gear shift into drive and accelerated forward, slamming on the brakes almost immediately. He'd already rolled down his passenger side window. He picked up the Remington Tac-3, held the barrel with the strap tight under his left hand, his right hand gripping the bird-shaped stock, his finger on the trigger.

Monster-Boy was more than strong enough to hold, point, fire the shotgun, and bring it back into position for the next shot, even with the heavy recoil from the Winchester Defender shells.

He fired off two blasts, aiming at the driver's side window of the Mercury Marauder. Then, assuming he'd knocked down the Italian, he angled the shotgun downward, firing another blast aimed at the seat. The one-inch slug caught the top of the door and blew a chunk out of it. Monster-Boy kept shooting at the downward angle. Slugs and buckshot blew past the door, tearing apart the interior of the Mercury. Beck had installed ceramic armor plates in both doors strong enough to stop bullets from a range of handguns, but the shotgun ammo never hit the center of the door.

The sound inside the van was deafening. Monster-Boy realized he should have worn ear protection. Fuck it. He kept blasting away. The bigger problem was the gun smoke. Monster-Boy fired off shot after shot, the semi-automatic shotgun performing flawlessly, and with each blast, the interior of the van filled with more gun smoke, blinding him. Half-deaf and blind, he blasted away without mercy, grinning at the image of a human body inside the car blown apart by the deadly ammunition.

But there was nobody inside the Mercury to be torn apart.

The light from the strobes and flashers in Brennan's SUV had been enough to intermittently illuminate the interior of the van parked down the block. When Monster-Boy leaned forward to put the van in gear, Ciro caught the motion in his rearview mirror. He barely had time to reach up, turn off the interior light, and get out of the car before Monster-Boy pulled up and started shooting. By the time the first slug from the shotgun blasted through the driver's side window, Ciro had made it out the passenger door and dropped to the ground. But he hadn't had time to close the door behind him. There was nothing to protect him from shotgun slugs and buckshot that made it out the open passenger door.

As Ciro crawled around the open door and toward the front of the car to get behind the cover of the Mercury's tire rims, Monster-Boy continued blasting shots into the interior of the car. Some of the slugs and 12-gauge buckshot penetrated the floor and smashed into the street below the car. One slug just missed the bottom of the passenger side door frame and flew past Ciro, but one of the 12-gauge balls caught the back of his left calf, ripping away a chunk of muscle and skin, followed by a second ball of buckshot that hit the same leg, severing Ciro's Achille's tendon.

Even crippled, Ciro managed to get up on one leg and fire off five shots from his Smith & Wesson at the disappearing van before he fell back onto the ground.

56

At the sound of the shotgun blasts, Beck ran out of Montello's house.

At the same time, the Worm stepped out from his hiding spot in the hedges, aiming his knife at Demarco Jones's kidney. If there hadn't been a shotgun firing, Demarco would have heard the Worm sooner. Even so, he either heard him or sensed him in time to turn as the first blow from the knife hit him. The blade entered between two of Demarco's lower right ribs. The Worm pulled out the blade to strike again. Demarco knocked him away with a sweeping blow of his forearm. As he fell, the crazed ex-con buried his knife in Demarco's right thigh, splitting the long sartorius muscle, just missing the femoral artery, which would have killed Demarco within a minute or two. The Worm tried to pull the blade out and stab again, but Demarco put two rounds in the Worm's head and one into his heart. His attacker died, leaving his knife in Demarco's thigh, but his grip held on long enough to pull the blade downward.

Monster-Boy had taken a little over six seconds to empty his shotgun. Beck made it across the lawn and to the sidewalk as Monster-Boy shoved the van into gear and floored the accelerator. Without a gun, Beck stood helpless, watching Ciro's shots go wide, missing the van. And then he saw the horrifying, crooked-tooth smile from the behemoth driving past him.

Beck stifled his rage and sense of impotence as he ran toward where Ciro had fallen. Ciro had to be dead or seriously injured from those shotgun blasts. When he got to where Ciro had fallen, he saw his friend pulling himself up off the ground, trying to get into the back seat of the Mercury.

Beck grabbed Ciro around his torso to lift and steady him. "How bad?"

"I saw him before he opened fire. Just my leg. But can't use it, and it hurts like hell."

"All right." Beck helped the big man into the back seat. "Give me your gun."

"What about D?"

"Going for him now."

Beck wrenched open the driver's side door. Shattered glass and pieces of the door were all over the torn-up seat. Beck tried to sweep what he could off the car seat with his foot. Most of the interior damage was on the passenger side. The keys were in the car. He started the Mercury and pulled out fast, driving past the house to get to the backyard. He saw Brennan standing outside the house. He didn't even think of stopping.

He slowed down as he came parallel to the backyard and saw Demarco appear out of the darkness. He was limping, holding a hand to his side. The glare of the headlights showed blood from the right side of his torso down to his foot. Demarco had left the knife in his thigh.

Beck braked, slammed the car into park, and helped Demarco into the back seat next to Ciro.

"What happened?"

"I guess the sneak who got Manny's friends just got me. Didn't hear him with all the shooting. He got me twice. I got him three times. He's dead. I'm not."

"Good."

Beck pulled out his phone and got directions to the nearest hospital. Six minutes away. Beck determined to make it in four.

He drove, saying nothing. Thinking it through. His first call would be to their lawyer, Phineas Dunleavy. Then to his doctor friend, Brandon Wright.

Bullet wounds in Ciro would bring the cops.

The dead body in Montello's backyard would bring more.

Somewhere in the mix would be Dianne Brennan.

His entire crew was out of it now. They'd walked into a setup. How had that happened? How had they fallen for that?

For the moment, Beck forced his attention on two things.

Get medical treatment for Demarco and Ciro. And stay free.

Beck drove so fast that he nearly spun out as he made the last turn toward the Staten Island University Hospital emergency room entrance. He leaned on the horn, jumped out, and opened both rear doors.

Beck ran into the emergency room, yelling for help. He came back out and leaned into the car.

"You know the drill. I'll get Phineas on the way. Let him handle the cops. I'll call Brandon, let him handle the doctors and hospital. Just don't fucking bleed to death or anything."

Emergency room personnel were coming out now with gurneys and equipment.

Beck stood back while Demarco and Ciro were quickly examined and then lifted onto gurneys. As they head toward the emergency room entrance, Beck drove away.

57

Brennan stood for a moment on the front porch of the Montello house. She yelled back into the house and told Jablonsky, "Keep everyone in there. Nobody moves."

She'd heard gunfire in front and behind the house. She pulled her police radio off her hip, hesitating, knowing that whatever control she had over the situation would diminish once other police personnel arrived. She assumed neighbors were already dialing 911. She'd come out onto the front landing just in time to hear Monster-Boy's van leaving and see Beck getting into a black car with bullet holes in the driver's side door and no window. He took off with wheels squealing and the car fishtailing down the street.

She ran around to the back of the house and quickly found the body lying inert in the backyard. She pulled a mini Mag-lite from her jacket pocket and approached the dead man dressed in dirty jeans and a dark hoodie. He had long, unkempt hair, neck tattoos, and two bullet holes in his forehead. She ran the light over the body and saw a third bullet hole in the chest. She pictured the exit wound on the man's back but didn't turn him over.

Christ, what had Beck gotten her into?

He'd busted down the front door of a cop's house in the middle of the night, followed by a shootout in front of the house and a dead man in the back. Roth was going to lose his shit over this mess.

Now what?

240

She still had her police radio in her hand. She clipped it back on her hip and pulled out her cell phone, punching the speed dial for Grimaldi.

He answered quickly.

"Yeah."

"Where are you?"

"At the precinct on Hylan with Dave. Something's waking this house up, boss. Calls about multiple gunshots."

"Yes. One dead. It's a mess. Get over here as fast as you can. We'll have to see if we can control the scene."

"What happened with Beck's lead?"

"I'm about to find out."

"Is Beck still there?"

"No. My bet – he's at the nearest hospital. Get here as fast as you can." Brennan hurried toward the front of the house.

Grimaldi asked, "Where's here?"

"Shit." She realized she didn't know the address. Beck had never given it to her. When she reached the corner, she read off the street signs. "Hurry. It's the house on the corner. You'll see my SUV lights and the front door busted open."

Brennan hurried into the house. Jablonsky had turned on more lights. Richard Montello sat in his underwear and robe, still in the Lay-Z-Boy chair, scowling, massaging his wrist. His wife, also in her bathrobe, sat at the dining room table looking angry and confused, and scared. Brennan hoped her fear outweighed everything else. The son leaned against the wall near the stairs, no expression. He wore sweatpants and a N.Y. Mets t-shirt. The parents were in their fifties. Brennan figured the son for twenty-something.

Brennan had to take control and get answers, now.

"All right, I need your attention. A lot can go wrong in the next few minutes that could cause serious problems for you. Right now, I'm the commanding officer on the scene. But if I leave here without settling things, I can't help you."

Brennan didn't pause for a response. "So far, the only thing you've done wrong is disregard a lawful order to open your door. I'm not going to quibble about the gun and rifle. As for what happened outside, at this point, I'm willing to say none of that is your fault, so I'll do what I can to help you avoid trouble. But the only way I can do that is if you act smart and cooperate."

Police sirens sounded in the distance.

Brennan turned to Jablonsky. "Officer, I want you to stand outside and intercept any police personnel who show up here. Tell them a deputy inspector is in here interviewing the residents and doesn't want to be interrupted. Tell them there is a dead body in the backyard and advise them to follow proper procedures. We need their precinct sergeant on the scene for starters. Understood?"

Jablonsky said, "Yes, ma'am," and headed outside.

Brennan turned to the family.

Richard Montello asked, "Did you say there's a dead body in my backyard?"

"Yes. Shot three times. I'm assuming you know nothing about that."

"You assume right."

"Okay, let's all sit at your dining room table and get through this."

The father and son joined the mother.

Brennan took out the gym membership she had shoved in her coat pocket. She smoothed it out on the dining table.

"This is an application for membership to a gym on Staten Island. The name on the application is Billy Lindberg. The address is your address. Do any of you recognize that name or know why whoever filled out this application used your address?"

Richard Senior picked up the paper, scowled, and looked at it for a second.

"That's total bullshit. Nobody by that name lives here. And we've been here twenty-eight years."

The other two said nothing.

He held up the application and said, "You telling me that's why you came busting into my house in the middle of the night? And what the hell is this about you being a deputy inspector? I been on the force twenty-one years, and whatever is going on here ain't kosher, I can tell you that."

Brennan narrowed her eyes at Montello.

"Twenty-one years?"

"Yeah."

"Montello. You were in the driver training unit at the police academy when I was there. I remember you as being loud and overbearing. I didn't like it then, and I like it a lot less now after that stunt you pulled refusing to open your door to me." Brennan leaned over the dining room table, her voice rising with anger. "You want to know who I am? I'm in command of a special investigation unit that reports directly to Commissioner Warren Roth. Officer Montello, you will never in your life reach my rank. And you will never come as close as you are right now to losing your job and your pension. Not to mention bankrupting your family with legal fees that could crush you. Giving me attitude is a mistake. Don't do it. For the last time, are you going to drop the attitude and cooperate or not? Yes or no. I don't have time to argue."

Montello pursed his lips and nodded.

"I can't hear you. Yes or no."

Brennan got a begrudging, "Yes," seconds before she was about to make good on her threat. She'd be damned if this half-a-cop asshole was going to make her life more difficult. Even with Montello agreeing, Brennan considered having Alphonse and Dave take him in for questioning. And then the son spoke.

"I knew a guy named Lindberg."

Brennan turned to him.

"You did?"

"Yes."

"How did you know him?"

"I went to high school with someone named Lindberg. He was a couple of years ahead of me. I was in a driver's ed class with him. I think his name was Wayne. Wayne Lindberg. Not Billy."

Montello Senior broke in. "See, we don't know any Billy Lindberg. It's got nothing to do with us."

Brennan raised a hand for Montello to keep quiet. She asked the son, "What did Wayne Lindberg look like?"

"Kinda skinny. Long face. A swede. He had blond hair, blue eyes."

Brennan pointed to the address on the application.

"Why is your address on that application?"

Richard Junior shrugged and then said, "I don't know. Maybe the guy used my address and Wayne's name."

"How would he know your address?"

"I don't know."

"But you went to school with someone named Lindberg."

"Yeah. High school."

"Where was that?"

Again, the father started to answer, but Brennan held up her hand and kept her attention on the son.

"Saint Thomas."

"And somebody named Wayne Lindberg was there with you."

"Yeah. But like I said, he was a couple years ahead of me."

"What year was that?"

"I graduated in two thousand six."

"Did you know where Wayne lived?"

"No."

"Someplace near the school?"

"I don't know."

Brennan sat back and picked up the gym application.

"All right. Thanks for your cooperation."

She heard vehicles stopping outside. She looked out the broken front door and saw more flashing lights. Then turned back to the Montello family.

"So, here's the situation. The man who filled out this application is wanted for multiple murders, abduction, extortion, arson, and other crimes. I don't have time to explain more except to say the murders were committed in horrible ways.

"I have two choices. I confiscate your weapons, and we get into a long process that ends up with you being charged as failing to obey a lawful order, obstructing an investigation, brandishing weapons, endangering the lives of police officers, and I'm sure more charges that IAD and the DA's office can come up with." She pointed at Montello Senior and said, "You, Officer Montello, are in double jeopardy. Even if you don't go down on criminal charges and go broke paying lawyers, unless I make a very good case for you to Commissioner Roth, he could easily decide to fire you. He doesn't even need to bother with a hearing. And trust me, the union isn't going to make a big stink if he cans you."

Suddenly, Elaine Montello spoke. She said one word, "Or?"

Brennan turned in her direction, deciding she was the smartest of the three.

"Or, you put your guns away, play down the broken door, say there was a misunderstanding, and I leave." Brennan placed one of her business cards on the dining room table. "Any investigators who show up here who want more information about why I was here and what I asked you, you tell them to contact me. As for everything else, you tell them the truth, which I assume is – you don't know why there was a shootout in the street outside your house or how a dead man ended up in your backyard."

Elaine Montello said, "Agreed. We do not know anything about the shootout or the dead body."

Richard Montello frowned. He scowled at Brennan, but he kept his mouth shut. Brennan gave him a look.

"Are we agreed or not? If not, tell me now. I'll have my detectives take all of you to the local precinct, and we'll sort everything out there."

Montello couldn't keep the disgusted look off his face, but he said, "Yes. Yes, we're agreed."

Without another word, Dianne Brennan left, moving fast, figuring she was one step away from identifying the only man in the world that might save her career – Wayne Lindberg, whoever the hell that was.

58

Beck hadn't driven far from the hospital when he pulled onto a dead-end street, drove past the houses, and shut down the bullet-riddled Mercury.

He stared out at a dark expanse – Ocean Breeze Park. Behind him stood a slumbering neighborhood of modest homes.

Beck listened to the Mercury's sheet metal pinging as it cooled down in the cold March air, struggling to figure out his next move. Too much was spinning in his head. He concentrated, taking slow breaths and trying to clear everything from his mind. Anger and anxiety pulled at him. Where was he right now? What was going on?

The likelihood that Manny was dead had increased. Ciro might be permanently injured. Demarco? Beck didn't know. He'd been stabbed twice. If one of those cuts had punctured his colon, the results could be devastating. Best case, both men would be looking at a long recovery.

His home was gone, at least until he could deal with the restoration. How much damage had been done? Just soot and smoke, or structural? Would he have to rebuild? Did he even want to rebuild? And was it even possible to remain unknown and under the radar in a neighborhood becoming more gentrified every day?

And what about Brennan? The odds were that she would arrest him now. He'd defied her order to stay in the SUV, busted down a door belonging to a police officer, and left her dealing with a shit-show of shots fired and a dead body.

If Brennan didn't find him, driving around in a car shot to hell would attract the attention of any cop that spotted him. And how long would the Mercury last? The transmission was barely functioning.

Thinking about the car brought to mind the ambush. How the fuck did that killer set that up? Beck concentrated, tracking back the steps that brought him to Maple Street in Dongan Hills. It seemed inevitable they would have tracked Eugene or Monster-Boy or whatever his name was to that gym. The Bolo brothers had already discovered that the transmission from the surveillance camera ended up in Staten Island. Even if Joey B hadn't led them to Monster-Boy's drug dealer, they would have found the Xtreme gym just by looking for someone who fit Catherine Hodge's description. Even without her description, the image of Monster-Boy the Bolos had uncovered would have led them to that gym.

But why that address on the gym membership? Did Monster-Boy know that Montello was a cop? Beck had to assume he did. And that Montello would come to the door armed. Dealing with that had given Monster-Boy and his partner a chance to ambush them.

Beck asked himself, but how did Monster-Boy know when we'd show up? He had to know, or else he would have had to stake out the house for hours and hours. And who the hell is Billy Lindberg?

Before Beck could begin to form answers, an explosion hit the back of his car as a van slammed into the rear of the Mercury. Beck was whiplashed back and forth. He had his seatbelt on, so he avoided smashing his face into the steering wheel. And the seat headrest cushioned Beck's head as it snapped back. But the impact still almost knocked Beck unconscious.

Monster-Boy was out of the van and striding toward Beck, intent on getting his hands on Beck.

Monster-Boy tried to yank the car door open, but the collision had compressed the car body and jammed the door into the

248

frame. He reached through the empty space where the driver's side window had been, but Beck leaned away, released his seatbelt, and scrambled over the center console.

Monster-Boy grabbed the car door and pulled and pulled with enough strength so that the entire car rocked back and forth.

Up close, he looked enormous. Crazed and out of control.

Beck ripped open the center console between the seats and pulled out Ciro's Smith & Wesson and Demarco's Glock. He turned and fired twice just as Monster-Boy ripped open the driver's side door. Both shots missed as Monster-Boy lost his balance and staggered backward when the door popped open.

Beck fired twice more, shouldered open the passenger door, and half-fell out of the car, realizing that the rear-end collision had taken away his balance.

He heard a ripping crunch sound, looked over, and saw that the hulk had pulled off the side view mirror. Monster-Boy threw it at Beck, who ducked, but the mirror hit the left side of his head, and he went down hard. From the ground, he shot blindly at his attacker, then rolled over and tried to get to his feet, head spinning, off-balance, struggling to stand up while holding two guns.

By the time Beck was on his feet, Monster-Boy was back at his van reaching for his shotgun. Beck, still wobbly, fired off another shot that went wide. Monster-Boy finally got the Remington, turned, and fired a blast at Beck, who was already heading toward Ocean Breeze Park. Monster-Boy loaded more shells into the shotgun as Beck half-ran, half-stumbled into the darkness of the park.

Monster-Boy yelled, "Fuck it, I'm gonna kill you now. I'm gonna kill you and cut you up in pieces and feed you to the spic, and then set him on fire."

Lights were going on in houses. The sound of the car crash and gunfire had awakened people, but Monster-Boy didn't care. He was muttering now, something incomprehensible, his voice pitching higher as he stomped toward the park.

Out in the dark, Beck stood behind a cluster of three merged oak trees that had grown and formed a single, eight-foot-wide, three-part trunk. He tried to clear his head, blinking and wiping away blood dripping into his left eye. He counted the shots he had fired from Demarco's Glock 17. Four. Demarco had shot three. That left eleven shots. Ciro's gun held eleven rounds. It sounded like he had pegged six shots at the van driving away from Montello's house. Beck had fired one. Four left?

Beck leaned out and fired two more shots from the S&W in the direction he had come. The gun clicked empty.

Beck cursed. He'd forgotten about the shots fired at the Xtreme gym. He shoved the empty gun into his waistband.

He yelled back, "Come and try it, asshole. Come kill me. Come on!"

In the dark, he pulled out his phone as the first shot from the Remington Tac-3 rang out. Tree bark and splinters sprayed as the Defender shotgun shell ripped into the tree on Beck's right. He'd given up his position when he fired the Smith & Wesson. He was about thirty yards away from the shooter. When the ammo hit the tree, Beck realized his enemy was shooting a combination of slugs and buckshot.

Beck gripped Demarco's Glock, dropped into a crouch, moved right, fired twice, and dove back left behind the trees just before the return fire ripped through the space where he'd been. The monster knew how to use a damn shotgun.

Beck punched the speed dial on his phone as he yelled, "Fuck you, asshole. You'll never hit me from there with that shotgun. Come out here and get me."

Beck listened to the phone ringing, cursing, determined to use the only resource he had left – Dianne Brennan.

Monster-Boy answered with three more blasts. All three slugs hit the tree trunks, but some of the 12-gauge buckshot spread wide enough to zing past him.

Beck pressed the phone hard to his ear, listening for Brennan to answer. Fucking voicemail.

Beck ran farther into the dark to a lone hickory tree that barely covered his body. He pushed speed dial again and leaned out, trying to spot Monster-Boy. The police sirens sounded closer. He had to keep that big bastard here. He leaned out, and, instead of firing at the shooter, he shot two rounds aiming at the front tire of the van, knowing there was little chance of hitting a tire from where he stood, shooting with one hand.

Just then, he thought he heard a voice on the phone. He put the phone to his ear.

"Brennan?"

"Yes. Beck, where are you?"

"Shooting it out with the killer."

"What? Where?"

"I'm on a dead-end street near Staten Island University Hospital, near a park. Seal the area. He's in a…"

Another volley of shotgun blasts made Beck duck. A chunk of the tree hit the side of his right shoulder. It tore out a piece of his shirt and skin. It made him drop the phone.

He heard Brennan's voice from the grass. He yelled back at the phone, "Get over here. Now. Blue and white van. Flood the area."

59

Monster-Boy knew the cops were closing in.

No time to shoot it out with fucking James Beck. Fine. That wasn't the plan anyhow. Knowing Beck was heading toward the hospital had given him a chance to fuck with him that he couldn't resist, but it was time to get the hell out.

He ran to his van. The engine was still running. He jumped in, backed away from Beck's Mercury, made a U-turn, and pulled out. Something was squealing under the hood, and he thought he smelled antifreeze hitting the hot engine. Fuck it. Time to get rid of the piece of shit van anyhow.

He made the first right, a left two blocks later, and then kept gunning down the quiet streets, making whatever turns that took him away from the sounds of approaching police.

He raced past a cemetery, slowing down as he approached a commercial area.

He thought about finding an entrance into the cemetery and dumping the van in there but rejected the idea. He'd have to walk a long way to get to transportation, and that was dangerous. His size made him easy to spot.

And then Monster-Boy passed a parking lot filled with trucks and vans, adjacent to a Nissan commercial truck center. New and pre-owned. He had to pull around the corner to get into the lot but managed to find a space where he could hide the Econoline amidst the other trucks and vans. His van ended up blocking a cluster of vehicles, but so fucking what.

He parked and shut down the engine. There was a small duffle bag on the front passenger seat. The bag held extra ammunition for the Remington, a ball cap, a blue windbreaker, and sunglasses.

Monster-Boy jumped out of the Econoline, put on the ballcap and windbreaker, and walked out onto Hylan Boulevard. He found himself standing at a bus stop. Holy shit. Am I that fucking lucky? He peered down the street, looking for an approaching bus. No, not at one-fifteen in the morning you ain't.

Monster-Boy stepped away from the bus stop, pulled out his cell phone, and checked for an Uber. Son of a bitch. Some poor bastard named Amir was working. A fucking sand nigger. Well, those shitbags could be useful. Eleven minutes away.

Monster-Boy went back to the Nissan lot and hunkered down between two trucks as he ordered the car service. He watched the little black figure of a car on his phone heading his way. He listened to the sounds of police sirens ripping through the surrounding streets.

He wondered if he'd make it out of the area.

Well, he thought, still have my shotty. I don't make it; a lot of other assholes won't. He rummaged around in his bag and found the last of his Winchester PDX1 ammunition. He began reloading the shotgun, thinking about his plans for Beck. He was happy with what he'd done tonight. It was nothing compared to what was coming, but good enough for now. Now all he had to do was get back to the house.

Monster-Boy saw the headlights of Uber approaching. He smiled, revealing his mouthful of misshapen teeth, still thinking about how Beck had no fucking idea what was in store for him. Monster-Boy walked to the curb, waved down the Uber, and climbed in. He said hello to Amir, gave him an address within walking distance of his house, and then pulled out his cell phone.

Time to fuck with Beck a little more. He dialed a number on his cell phone. Time to call another man who shared his desire for revenge against James Beck.

60

Beck stood looking at his wrecked Mercury Marauder as the first NYPD patrol cars skidded to a halt. He'd hidden his guns under a bush about twenty yards inside the park along with his brass knuckles. He was clean.

There was also a Mossberg shotgun and $5,000 hidden in a secret compartment in his car's trunk. There was no way anybody would be getting the crumpled trunk open, so he didn't have to worry about that for now. He'd already called Joey B and told him to arrange for a tow truck to get the car and take it to one of the body shops Ciro used and most likely owned part of it.

Beck wanted to call Brandon Wright and Phineas to make sure Ciro and Demarco were okay, but he didn't want to interrupt them. They would call him.

He assumed the Mercury Marauder had seen its last day. It seemed like the shotgun's blasts had penetrated the floor of the car and damaged the transmission. He suspected the impact from the rear-end collision had bent the frame. Maybe they could salvage the engine and the suspension system and other parts. Over the years, Beck had put a lot of work and attention into the car. Maybe it was time to put his attention elsewhere.

Tires squealing and cops shouting interrupted Beck's thoughts. He hated that fucking shouting. All that hands up, hands up, show-me-your-hands bullshit. It just made everything more confusing and dangerous. Maybe one guy should have that job. Do all the fucking shouting while everybody else shut up and watched.

Beck stepped into the glare of the patrol car's headlights with his hands over his head and his fingers spread. His neck hurt like hell. His back was stiff. His shoulder hurt where the tree splinters had hit him. His head ached where the side view mirror had clocked him. He was exhausted, angry, anxious to know about his partners. He had no jacket to ward off the cold night air, which meant he had to fight to keep from shivering. And if he made one wrong move, all these assholes yelling at him would shoot him.

Two more cars arrived.

Someone in the dark yelled, "Down on your knees!"

Motherfuckers. Where the hell is Brennan?

Beck dropped to his knees, realizing that none of these bozos was looking for the sonofabitch who had killed Manny's friends, tried to kill him, and Demarco and Ciro, set his home on fire, and ruined his car. Not a goddamn one of them.

Beck imagined getting off his knees, running back into that park and disappearing. Finding that crazy, juiced-up maniac, and killing him.

Instead, he kept his mouth shut and head down so the glare of the patrol cars' headlights wouldn't blind him. He felt his right hand wrenched down and pulled behind his back. He lowered his left hand to avoid that arm being manhandled, too. There were three cops around him and one cop doing the handcuffing, the largest among the four. He was black. Had a deep, loud voice and was intent on trying to cow Beck.

When Beck's hands were cuffed, the big cop pulled him to his feet. The other uniforms had finally holstered their weapons. Two of them shined their flashlights in Beck's face.

Beck had yet to say a word. No questions. No protests. No reaction to the tight handcuffs. Now that they had Beck standing in the glare of headlights, it was clear from the blood and torn clothes that Beck was injured. It didn't matter to the cop in charge. He yelled at the cops around Beck, "Get him into my patrol car."

Finally, Beck pulled away and yelled back, "Hold it! A man wanted by the NYPD for multiple murders attacked me. He escaped in a blue and white van. He could still be in the area. You need to find him."

The cop shoved Beck toward the patrol car and said, "Shut up."

Beck's last shred of patience evaporated. He turned and tried to break free from the cops holding him. "Don't be a moron. You're fucking up this crime scene and letting a murderer get away."

The cop yelled, "What did you just say to me?"

Beck yelled back, "You heard me!"

The cop grabbed Beck's hair, held his head up, and reared back to punch him in the face. Beck was a fraction of a second from launching a kick between the big cop's legs when a female voice yelled out, "Hold it!"

61

Manny Guzman finally rolled onto his back in the middle of the garage and closed his eyes. It had been over an hour, maybe two hours since he'd heard the van with the bad muffler drive away, the same vehicle he'd been transported in. He assumed both of his abductors had gone, but he didn't know for sure or care. All he cared about was finding a way to kill or maim them.

He'd crawled all over the garage floor, lightly brushing his hands over the gritty concrete floor, trying to find something he could use as a weapon. He couldn't search beyond the four-foot length of his chain and his extended right arm. A little over a hundred square feet. A hundred square feet of nothing. There wasn't a nail, a rock, a piece of broken glass. Nothing.

Then he'd spent time twisting the chain around the forged-steel eyebolt embedded in the concrete floor, trying to break the chain or loosen the eyebolt. Same result. Nothing. Nothing except tearing up the skin on his wrist.

Now he lay on the dirty floor, eating a power bar, thinking it through. They'd taken his belt, his shoes, and emptied his pockets. Manny sometimes carried a knife in his back pocket but usually relied on his revolver – a Charter Arms six-shot Bulldog that fit in his right pants pocket. He carried it whenever he left the Conover Street place. They'd quickly taken that from him.

Manny Guzman was a patient and methodical man. He didn't let pain or frustration deter him. He sat up and drank lukewarm water from the plastic jug, mostly because he felt it would help his headache and keep him more alert. Manny had been through countless episodes of suffering in prison. Beaten more times than he could remember and thrown in solitary housing units more times than he cared to think about. Left alone, angry, hurting, feeling helpless. He'd learned that the worst of it was the helpless part. That's why as soon as he was isolated in one of the bare-bones, stinking, separate housing units, as soon as his pain or injuries subsided, he began making his environment better. Checking out the condition of the cell. How much toilet paper was there? How much soap? His bedding, his mattress. How dirty? How clean? Did the toilet work? His sink. Whatever he could clean, he cleaned. Whatever he could fix, arrange, organize, he did. Anything to push down and defeat feeling helpless.

He told himself he'd been in worse situations than this. He was not helpless.

His eyes had adjusted to the darkness. As he ate, he looked around every part of his makeshift prison. The wood beams and plywood ceiling, the boarded-up windows, the chair he had been sitting on. The walls. For the second or third time, he thought about breaking apart the chair and using a leg or handle for a weapon. And he rejected the idea for the same reason he had before. He needed the element of surprise. If his captors entered and saw the broken chair, it would be over.

He'd been through all of this before, but he went through it again.

And again, he missed it. Almost.

It was the power bar that gave him the idea. The weapon had always been there, lurking just below the surface. He sat up. So goddamn obvious. It was disgusting in its way. It would require work. Work that might make him gag. But it could be a weapon. Maybe two weapons. Why the hell hadn't he thought of it before? Hopefully, he still had time.

62

Dianne Brennan didn't waste time. She showed her credentials to the cop manhandling Beck, told him to take off the cuffs, told him Beck was now in her custody, and then hustled him to her SUV. She didn't speak to Beck, nor he to her. As soon as the doors to the SUV closed, she told Jablonsky, "Go. Head over to that address."

Beck said, "What address?"

Brennan was so angry she grimaced at the effort it took for her to keep her reaction in check. She reminded herself of what she had realized shortly after Beck's phone call.

She turned to Beck.

"There's only one reason I'm not arresting you and throwing you in a cell."

Beck didn't give her the chance to tell him.

"Because you need me for bait."

"You may be annoying, uncontrollable, dangerous, and intent on breaking the law every goddamn chance you get, Mr. Beck, but at least you're not stupid. Yes. I need you for bait. It's obvious the fastest way to get to this murderer is to be around you. He's coming for you. I'd like to tie you to a stake and wait until he crawls out of his hole and tries to kill you."

"That's one plan."

"How did he find you?"

"I don't know. Maybe he figured I'd take my guys to the hospital, and he followed me when I left. I pulled into that dead-end street to try to figure out what the hell happened. I didn't see anybody following me, but I'm not exactly at the top of my game. He rear-ended me and tried to shoot me. I don't suppose you have anybody out there looking for him."

"Two of my detectives."

"That's it?"

"I'm not in command of the precincts here. By the time I could get those people mobilized, our suspect wouldn't be anywhere near this area."

Beck almost said, so much for the all-powerful NYPD, but kept his mouth shut.

Brennan said, "How did he set up that ambush?"

"Best guess, about a month ago, he planted the address of Montello's house at that gym. Probably started watching my place around that time to figure out when and how to snatch Manny. When to torch my place. He knew I'd come after him. He wasn't hard to track down to that gym. I took the bait."

"How'd he know when to be at that house?"

"I don't know." Beck checked his watch. 2:21 a.m. "This whole thing started this morning. Well, yesterday morning. He set my place on fire around three or four o'clock. Staked out that house a few hours later? Seven hours later, I show up with you. I'm sure people have staked out places for a lot longer than that."

Brennan considered Beck's theory. It sounded feasible, but as usual, she sensed he wasn't telling her something.

"Did you say he watched your place for a month?"

"I said he planted that membership application a month ago. But clearly, he surveilled me long enough to figure out the best time and place to snatch Manny."

"How?"

Beck decided he didn't have to keep that information hidden.

"We found a surveillance camera focused on my building. It was mounted on one of the warehouses at the end of Liberty Pier. Sent the feed through the Wi-Fi used by one of the businesses in those warehouses."

"What business?"

"The one where Catherine Hodge works."

Brennan's frustration kicked up a notch.

"You didn't think it important to tell me that?"

"I figured the most important thing was to tell you what she told me. Give you the description of the suspect."

"But not about the surveillance camera."

Beck shrugged. "Sorry. I was focused on other things."

"How'd you find the camera?"

"Friends of mine."

"What friends?"

"Friends who know about that stuff. What did you find out from that family in Dongan Hills? Do they usually answer the door with a gun and rifle?"

"He's a cop."

Beck said, "You think Monster-Boy knew that?"

"Monster-Boy?"

"That's what they call him at that gym."

Brennan said, "Monster-Boy. Jeezus." She shook her head and refocused. "Montello being a cop might just be a coincidence. More cops live on Staten Island than in any other borough. And, frankly, it was lucky for you."

"How so?"

"I was able to pull rank. Browbeat him into keeping his mouth shut about you busting down his front door and assaulting him. Not to mention, I have to deal with why there was a shootout in front of that house and a dead body in the backyard."

Beck's frustration boiled over. He was cold. His head, neck, back, and shoulder hurt. He needed food and sleep. His entire crew was injured or in danger.

"For fuck's sake, Brennan, get your goddamn head on straight. You and your rookie assistant boy-wonder were on the other side of a door with a gun and rifle pointed at you by two idiots who could have opened fire on you. How many fucking times did you tell them to open the door? Four? Five? Neither of you could've knocked down the goddamn door and disarmed Montello, so stop busting my balls. And I'm not the reason there was a shootout or a dead body in the backyard. That's because there's a homicidal maniac on the loose responsible for the deaths of two people and injuring every person close to me and nearly killing me."

Brennan stared at Beck. She wanted to yell at him about getting his men involved, but what was the point? Beck was right. Despite his recklessness, he wasn't responsible for what had happened. And he'd clearly paid a terrible price. His men had been injured, most likely very seriously. He was bloody, banged up, and exhausted. Reading the riot act to Beck would just make him angrier and more crazed.

Brennan reached under the dashboard and pulled down a first aid kit. She told Jablonsky to pull over. Carrying the kit, she got out of the front seat, opened the rear passenger door, and told Beck to climb out.

At first, Beck thought she was going to dump him in the middle of nowhere and leave him. But Brennan said, "I'm too tired to fight with you. If we're going to do this next thing, you need to look human. Come out here and let me clean you up."

"What thing?"

"Take off your shirt."

"It's goddamn cold."

"I have to clean the blood off your head and do something about your wounds."

Beck did as she asked. Brennan laid the first aid kit on the ground, then took out a bottle of hydrogen peroxide and a wad of gauze pads.

"Lean over."

Brennan positioned Beck's head and squirted a stream of the antiseptic all around the side of his head, dabbing with the gauze and dousing the wound until the blood was off. She wiped off the hydrogen peroxide that had dripped onto Beck's neck and back.

"Okay, straighten up."

She shined her Mag-lite at the side of his head.

"It's not too bad. You could use a couple of stitches, but that's not happening. And I can't cut away your hair and shave your head so a Band-Aid will stick."

She squinted at the wound.

Beck said, "You got any Krazy Glue in that first aid kit?"

"No. It's not bleeding. Just let it be for now. Let me see your shoulder."

She performed the same treatment, having Beck lean sideways so the hydrogen peroxide wouldn't hit his pants. This time she covered the ragged cuts with a gauze pad and taped it in place. While she tended to Beck's wound, Brennan explained where they were at.

"Richard Montello is an asshole. Not worth talking about. He's a cop, but barely. He's lucky his wife and son have half a brain between them. The son recognized the name on the gym application. He went to high school with someone named Lindberg, not Billy Lindberg. Someone named Wayne Lindberg. Based on his memory of Wayne and his description, it doesn't sound like this Monster-Boy maniac. So, the only move, now that we missed capturing our suspect when he attacked you, is to track down Wayne Lindberg."

"Okay. How?"

"Fortunately, there is only one Lindberg listed on Staten Island. Name of Walter Lindberg. We were heading toward that address when you called."

"Okay."

Beck had his torn flannel shirt back on, but he couldn't hide the fact that he was shivering. He climbed back into the Chevy. Brennan took the first aid kit and returned to the front passenger seat.

Beck said, "Thanks."

Brennan said, "You're welcome."

"Sorry about my yelling."

Brennan said, "It's understandable. And you happen to be right."

"About what?"

"Jablonsky is a rookie."

Beck smiled. Apparently, Dianne Brennan had a sense of humor underneath all her deputy inspector bullshit.

63

It was the stench of the burned pig meat nauseating him while he was eating his power bar that made Manny sit up and realize he might be able to turn what was left of the pig limb into a weapon. Maybe two.

Manny sat in the chair next to the pig shank lying on the piece of plywood placed on the chair's arms. His captor had left the foreshank and hoof in one piece because together, they mimicked a human forearm and hand. The first job was to separate the hoof from the shank. Manny didn't have a knife to cut through the skin and ligaments, so he used his teeth, gnawing through the rubbery skin and raw meat surrounding the joint. He tried to ignore the burnt taste and feel of pigskin and raw meat in his mouth. He thought about rubbing the hoof joint against the edge of the plywood, but he knew chewing was faster.

Gnawing at the pig joint disgusted him. He distracted himself by imagining how he would use the weapons he was trying to make against the big bastard who had imprisoned him, tortured him, threatened him. Manny had to growl to fight against the revulsion caused by using his front teeth and incisors to chew through the skin, fat, and meat surrounding the hoof joint. He switched to bending and twisting the hoof to tear apart the flesh that covered the joint. The foreshank slipped in his hands. Manny propped the piece of meat against the edge of his chair's arm, feeling for the joint. He positioned it so that the joint was on the edge of the plywood and held the shank in place as he pushed down on the hoof. The skin and ligaments tore, and the joint cracked. He kept at it until he finally pulled the hoof free of the shank.

He quickly removed his socks. He slipped the hoof into one sock, and then that sock into the second one. He tied a knot as close to the top of the socks as possible. He wanted as much length on his improvised blackjack as he could get. He spun the doubled-up socks slowly, one time, and lightly slapped the encased hoof against his thigh. The pain, even with a modest hit, told him he had something to fight with. The hoof was hard. The extra flesh and tissue added enough weight and density to do damage.

Now, he attacked the shank. The monster had poured most of the thickened gasoline on the shank. It had burned out hours ago, but not before it had also burned much of the skin, fat, and meat on the shank bone. Manny worked furiously to peel and strip away everything he could from the bone. He used his hands, fingernails, teeth, even the edge of the plywood board. Within ten minutes, he'd removed enough skin, fat, and flesh from the bone to begin the real work – sharpening the knob of bone at the end of the shank into a point.

He began scraping it against the concrete floor. Turning the greasy pig bone back and forth as he tried to sharpen the edge, but the hard floor chipped pieces off rather than grinding the bone into powder. So instead of trying to form a point, Manny began scraping the knob of the pig shank bone, turning it, scraping it until he had sharpened the whole edge.

Manny's hands were cramped, his knuckles bleeding, his right wrist raw from the handcuff. He found himself short of breath. He stopped. And that's when he heard a car outside braking and a door slamming.

64

Beck asked Brennan, "So where is Walter Lindberg located?"

"Palmer Avenue on the north section of the island. Port Richmond area."

From the driver's seat, Jablonsky said, "About ten minutes."

Beck said, "Think we might be walking into another ambush?"

Brennan said, "Do you?"

"Well, that maniac is still out there."

"Because we didn't catch him?"

"I didn't say that."

"You didn't have to."

"Okay, but maybe we should take a look around that address before we step out."

"Agreed."

Beck said, "And it's almost three o'clock in the morning. Be nice to talk to these people without another confrontation."

"Montello's number was unlisted. Usual for cops. Lindberg's isn't. I'm going to call him now before we barge in."

Beck wondered how Mr. Lindberg would react to a phone call at four in the morning.

The first attempt went to voicemail. Brennan didn't bother leaving a message. She waited a bit and called back. This time somebody answered. Beck could only hear Brennan's side of the conversation. The exchange didn't take long. Brennan was professional and to the point. More importantly, whoever had answered believed that Brennan was with NYPD investigating a murder and agreed to meet her despite the hour.

The last part of the call was the most important.

Brennan said, "Mr. Lindberg, one last question before I see you. Do you have a son named Wayne who went to Saint Thomas High School?"

Brennan listened to the answer, nodded once to Beck, and finished the call.

"Okay, sir. Thank you, we'll see you in about ten minutes."

She turned to Beck.

"He has a son Wayne. Went to Saint Thomas. Lives in Phoenix. We'll talk to him, too, if we have to."

After cruising around the neighborhood and checking every vehicle nearby, Jablonsky stopped in front of a compact wood-frame, shingle-sided house in a row of similar houses on a one-way street. It was the only house with the lights on.

Brennan told Jablonsky, "You might as well stay here, William. Leave your flashers on just so we look official." She said to Beck, "Let's go."

There was a streetlight near the Lindberg house. Brennan paused to look at Beck.

He said, "What?"

"Christ, you're a mess. Your shirt is torn, bloody…"

Beck shrugged. "I'll tailgate on your good looks."

"Yeah, right. Hold on."

Brennan told Jablonsky to pop the hatch and went to the back of the SUV. She opened a small storage space behind the last row of seats and rummaged around until she found a dark blue NYPD Tact Squad raid jacket. Brennan wasn't happy about all the NYPD insignia on it, but she handed it to Beck.

"Put this on."

"You gonna arrest me for impersonating a police officer?"

"And fix your hair."

Beck ran a hand through his thick, dark hair.

"And try not to look so pissed off."

Beck forced an insincere smile.

"And let me do the talking."

Beck held out the image of a generic NYPD badge on his jacket and said, "Why not? Apparently, you outrank me."

"Keep that in mind."

"I will unless you fuck up trying to find the connection between Wayne Lindberg and a murderous, six-eight, overgrown juicer maniac."

"Six-eight? Is he growing?"

"I saw him."

Brennan didn't comment.

As they approached the house, the door opened before they ascended the three steps that led to the front door. A tall man with a fearsomely pronounced chin, thick gray hair disheveled from being awakened at the late hour, and a matching mustache cut square at the ends stood in the doorway. Walter Lindberg looked like a 19th-century lumberjack. He was barefoot and wore faded jeans and an old shirt with paint stains on one sleeve.

Brennan extended her hand, apologized for the intrusion, showed her credentials, and introduced herself. Beck stood behind her, keeping out of her way.

Lindberg accepted Brennan's handshake but said, "What's this all about, and who's he?"

Brennan tipped her head toward Beck without turning around.

She said, "Officer Beck," and left it at that.

Beck nodded and tried to look friendly.

Lindberg motioned them into an entranceway too small for all three of them. He pointed to a modest living room on the right. He let Beck and Brennan enter the living room and followed behind them. A tall, trim, white-haired woman sat ramrod straight in a wingback chair. She had pulled her hair back in a ponytail and wore an old blue and green plaid Pendleton bathrobe with moccasin slippers. The furniture was basic, old, and sturdy. A Toshiba 27-inch cathode-ray tube TV sat on a corner table behind the couch. Beck wondered how long it had been since anybody had turned on the TV.

Emma Lindberg was a handsome woman, her skin marred by a network of fine lines. Beck thought she must be a smoker or had spent a lot of time in the sun.

She, too, asked, "What's this all about?"

Her husband's Nordic accent was slight. Hers was more pronounced.

Walter said, "This is my wife, Emma."

Beck stepped forward and offered his hand. "Sorry to be disturbing you at this hour. My name is Beck."

Emma Lindberg frowned slightly and conceded to the handshake, but it didn't seem to mollify her much.

Brennan's introduction was more official. Again, she showed her credentials. Recited her title. Didn't apologize but explained they were conducting an investigation that involved multiple homicides, and, despite the late hour, they needed their help.

She showed them the gym membership. Pointed out the name, but before she could ask the Lindbergs about it, Beck stepped forward with his phone and held it out to the couple.

"This is a photo of the man who filled out that membership with your last name."

Brennan looked at him with a mixture of anger and confusion.

Beck said, "Sorry, Inspector. It just came through."

Brennan took the phone from Beck, glanced at the image of Monster-Boy, and handed the gym membership form to Walter and the phone to Emma Lindberg, who had stood up from her chair to join her husband.

Emma knew how to expand the image on Beck's phone. She said, "That is not our son."

Brennan said, "Yes, we already know the man pictured there is not your son. And unless your son used the name Billy as a nickname or something, we know the person in this photo only used your last name. We think he used your last name because he went to school with your son at Saint Thomas and presumably remembered your son's last name. Do you recognize him? Do you have any idea who he might be?"

Walter handed the gym membership to Emma. She gave him the phone. Beck could see it was taking time for the Lindbergs to process everything.

Walter said, "There's nobody related to us named Billy."

Emma seemed accustomed to her husband not quite getting the point of something.

"It's the last name they're wondering about, Walt. The first name doesn't matter. Go get your glasses." She took the phone back and squinted at the picture. Beck wondered if she needed glasses, too.

"This face actually looks familiar somehow. It's a strange face."

Beck forgot about Walter and focused on Emma Lindberg. He glanced at Brennan, willing her to keep quiet and let Emma work it through.

Walter returned with his reading glasses. He'd found them on a side table near their couch.

Emma continued looking at the image of Monster-Boy.

Walter propped his glasses on his nose and, for the first time, looked at the image on the phone.

"It's not a very good picture." And then Walter Lindberg said to Beck, "He looks big."

Brennan tried not to appear to be annoyed at Walter addressing his comments to Beck. Typical. He was the other man in the room. At least Beck kept his response simple, avoiding leading the witness.

"Yes. Around six-seven."

And then something clicked in Walter Lindberg's memory. His prominent chin jutted out farther.

"I know who that is, Emma. They're right. He was in high school with Wayne. A big kid. Big but looked young. Wayne tried to get him to play on the football team."

Still thinking about the photo, Emma spoke softly, more to herself than to her husband.

"I seem to remember something like that."

"Sure. Wayne played fullback. He asked the big kid to try out for football because he wanted somebody with size blocking for him. But the kid wouldn't. He pointed him out to me in the parking lot after a game. What the hell was his name?"

Emma kept looking at the picture, eyes narrowed, trying to remember the name.

She said, "I wish Wayne was here. Should we call him?"

Walter Lindberg was now fully engaged by the picture and his effort to remember. Beck didn't want them to bail out and call the son. He wanted him to keep working at it.

"Course he was younger then. Not built up like this guy looks to be. A big, heavyset kid. Kind of a baby-faced kid. With hair, obviously. Long hair, hanging down. Like he wanted to cover his face." Suddenly Walter stabbed a finger at the phone.

"I remember. It's that Cederland kid. Something Cederland. What the hell was his first name? Something unusual about the first name. I don't..."

His voice trailed off, but now Emma's memory kicked in.

No, Walt. No. Not Cederland. I know who you're talking about."

"Not Cederland?"

"No."

Emma got a far-off look. Beck watched her blink. Her eyes went up and to the right as she tried to picture Monster-Boy when he was in high school. They were close now. Beck narrowed his gaze at Emma, willing her to remember. There was nothing in the room now except him and Emma Lindberg.

Walter asked, "You sure? Not Cederland?"

She waved Walt off, not wanting to be distracted. Beck suppressed the urge to tell Walt to keep quiet. Let her think.

Emma said, "His father died when he was young. I remember

that. I think his mother remarried. Not sure. But…" And then she had it. She pointed to the picture and said, "Nederland. Nederland, not Cederland. Ronald Nederland. Not Ron or Ronnie, Ronald. Always Ronald. Kind of formal."

Walter snapped his fingers.

"Right. Right. A weird kid. Didn't they call him Nerdy-land? Nerd something. Ronald Nerdy-land."

"I don't know about the nickname," said Emma. She handed the phone to Beck and the gym application back to Brennan. Very precise. Returning things to the appropriate person.

"That man is Ronald Nederland."

The way Emma Lindberg looked at them said there was no need to ask her if she was sure.

Brennan asked, "How did he spell his name?"

Emma said, "I assume like it sounds, n e d e r l a n d. Pronounced needer. Like cedar. With the one e."

"Do you remember where he lived?"

Emma thought for a moment and said, "No. I don't think I ever knew. Kids came from all over the island to go to Saint Thomas."

"What years did your son go to high school?"

Walter broke in so as not to be left out. He knew this answer.

"From two thousand to two thousand four. But that Nederland boy was one year ahead of him. I think."

Brennan was already planning on how to get the school records from 1999 to 2005. She'd call Grimaldi and Metuchen and put them on it as soon as she got out of this house.

She extended her hand to the couple, realizing now how handsome and wholesome these two people seemed to be. They ought to be living in Maine. Their son shouldn't have gone to school with someone like Ronald Nederland.

"Mr. and Mrs. Lindberg, we can't thank you enough. This is extremely helpful. I'm sorry we can't provide more details. We're running nonstop to locate this individual."

"Oh yes, well…"

"Please keep this visit and our conversation confidential."

Walter Lindberg nodded, distracted. But his wife, still the sharper of the two, said, "Why?"

Beck watched Brennan try to brush off her comment. She had made a mistake. Now she had to fix it.

Brennan shook her head as if it were nothing. "We ask everyone to keep our interviews confidential. It lessens the chances for confusion."

Emma wouldn't let it go. "What does that mean?"

"We just have to be careful, Mrs. Lindberg."

Beck cringed. Brennan might be making this worse. Emma Lindberg had good instincts. She realized that somehow, she and her husband had become linked to someone who had committed multiple homicides. Beck wondered if the Lindbergs might actually be in danger.

Brennan changed tactics. "I assume keeping our interview confidential isn't a problem. Is there someone you'd need to talk to about this?"

Emma thought about it. Finally, she said, "Well, I suppose our son, Wayne."

"Oh, well, I'm sure that would be fine. But it would be better after we finish our investigation. If you don't mind. As I said, it's just standard practice to reduce the chance of confusion, rumors, things like that."

Emma said, "We're not in any danger, are we?"

Brennan answered quickly. "No. Not at all. Particularly if nobody else knows about our conversation."

Walter said, "Okay, then."

Emma nodded, but she didn't look entirely convinced.

They left with a quick round of perfunctory handshakes.

As they walked to the SUV, its lights still flashing, Brennan said to Beck, "When did you really get that photo?"

"Awhile back."

"How?"

"One of my guys pulled it off my security camera and sent it to me. I didn't have time to show it to you. I'm sorry."

"Anything else I don't know?"

"Haven't we been through this already? There's nothing you don't know that will help you with the case. Is there anything I don't know?"

Brennan waved a hand. "I'm so fucking tired of…never mind."

Beck said, "Emma Lindberg is no dummy."

"Why? Just because she didn't like a murderer using their last name?"

"No. Because she's worried they might be the focus of somebody no one in their right mind would want knowing about them."

Brennan said, "He doesn't know them. He pulled that information for the gym membership out of his ass. An address from here. Half a name from there. Another half from somewhere else."

Beck wondered if Brennan really believed that. He didn't. Someone might remember a high school classmate's name. But an address? Unlikely. Beck didn't believe that Monster-Boy Ronald Nederland had done anything without a reason.

Beck trailed behind Brennan as she walked to the SUV. The slight distance from her seemed to give him room to think. He had to figure out his next moves. But to do that, he had to know more about what Brennan was thinking. She acted like she had the lead she needed. She looked like she believed she was one step away from finding her prey. Fire up the big NYPD machine. Scour the databases. Call out the troops. She had the monster's real name. The fact that he'd lived on Staten Island. The high school he went to. A picture and physical description. She believed she had him. Beck didn't.

Whoever Monster-Boy Ronald Nederland was, everything he had done, he'd planned in advance. And all of it for a reason. He'd led them to the house on Maple Street so he could ambush them. He had to know they would eventually find the Lindbergs. And that meant he had to know there was a good chance they'd find out his true identity. Why? To lead them into another trap?

And who was working with Nederland? Demarco had killed one of them. Were there more? Who?

Most important, why was Ronald Nederland, a.k.a. Monster-Boy, doing all this? What had turned a nerdy fat kid into a juiced up, crazed, super-strong, vicious killer?

Beck had no problem with Dianne Brennan racing around Staten Island, looking for her suspect. He just didn't want to be with her as she did it. He wanted to cut loose from her. But how?

65

Manny heard the car pull away. He felt the heart-pounding adrenaline rush that comes before a fight. He knew nothing would happen until the freak came to him. He was chained, confined. He somehow had to turn that to his advantage.

He laid down on the concrete floor, close to the eyebolt so he could extend the five-foot chain as much as possible. He breathed deeply, concentrating on what he was going to do to the maniac who had killed Ramon and Eduardo. Who had abducted him, tortured him, and chained him. Picturing it until his fury replaced his fear.

His only chance was to catch the freak by surprise. Fake sleep. Hide his pig hoof sap under one leg, his shank-bone shiv under the other. Wipe off his greasy hands on his pants and be ready to attack as soon as the big fucker came toward him. But what about the second guy? What if he came at him first?

Fuck it, Manny told himself. You ain't getting out of this alive. You're chained to the goddamn floor. Just try to fucking kill whoever gets close to you and keep fighting until they kill you. And then, he realized, what if they see how he had separated and stripped the pig shank they'd left on that piece of plywood?

He thought about getting up and kicking the plywood off the other chair. Make them figure I just wanted to get that disgusting burned meat away from me.

Manny was about to get to his feet and do that when the side door to the garage burst open, and the overhead light went on. Manny twitched but quickly went motionless.

At first, Ronald Nederland didn't see the spic. Then he saw him on the floor.

"Rise and shine, asshole. Time to die. I got no more use for you."

Manny sat up, trying to look confused. He raised his right forearm in front of his eyes as if he had to block the feeble overhead light but looked intently at his captor to see if he was alone.

The freak had nothing in his hands. No knife, no gun, no gasoline. He wore dark canvas work clothes and black leather work boots with heavy treads.

Without another sound, Monster-Boy rushed at Manny. Manny knew the freak's plan. Stomp him. Kick him. Feel the crunch of bones breaking and hear cries of pain. Manny had seen depraved men revel in the joy of beating another human with their own hands and feet. This evil bastard was one of them.

The adrenaline surged through Manny, making him fast and strong. Blowing away his pain and discomfort. The huge boot came down toward his face. Manny rolled away, gripping the shank bone his leg had been covering. Monster-Boy's foot missed. Manny rolled back and stabbed upward, driving the sharp edge of the shank bone into the bottom of Monster-Boy's thick, hard gluteus maximus muscle.

Monster-Boy roared at the sudden pain and surprise caused by the sharp end of the bone. He lost his balance, teetering on one foot, giving Manny a chance to spring up and ram his shoulder into Monster-Boy's right hip, knocking him off balance. Monster-Boy fell hard on his left side.

Manny dove at him, swinging his hoof sap at Monster-Boy's face, hearing more than feeling the impact. He landed on his knees next to Monster-Boy, swinging the sap again and again, aiming for the nose, eyes, temple – hitting him four times before Monster-Boy swung his massive right arm at Manny, knocking him away.

He roared, "You motherfucker!"

Manny sprang up on his bare feet. Before Monster-Boy could stand up fully, Manny flew at him, stabbing at the massive body in front of him with roundhouse swings aiming the edge of the shank bone at the ribs on Monster-Boy's right side, then he whipped the pig hoof sap aiming for the side of Monster-Boy's head.

Monster-Boy took the blows on his hardened body, blocked some of them, and then kicked Manny. Manny flew backward until the chain caught, and he landed on the floor.

Manny quickly scrambled to his feet. His blows had stunned and hurt Monster-Boy. He watched the hulk touch his face and head where the sap had connected, looking at his side, blood staining his shirt. Monster-Boy felt behind him. Manny's first stab drew blood there, too.

"Jeezus, you sneaky little spic piece of shit. What'd you do? What've you got there?"

Manny held his weapons at his sides. "Come and find out, asshole." He yelled, "Come on!" knowing he would never defeat the massive, muscled-up force standing in front of him.

Manny held up the pig shank. He saw that part of the edge had broken off. The sock had begun to rip. This wasn't going to last too much longer.

He taunted Monster-Boy.

"Come on. I'm chained up here. Come on!"

Monster-Boy lifted a finger and wagged it at Manny.

"Nah. I won't dirty my hands on you. You stink, you know that? You stay right there. I'm gonna blow you to bits, chop off your fucking head, light it on fire, and send what's left to that asshole Beck."

Monster-Boy disappeared out the side door of the garage.

Manny believed every word the freak had said. Now he would be facing a gun and a meat cleaver.

He pushed down his panic. He had to get out. Now.

He dropped the sap and took the bone end of the pig shank. He began rubbing the greasy meat end on his manacled hand

and wrist, furiously trying to work the slippery fat under the handcuff. But he knew that wouldn't be enough. He knew he'd never pull his hand out of the cuffs, so he placed his right hand sideways on the concrete floor, gritted his teeth, roaring against what was to come, Manny Guzman rose up and dropped his right knee down on his right hand once, and then, despite the unbelievable pain, did it again, and again, dropping all of his body weight on his hand, breaking and dislocating all the metacarpal bones in his thumb, little finger, and forefinger from the carpals and ligaments and tendons – crushing his hand.

Then, nearly passing out from the horrendous shock and pain, he stood up and stepped back, pulling the chain taught. Standing sideways toward the eyebolt, he leaned right and then suddenly lurched backward with all the force he could muster, and then again. Lean and jerk back, and again, pulling his mangled hand farther into the cuff, scraping off skin, screaming and tugging until he finally tore his hand free.

Nearly passing out from the ordeal, Manny turned and stumbled his way out of the garage side door. He looked to his right and left. No sign of the freak. Manny turned left and ran barefoot through the backyard of Monster-Boy's house. He had no idea where he was or what he was running toward.

Nederland burst out his back door, having shoved his last three Defender shells into his Remington Tac-3 shotgun. He saw Manny disappear into the scraggly hedge that separated his property from the overgrown empty lot behind his house. He fired a blast from the Remington, but too late to hit Manny, who had already burst through the hedge and turned left on a dead-end street.

Manny saw two houses nearby. Both dark. Ahead of him, an empty, dense expanse rose to fill the space at the end of the road. Manny had no idea he was facing the William T. Davis Wildlife Refuge, 82 acres of scrub forests and salt marshes. He stumbled and ran toward the refuge. Despite his bare feet and the excruciating pain in his right hand and arm, Manny ran for his life.

Monster-Boy stormed through his yard and through the scraggly hedges in pursuit. He couldn't believe he was going to lose the spic. That wasn't going to happen. The guy was half-starved, beat up, and barefoot. How the hell did he get free of that handcuff?

Despite the annoying wounds and bruises from Manny's attack, Monster-Boy moved very quickly for his size. He came out onto the adjoining street just as Manny ran past a guardrail blocking the entrance to the refuge.

Monster-Boy fired another sharp blast from the Remington, knowing his aim had to be good even though the single slug and three 12-gauge balls of buckshot weren't going to spread much.

He thought he saw the spic knocked down just as he entered the overgrown marsh. He lost sight of him amidst the grass, reeds, bushes, and trees. Monster-Boy ran as fast as he could. He had to make sure that piece of shit was dead. He wanted the goddamn body so he could send the head to Beck.

Monster-Boy's aim had been on target, but Manny's bare feet had saved him from death. They gave out as he'd tried to run over the sharp cordgrass growing in the refuge. He'd stumbled and fallen into the dense foliage just as the shotgun fired. The one-inch slug missed his head by inches, but one of the 12-gauge balls hit him as he was falling forward, coming in at an angle, striking his right shoulder blade, cracking the bone, tearing out a trough of skin and muscle, and knocking him forward.

Manny hit the ground hard.

The pain and shock were instant, but Manny forced himself to keep moving, crawling through the reeds and bushes. His right arm and hand were nearly useless, so he used his right elbow, left hand, and knees to move forward. He couldn't crawl in a straight line. He veered off to the right. He had no idea where he was going. All Manny knew was that he had to get away from that shotgun.

And then he heard the sounds of a large body bursting into the dense foliage behind him. The freak. Upright. With sturdy boots. Pushing and shoving his way through the salt marsh.

Manny knew the monster would find him soon. Even though the night was cold and dark, he had to be leaving a trail of bent grasses and foliage as he crawled. He thought he heard the freak closing the distance. He didn't know Monster-Boy had only one shell left in the Remington. All Manny Guzman knew was that he had to keep moving. Keep trying. Fight to the end.

Behind him, Manny heard Monster-Boy grunting and cursing, getting closer. He had to move faster. Manny rose to his feet, staggered forward, trying to run, and then, without warning, it felt as if the earth had disappeared beneath him, and Manny Guzman was falling, falling into a dark, cold void.

66

Beck sat slumped in the passenger seat behind Brennan. He was exhausted. He felt his neck and back getting worse from the rear-end impact. More pain. More stiffness. The wounds on the side of his head and shoulder had stopped bleeding, devolving into dull, persistent aches.

He tried to figure out his next moves. The name Nederland meant nothing to him. He had never seen or heard of anyone by that name. Just like he had never seen anybody who looked like that man who had tried to kill him a short while ago.

Brennan sat in the front passenger seat. Jablonsky behind the wheel. Beck asked, "What are you going to do now?"

"Find Ronald Nederland. What are you going to do?"

Without thinking about it, Beck said, "Check on my friends."

"At the hospital?"

"Yeah."

Brennan said, "I'm not sure I want you running around loose."

"I don't mind if you are."

"Are what?"

"Running around loose."

"That's nice of you."

"Hey, you know everything I know. You don't need me now. Why don't you drop me off at the hospital? That should be a good enough reason to let me go. In case the big boss asks."

Brennan didn't respond to Beck's comment about the big boss. She told Jablonsky to head over to the hospital while she started making calls. The first call was to Grimaldi and Metuchen, telling them to get over to St. Thomas High School, wake somebody up, and get the school records for a student named Ronald Nederland. She recited the years he'd attended.

Beck thought about who he should call. Ronald Nederland knew Demarco and Ciro were at Staten Island University Hospital. He had to make sure they were safe. He pulled out his cell phone. The screen showed a whisper-thin red line in the battery icon and promptly shut off.

"Shit."

Brennan turned to look at Beck. He showed her his phone. "Dead."

Beck closed his eyes. After all that had happened, all the pain and anger and fatigue and danger and frustration, his dead phone battery sent him over the edge. For five seconds, he didn't speak or move.

And then he heard Brennan say to him, "Here."

He looked up. She held out an old flip-phone.

"It's a burner. And the phone number is a throwaway, too. Go on. Use it."

Beck hadn't expected this act of practical kindness from Brennan. He realized he didn't really know what to expect amidst their sniping and bickering, part of which he knew was a form of flirtation, part of which he knew was genuine animosity. They were on opposite sides in too many ways to think about, but Brennan's offer of help made Beck decide that at least for now, Dianne Brennan was not his enemy.

He nodded, said, "Thanks," but didn't take the phone. "The people I'm calling won't answer if they don't recognize the number."

Brennan said, "Jeezus, you're a pain in the ass." She took back the phone, pulled out a cord connected to a USB input in the SUV dashboard, and handed it to him.

"Here. Plug your damn phone in and make your calls. Don't take long."

Beck plugged in the phone but didn't call.

Brennan said, "Now what?"

"I don't think you want to hear any of this."

Brennan looked down, shook her head, and muttered a curse.

Beck smiled and shrugged by way of apology.

Brennan tapped Jablonsky on the arm and motioned with her head.

"Pull over, William."

They both stepped out into the cold, giving Beck his privacy. For a moment, Beck thought there might be a recording device in the SUV but decided he didn't give a shit.

Beck called Willie Reese first, and then Joey B. They both answered on the second ring. He told them quickly what he wanted them to do – get to Staten Island University Hospital and make sure Ciro and Demarco were safe. Bring enough people to cover every point of access into the hospital. He asked Willie to be in Demarco's room. Joey B to be in Ciro's. He told Joey B he needed a jacket or a sweatshirt, a car, a phone charger, and a clean gun.

Both calls had taken a little less than two minutes. Beck noted that Brennan was still on her phone. Jablonsky stood waiting and watching.

Talking to Willie and Joey B dispelled Beck's feelings of inertia and fatigue. Next, he called Alex Liebowitz. Despite the late hour, Liebowitz also picked up quickly.

"Alex, it's me. I want you, Ricky, Jonas, anybody else you know who can help to find every piece of information that exists on someone named Ronald Nederland. White, male, around 30 years old. He's the one in the CCTV photo Ricky and Jonas downloaded. Last name is spelled n-e-d-e-r-land. I want to know any place he has resided, starting with Staten Island. Find his criminal record. Known associates. What he owns. Relatives, employment history, where he shits, and where he breathes. Anybody connected to him. Anything and everything that will help me find him. Search wherever you have to, hack in wherever you need to."

"What else do you know about him?"

"Ronald Nederland attended Saint Thomas High School in Staten Island sometime between 1999 and 2005. Check property records around the area where Ricky and Jonas traced that surveillance camera transmission."

Liebowitz said, "Northwest section of the island."

"Yes, and it might be a good idea to start at a place called Xtreme Gym off Victory Boulevard. Just keep moving in a wider radius from there."

"Okay."

"You still have a backdoor into NCIC?"

"I think so. But just so I know, do the cops have this same information?"

"Pretty much. Not the geographic info we have."

"Then they'll be tapping into NCIC, too. I'd better move on that right now. Get in ahead of them."

"Right, good. And cover your tracks out."

"Always, but it's not a hundred percent. Everything leaves traces. Although they probably won't find any signs I was in unless they're looking for that."

"Do what you can. I'm convinced Nederland is an ex-con, but the cops came up with nothing in New York State. I don't know if you can research out of state prison systems."

"Yes. I can get into national databases. It'll go fast if he was in a federal pen. Otherwise, I have to go state by state."

Beck said, "Okay. High school. Property records. Out of state prison records. Are Ricky and Jonas still there?"

"Yes. And I got one other hacker lined up that I can use."

"Good."

Liebowitz said, "Anything else?"

"I'm sure I'll think of something, but that's it for now. Call me as soon as you find anything useful. He's the one behind all this shit. He's the one I have to find."

"Will do."

Beck cut the call. He looked at his phone. Four percent charged. Maybe he could get it up to ten percent on the ride to Staten Island University Hospital.

67

Monster-Boy tramped around the salt marsh getting his feet wetter with each step, pushing aside bushes, ducking under tree branches, shoving aside grass reeds slapping his face. With each step, he found nothing. With each step, he grew more enraged.

He wondered if any of his fucking moron neighbors had dialed 911 because of the shotgun blasts. Maybe. Maybe not. Probably.

Time for stage two, thought Nederland. A little early, but what the fuck. Be nice to find the dead spic's body to add to the festivities but can't have everything. He was almost sure he'd hit him with the last shot. Let him crawl off and die in this mess. Bleed out in the muck and cold.

Monster-Boy stopped and stood in the wetlands, remaining still, listening for any sound of movement. He held his breath so he could hear better. He heard the wind moving through the marsh, the soft scraping of dry reed stalks, the far-off insistent call of a great horned owl. But nothing that sounded like a human moving in the marsh.

He wiped down the shotgun with his shirtsleeve. Then he pulled out a stalk of dried reed, wrapped it around the barrel of the Remington, and side-armed the weapon as far as he could throw it. He heard the Remington land with a small splash about fifteen yards away. Good enough.

He walked out of the marsh and made his way back to his house, creeping slowly through dark backyards, staying out of sight as much as possible, listening for police sirens, and looking for flashing lights.

When he returned to his house, he spent an hour setting up his next move. First, he went behind the garage and pulled aside a tarpaulin, revealing a cache of material. He retrieved a 28-quart Coleman ice chest holding four gallons of gasoline, a thirty-pound propane tank, and a jerry can filled with 20 liters of gas. He carried the ice chest under his left arm, the jerry can in his right hand, and the propane tank in his left.

He had no trouble with the weight or worries that the gasoline in the ice chest would slosh out because he had sealed the lid with WaterWeld plumber's epoxy.

Once in the garage, he set the ice chest down in the middle of the garage. He had epoxied a 6V lithium battery on the lid and a simple timer switch hard-wired to the battery. Plugged into the switch was a sixteen-gauge extension cord Ronald had cut down to five inches long, with the female end clipped off and stripped bare. The short extension cord had been pushed through a hole drilled in the lid of the ice chest and secured in place with hardened epoxy. Ronald had wrapped heavy-duty steel wool around the exposed ends of the extension cord before he had sealed the lid shut.

It was a primitive but effective and reliable firebomb. With the male end of the extension cord plugged into the timer, once the switch clicked into the on position, the 6-volt battery would send a charge through the extension cord and create a crackling spark at the other end. When the electric spark hit the steel wool, it would ignite the gas fumes gathered in the cooler. The exploding vapors would ignite the four gallons of gas. There would be a muffled whump, followed by a boom as a ball of flaming gasoline burning at 1,700 degrees Fahrenheit filled the garage.

He placed the propane tank on top of the Coleman cooler. The firebomb would engulf the tank in flames and ignite the twenty-two gallons of gasoline Monster-Boy poured onto the floor and walls of the garage, further adding to the fire and heat. Within minutes, the propane in the tank would boil. Pressure would build in the tank because the safety valve was sealed with the same plumber's epoxy. Monster-Boy wished he could be there when the propane tank exploded.

Ronald set the timer switch to turn ninety minutes. He made sure to close the side door to the garage as he left.

Then he went into the house with two more twenty-liter jerry cans filled with gasoline. Pulling his shirt up over his nose to cut down the stench of Brian Bozek's decomposing body, he poured gasoline from one jerry can over the corpse, making sure to soak the battered head and stupid pigtail, then around the room and out into the hallway. He doused the other rooms upstairs, the stairs, and the walls downstairs with the second twenty liters.

He checked his watch. He had forty-seven minutes before the firebomb in the garage ignited.

Ronald hurried through his shower, examining the wounds the spic had inflicted on him. There was a bothersome three-inch cut in the crease where his right buttock met his leg and three similar wounds along his left side. These, in addition to the deep cut on his arm, inflicted by Brian Bozek. All of them annoying, but nothing that would stop him from doing what he had to do.

He covered each wound with an antiseptic ointment and gauze pads and bandaged everything in place with adhesive tape while standing naked in the small second-floor bathroom. He looked at a lump on his forehead, a bruise under his left eye, and another at the bridge of his nose. He had to hand it to the spic. He put up a good fight using that stinking pig shank. He wondered again how the fuck he'd gotten out of the handcuffs. Must've done a number on his hand. Fuck it. Son of a bitch had heart. A righteous con. Now dead for his trouble. Should've stayed clear of asshole James fucking Beck.

Clean of the stench of gasoline and the muddy mess from the marshland, Monster-Boy left his dirty clothes on the floor and changed into loose-fitting black jeans, a t-shirt, and a gray XXXL hooded sweatshirt.

He had already placed a large rolling duffel bag with his belongings on the back steps, along with a backpack holding two Sig Sauer 9-mm semi-automatic handguns with a hundred rounds of ammunition for each and a little over $18,000 in cash.

He checked his watch one more time. 4:48 a.m. Fifteen minutes left.

He carried his duffel bag and backpack and loaded them into his Ford 150 parked on the next street over.

Again, he checked his watch. Ten minutes.

This last part had to be done right.

He hustled back to the house, up the stairs, and three steps into the room where he had set up Genghis Khan. There was a small puddle of gas pooled in Genghis Khan's lap. Monster-Boy edged closer. He had a book of matches in hand. He struck a single match and used it to ignite the entire book. The matches hissed and flamed. He took another half-step and underhanded the flaming matchbook toward the soaked corpse. The toss was perfect. The burning bundle of sulfur and cardboard arced through the air and landed with a soft plop in dead Brian Bozek's lap. Monster-Boy had to stay for just a moment to make sure the gasoline ignited. It wasn't a sure thing. The puddle of gas could have doused the flames, but there were enough fumes and vapor to feed the burning matches. There was a soft whump, and flames blossomed up and around the corpse. Monster-Boy turned and ran.

68

Elliot Tanner parked his car on Seaview Avenue close enough for a relatively quick exit out of the area.

Elliot was 36. He was a reserved, deeply angry young man, made more so in the four years since he'd been shot during the gun battle behind James Beck's building. A 9 mm bullet hit him just below his bulletproof vest at the top of his right hip, shattering his pelvis and twisting him around so violently that he'd torn the ligaments in his right knee. He ended up with a permanent limp, consigned to desk duty for the rest of his police career.

Tanner was from Scotch Irish stock, wiry, strong, raised by parents who grew up in east Texas. His entire clan was racist and bigoted to the bone. His mother and father had inculcated him in a value system devoid of empathy for anyone other than their kind.

Elliot Tanner hid his bitterness and resentment well. He did not attract attention. He dressed neatly in chinos, tie-shoes, collared shirts. Kept his hair trimmed neatly. Had no visible tattoos. He did have a confederate flag tattooed over his right pectoral muscle.

When Ronald Nederland reached out to him, having picked his name from the police reports in the Esposito file, Elliot quickly agreed to help in any way that would cause pain and trouble for James Beck.

When Nederland told Elliot that he wanted to know about the whereabouts of Beck's men at Staten Island University Hospital, Elliot said, "No problem."

Tanner did fantasize about slicing the throat of Beck's nigger and putting a bullet into the wop, but imagining it was as far as it went. Elliot Tanner was still a cop and knew the chances of getting away with a double murder in a hospital were non-existent.

Elliot figured the emergency room was the best place to start locating Ciro Baldassare and Demarco Jones. He didn't figure that James Beck himself would be doing the same thing. When Tanner entered the emergency room area, he saw Beck standing at the intake counter talking to the clerk.

It only took Tanner a second to turn and walk right back out, but he kept near the entrance so he could keep an eye on Beck. Just then, he saw two uniformed cops enter the emergency room lobby and head for the exit.

Beck continued talking to the woman at intake, acting like he hadn't seen the patrol cops. He figured the two cops were on the premises because the hospital had reported a gunshot injury. Fuck 'em. Let them file their reports. Phineas would handle it.

When the cops came out of the emergency room and turned toward their patrol car, Elliot Tanner approached them. He pulled his ID wallet and flashed his badge, trying not to think about Beck as he smiled and introduced himself. If these two had been here because of Beck's men, he wanted to find out whatever they knew.

Beck thanked the woman at the counter and turned away, heading for the emergency room waiting area. The intake clerk had told him that Demarco was in surgery, and Ciro was still in the emergency room holding area waiting to see an orthopedic surgeon.

The woman had made it clear to Beck that he could not visit Ciro. He didn't argue the point. He intended to find out what he needed to with or without her permission.

As soon as he entered the waiting area, he spotted Joey B standing near the swinging doors leading to the treatment area. Beck raised a hand and came toward him.

"Joey, what do you know?"

At five feet six, Joey B was almost as wide as the double doors he stood in front of. Beck had always liked Joey. He listened carefully, made a decision, and stuck with it no matter what. Beck knew Joey B would go down fighting before he left his spot.

Joey answered Beck's wave by pulling a key fob out of his pocket.

"There's a red Nissan Maxima parked in the first row in the parking lot on your left as you go out. The lot is for doctors, but what the fuck. In the cupholder is a portable phone charger. Good for at least two charges. And there's a down jacket on the passenger seat. You know, one of those light ones. Not as good as that Burberry thing you like, but good enough."

"Thanks. You're the best. How's Ciro?"

"Uh, I talked to your doctor friend. He's in there with the lawyer dude. Ciro ain't going to die or anything, but I couldn't really follow what the doc was saying."

"What about Demarco?"

"He's in surgery. That's all I know."

"Right. What happened with those cops I just saw leaving?"

"Nuthin. Phineas took care of it."

Beck knew that meant Phineas told the cops Ciro was his client, and any questions had to come through him. Probably also said his client was too sedated to answer anything. So far, so good.

"Okay. You got people looking out for things?"

"Yeah." Joey nodded toward the waiting area. "Got two guys from a crew Ciro is tight with waiting out there. And two guys I know circulating around outside. Checking entrances, generally looking around. Like that."

"Good. As soon as Ciro gets a room, you set up in there. And have a guy right outside. The woman I talked to said they allow family members to visit twenty-four, seven."

"Good. Ciro's got a big family. You think there might be trouble?"

Beck paused for a moment before he answered.

"I can't say there won't be."

"Who're we looking for?"

Beck couldn't imagine Ronald Nederland walking into the hospital to do something. He'd be spotted immediately. But that didn't mean Ciro and Demarco would be safe. Nederland had used at least one ex-con to attack Manny and stab Demarco. Beck had to assume there could be others working with Nederland.

He said to Joey B, "You're looking for anybody who gets anywhere near Ciro who you don't know. Anybody."

Joey B said, "That would include a lot of doctors and nurses."

Beck nodded. "Just make them introduce themselves to you before they get near Ciro. And show you their ID."

"Doctors are going to love that."

"Tough shit. Be upfront. Tell anybody who balks that somebody tried to kill your uncle, and you gotta make sure nothing happens to him."

"Okay."

Beck realized it might be safer to get Ciro and Demarco treated someplace Ronald Nederland didn't know about. He'd have to talk to Brandon about that.

"Let me go back there and see if I can get an update from Brandon and Phineas before they kick me out."

Joey B stepped aside.

"Good luck."

Beck didn't get more than twenty feet into the treatment area before a nurse at the central workstation called out to him.

"Sir, you can't be in here."

Beck stopped, raised a hand, and nodded at her. He looked around until he spotted Brandon Wright and Phineas Dunleavy outside a curtained-off space at the far end of the treatment area.

The nurse raised her voice.

"Sir! You have to leave."

Beck turned to her and barked, "Just a minute."

It wasn't just Beck's size and demeanor or the bloody bandage on the side of his head that shut her up. It was the look in James Beck's eyes. He had reached his limit. Nobody was going to yell at him or order him around. Not now.

Beck didn't have to wave over Phineas and Brandon. They came to him quickly, both wanting to stave off an explosion.

Brandon spoke first, carefully eyeing Beck's condition as he gently led him to the exit.

"James, let's step out here for a minute."

Phineas said, "We can fill you in out there as easily as in here."

The three of them walked out past Joey B, nodding to him as they led Beck to a small alcove down the hall from the main reception area. They continued to a quiet spot near two vending machines, one dispensing drinks, the other snacks.

It was nearing five in the morning, and although both men had been at the hospital dealing with the situation for a couple of hours, they looked alert and relaxed. Phineas wore a green cashmere turtleneck and wool slacks. Beck thought the color might be called sienna. And, of course, a great looking pair of wing-tip shoes. The colors went well with his dense, unruly white hair. The clothes perfectly fit his short, stocky frame.

Brandon Wright wore custom-made brown half-boots, faded blue jeans, a fitted white shirt, and a dark blue Vicuna sweater. The clothes looked both casual and expensive.

Beck said, "What's the bottom line?"

Phineas spoke first and succinctly.

"Demarco and Ciro are fully lawyered up with me. Not a word to be spoken to anybody. Of course, both lads know that without me telling 'em. So, the operating story of the moment is that both are victims of violence. Demarco's case will obviously be more complicated because he had to shoot somebody. The wounds he incurred are evidence that he acted in self-defense. I've already started negotiations with the district attorney's office.

That's where the work will be done, James. Nobody is about to be arrested. We'll do whatever we have to do."

"Good. Brandon?"

Brandon Wright paused before he answered. Beck waited patiently. He knew Brandon was sorting through a complicated set of medical facts, including sifting through what he had been given access to and what he hadn't.

"Let me talk about Ciro first. I haven't been able to examine him. Nor have I seen the ultrasound results. I don't have any affiliation with this hospital, but I made sure to get on record as the primary care doc for both of them. Ciro had two wounds. Neither life-threatening. One is soft tissue. The other is damage to his Achilles tendon. My preference is to get it treated as soon as possible. The emergency doc's notes said a bullet severed the tendon. I can't really tell how badly until I see the ultrasound. It might only be partially torn. If so, it should be a straightforward repair. After I talk to the orthopedic surgeon, I'll decide if there's a need to move Ciro to somebody I think can do the best repair."

"Okay. And Demarco?"

"More complicated. Stab wounds. Again, haven't examined him. But the surgeon was cooperative. He agreed to take the right type of CT scan and let me see the results. I've seen my share of that type of wound in my ER days. Life-threatening if you don't get to a hospital, only a five or six percent chance of death or serious complications if you do. I don't think the wound punctured the colon, so peritonitis probably isn't a factor. I'm almost certain it did cut the liver. There's a good deal of blood pooling internally. Won't know until the surgeon gets in there and takes a close look. I hope the guy is as good as he says he is. He's doing it laparoscopically as we speak. Should be okay. Fairly long recovery. We don't want to move Demarco for at least a week post-op unless it's absolutely necessary. Are they in danger here?"

"More than they would be elsewhere, but I think we've got that covered. Joey B has people here already. Willie Reese is bringing in his guys to watch over Demarco. It sounds like Demarco isn't going anywhere soon, and Ciro would be better off treated here."

After a pause, Brandon said, "Yes. I think so."

Beck said, "So they stay put. You guys can hang in for a while longer?"

Brandon said, "Of course."

Phineas said, "Absolutely. What about you, James, what's going on? What can you tell us?"

Before he could answer, Beck's phone rang. He had four percent left on his phone's battery. It was Alex Liebowitz.

69

As soon as Brennan dropped Beck off at the hospital, her focus turned to finding Ronald Nederland. She wasn't sure if she should head back to One Police Plaza in Manhattan or stay in Staten Island. She made the decision quickly.

"William, find a place to get coffee and park."

Jablonsky quickly located a 24-hour 7-Eleven on Hylan Boulevard. Three minutes later, he had the big Chevy Tahoe tucked into one of the eight parking spots in front of the store.

While Jablonsky drove, Brennan called Nina Solowitz's cell phone. She checked her watch. 5:34 a.m. She wondered if Nina was awake. She assumed she was at home in Jersey City, a quick commute to police headquarters.

Nina answered on the first ring.

"Yes?"

"Nina, did I wake you?"

"Yes."

"Where are you?"

"On your couch."

"Oh, great, you're there. Did you get any sleep?"

"Some, what do you need?"

Brennan smiled. That was just like Nina. Right to the point and ready to go.

"Okay, we're getting close now. This could be the last push. I've got a name."

Solowitz told Brennan. "Hold on a second. Let me get my AirPods in."

She was under a blanket wearing only her underwear and an NYPD sweatshirt that fell below her hips. She'd locked Brennan's office, but there were no blinds or curtains to cover the glass wall. She tossed aside the blanket, scurried behind Brennan's desk, and grabbed a pen and a legal pad. "Okay, go on."

"The name is Ronald Nederland. White male. You already have a description. He went to high school on Staten Island at Saint Thomas High between two thousand and two thousand four. Most likely grew up on Staten Island. I've got Alphonse and Dave over at that high school figuring out who to wake up to get whatever information the school has. As soon as I hear from them, I'll fill you in. Where's Phil?"

"Sleeping somewhere. I'll find him."

"Okay. You two go downstairs to the RTCC. You know the drill. Scour the databases for anything that will help me locate Ronald Nederland. Criminal record, previous addresses, known associates, hangouts, family members, significant others, whatever. As fast as you can."

"Got it."

"Before you get on that, text me the names and contact numbers of the three precinct commanders on Staten Island."

"You still out there?"

"Yes. Hold on." Brennan covered her cell phone and told Jablonsky as he got out of the Tahoe, "Get me two yogurts. Something with fruit."

"Okay."

"And a bagel."

"What kind?"

"I don't know. Sesame if they have it. Or poppy. Or plain. Toasted if you can. With butter."

"Got it."

She didn't have to tell Jablonsky what size coffee or how she wanted it. He already knew. The biggest he could get with whole milk and two sugars.

Suddenly, Brennan felt ravenous. She wished she could eat a full breakfast. Ham, eggs, potatoes, toast, all if it, but there wasn't time for that now.

Solowitz got her attention back.

"Anything else?"

"Just work as fast as you can. If anybody tries to give you flack at RTCC, call me."

"How do you spell Nederland?"

"N-e-d-e-r-l-a-n-d. Pronounced neederland. I'm going on the assumption that he's been incarcerated. I know you've already scoured New York State, so I assume he served time out of state. You'll have to check the national databases."

"You think it could be federal?"

"I don't know."

"Okay," said Solowitz, "that should be more than enough for now."

"What have you heard from the big boys?"

"Nothing, but I just woke up. Everyone you thought would be at the meeting showed up, plus the usual underlings. I don't know who's doing what yet. I'll call around and tap into the girls' network, but it sounds like you're way ahead of anybody else."

"Good."

Brennan's attention was already turning to how she should orchestrate all this with Roth. He'd be getting reports on the shootout and dead body found at Richard Montello's house, but Brennan figured she had at least a couple of hours before he connected that information to the Nederland case. Any conversation she had about it with Roth would go better if she had a solid lead on Nederland. Brennan knew that Roth would turn over everything she'd found out to the higher-ups when it came time to arrest Nederland. But she wanted to make sure she got full credit for identifying the prime suspect and finding him.

"What's the commissioner's schedule today?"

"The usual, as far as I know. I'll send it to you. But we both know he'll cancel whatever he needs to."

"Let's hope he stays busy on other things for a while. Get going, Nina. Keep in touch. Thanks."

Solowitz hung up just as Jablonsky climbed into the driver's seat with the food and coffee. Brennan smelled hot food. She leaned over to look at the bags in Jablonsky's hand.

"What did you get?"

"Some sort of egg and muffin thing. With bacon."

"Really?"

"Don't worry. I got you one."

"You're a prince."

"Actually, I got four if you want two."

"I knew hiring you was the right move."

"Don't get too excited. They're microwaved."

"Whatever. Unpack the food. I'm going to set up in the back."

Brennan jumped out of the front seat and onto the bench seat. She pulled out her notebook computer from the carry compartment on the back of the passenger seat. Jablonsky tore open the white paper bags carrying the food and laid the paper across the bench seat, placing everything within Brennan's reach

She took a long swig of coffee as she waited for her computer to boot up, organizing her thoughts for a memo to Warren Roth updating him on her progress. She had to be careful with the information. But she wanted the memo on his desk when he walked in at 8:00 a.m.

She waited for her notebook computer to connect to her phone's Wi-Fi hotspot signal, bit off a third of her ham and egg muffin sandwich, and began typing.

Jablonsky interrupted her.

"Anything you want me to do?"

Brennan thought for a moment and, with a mouthful of food, said, "Yes. Look in my briefcase. It's under the front seat.

Pull out the copy of Esposito's file. See if you can find any mention of anything that's connected to the name Nederland."

"Okay. I'm on it."

Brennan took another bite out of her sandwich. It was soggy and tasted dead, but she didn't care. It was food. And the coffee was good.

70

Beck stepped away from Phineas and Brandon to answer his phone. They took the opportunity to pull out their phones and get to work.

Beck didn't waste time with hello.

"What have you got, Alex?"

"How much time do you have?"

Beck stifled his immediate impulse to say, none. Liebowitz almost always overexplained, but Beck appreciated that he had asked first. He'd also learned there was always something in Alex's details worth hearing.

"My phone is about to die, but keep talking until then."

"Okay, first off, Nederland is an ex-con. But he wasn't incarcerated in New York State."

"Where?"

"Alabama. Got lucky there."

"How?"

"Started checking states alphabetically. Nederland was in a hellhole known as Saint Clair Correctional Facility in Springfield, Alabama. It's known as one of the worst prisons in the country. Barbaric comes to mind. Here's a quote: 'a total breakdown of the necessary basic structures that are required to operate a prison safely.' "

"Nice."

"I don't think anybody coming out of there could be normal."

"How long was Nederland in?"

"Seven years on a twelve-year bit for drug trafficking. Don't have much in the way of details. Got paroled four months ago.

Currently wanted for violating his parole five weeks after his release. Left the jurisdiction."

"Anything else?"

"Not yet. We're drilling down on it. I've got a colleague helping me. She's at my place now."

"She knows to keep everything tight?"

"Absolutely. And she's a whiz at breaching secure sites. She's got the software and the experience to get in just about anywhere. And she's fast."

"Sounds good. Do I know her?"

"No. Her name is Lucille. She's a little…"

"What?"

"On the spectrum."

"Oh."

"But it's like a superpower with her. Makes her way focused. All I have to do is point her in the right direction. I love working with her."

"Good."

"Lucille is helping me track down information that will lead us to Nederland. We've gone a couple of levels deep in the five boroughs, the towns in Jersey closest to Staten Island, and the southern half of Westchester. Surprisingly, we've come up with zero addresses for anybody named Nederland. I don't know what that means yet. Maybe just an unusual name, but there it is."

"Okay."

"The Bolos are pushing ahead with their needle in a haystack search to find clients using servers in that area of Staten Island they homed in on before. They haven't found anything connected to the name Nederland. Not surprising since it's doubtful our guy would use his real name, but they have narrowed down the service area a bit, which tells me we're looking in the right neck of the woods."

Beck said, "Okay," as he turned toward the doorway leading out of the hospital. He waved at Phineas to catch his attention and motioned to him that he was going. He was gone before Phineas could put his call on hold or come after him.

Beck held his phone with one hand and dug into his back pocket with the other. He pulled out the driver's licenses they had taken from the patrons at Xtreme gym. He thumbed through them, intending to track down the manager and smash his broken nose against a wall until he told him everything he knew about Billy Lindberg, a.k.a. Monster-Boy, a.k.a. Ronald Nederland. The manager's address on the license was near the Xtreme gym, but Beck didn't know Staten Island well enough to realize that.

As Beck headed to the parking lot to find the car Joey B had brought for him, he asked Liebowitz, "Anything else?"

"Yes. I'm almost done."

"Keep talking. I'll have a phone charger in a minute. If I lose you, I'll call you back."

"Okay. So, the deal is, I doubled down on the area around that gym like you advised. Starting with the thirty-seven hundred block of Victory Boulevard. The good news is there isn't much residential property around there. There's a wildlife refuge, an industrial park, and some kind of recreational area…point being, I'm halfway through."

"How long before you get all the way through?"

"I'm pulling Lucille in on searching property records now. Half hour, tops. Maybe less. Are you still in Staten Island?"

"Yeah."

"Then my advice is head over to the area near the gym. If we hit something, you might be in the right place to get to him faster. Where are you now?"

"Staten Island University Hospital."

Beck heard Alex clicking the keys on his keyboard.

"You've got some ground to cover. By the time you get there, we could have something."

Beck was about to answer when his phone died. He hurried toward a red Nissan Maxima, pushing the unlock button on the key fob Joey B had given him. Flashing taillights confirmed that was the right car.

He plugged in his phone to the portable charger. It was the biggest one he'd ever seen. Clearly, Joey B-for-Big appreciated large sizes.

His phone came awake as he pulled out of the parking space and headed for Seaview Avenue. He heard the signal for a text and smiled when he saw that Alex Liebowitz had sent him directions for the Xtreme gym. He hit the display and a voice came up, telling him to turn right on Seaview, taking the same route Jablonsky had driven to the 7-Eleven on Hylan Boulevard. He made a right turn and accelerated on Hylan toward the Staten Island Expressway, not realizing that Dianne Brennan was fifty feet away, working on her memo to Warren Roth.

Beck drove fast, but he knew not as fast as Demarco Jones would have. Strangely, it wasn't until that moment that Beck fully realized that if he did find Ronald Nederland, he'd be facing him alone.

He reached under the driver's seat, felt around, and pulled out a beautiful Sig Sauer P220 10 mm, semi-auto. Joey B had come through again. It was a heavy, stainless steel gun capable of firing ammunition that had enough impact to put down a bear. Hopefully, enough to put down a monster.

Beck laid the Sig on the passenger seat next to him. He didn't feel quite so alone.

71

Brennan finished the last bullet point on her memo to Roth. She'd played it reasonably straight, communicating every important step in the investigation. The only thing she fudged was Beck's busting in to disarm Montello and his son. She downplayed it by saying: *With assistance from informant Beck, gained access to home of Richard Montello.*

She told herself Roth wouldn't want her to document what had really happened. She'd tell him the details in person.

She scrolled up to the top of the page and skimmed through her work one more time. She wanted the memo to convince Roth she should stay on the case because she was coming up with more information than anyone else. She felt confident it would. Who else was out in the field running nonstop? Brennan figured Fernandez and his homicide cops at the Seven-Six knew Roth would be bumping the case up past his command, so why work when there was such a slim chance of getting credit?

Brennan wanted to call Nina to check her progress, but she decided to wait. Pestering Solowitz wouldn't make her work any faster. And it was better that she didn't know anything new from Solowitz when she sent her memo to Roth. Right now, Brennan could truthfully claim she'd told him everything she knew up to the time she sent the memo. If something came up, she'd tell him. After she'd found Ronald Nederland.

Her cursor was moving toward the SEND icon when Jablonsky turned to her and said, "Uh, did you bring the file on Beck with you?"

"Yes. In my briefcase. Why?"

"Just want to check something."

Brennan said, "Okay," and sent her memo to Roth's NYPD email address, hoping he wouldn't open it until he arrived at the office.

Brennan turned her attention back to Jablonsky.

"What do you want to check?"

Jablonsky answered as he simultaneously skimmed through the Beck file and Esposito's report. He had one file folder on his lap and the other on the passenger seat.

"Something caught my eye."

Brennan said, "Me, too. But I can't remember what it was. Something connected to Staten Island."

Jablonsky nodded. Now he had his phone out, pulling up an app.

He said, "Are you talking about the fact that the cop Beck killed lived on Staten Island?"

"Yeah. I think that was it. But I didn't put much thought into it. Tons of cops live on Staten Island. But I was curious about Beck running down a lead on Staten Island. Haven't had time to connect any dots."

Jablonsky said, "And there doesn't seem to be any connection between Charles Lawrence and Ronald Nederland."

"The cop Beck killed."

"Right. But something was nagging at me."

"What?"

Jablonsky turned another page. "Here it is."

"What?"

"I was looking for Charles Lawrence's home address. Esposito's file has some of the trial proceedings, but Lawrence's home address wasn't in there. I found it in the sentencing report, which is in Beck's file. Charles Lawrence, 168 Burke Avenue, Staten Island."

"So?"

"So that gym where Beck got the lead on Nederland…" Jablonsky held up his phone, showing Brennan a map of the Burke Avenue location. "…is located less than a mile from Charles Lawrence's address."

Brennan stared at the map. Her expression darkened. This was beginning to feel like one too many coincidences. Beck was connected to Charles Lawrence, who had lived near the gym where Ronald Nederland worked out and bought his illegal drugs.

"Okay, it could be nothing, but let's head over to that address. If it doesn't pan out, we'll drop into that gym while we're in the area. See if we can find out more about Monster-Boy."

Jablonsky placed all the files on the passenger seat and pulled out of the 7-Eleven lot.

Brennan hit her speed dial for Nina Solowitz.

"Nina, where are you?"

"In the RTCC, running down data on Ronald Nederland. First pass, I uncovered his criminal record. He was paroled from an Alabama prison…"

Brennan interrupted.

"Okay, good. But listen. I want you to shift gears. I want you to run down property records for 168 Burke Avenue, Staten Island. I want to find anyone who has ever owned that house. Names, relatives, everything. Start with the most recent owner. If it turns out to be a Charles Lawrence or anybody related to him, call me immediately."

Solowitz was not one to ask why. She re-read the name and address so that Brennan could confirm.

She said, "Got it," and hung up.

Brennan dialed Grimaldi's phone. A quick conversation confirmed that any information on Ronald Nederland during the dates he attended Saint Thomas High School would be in the Archdiocese office in Manhattan.

Brennan said, "Set that aside for now, Alphonse. I want you and Dave to meet me at 168 Burke Avenue, Staten Island."

72

Beck followed the voice directions on his smartphone so he didn't have to take his eyes off the road. He was nearing the exit that would lead him to Victory Boulevard when his phone rang. It was Alex Liebowitz, ten minutes before his estimate of a half-hour.

Beck punched the speakerphone icon. The first words he heard were: "Got him."

"Talk to me."

"Listen carefully, James. Where are you?"

"Coming onto Victory Boulevard. I guess a couple of miles east of that gym."

Liebowitz talked quickly.

"Okay, first…the address you're looking for is 168 Burke Avenue. Once you pass that gym, go to the fifth left turn. About a half mile. That's Burke. Turn left. It's a dead-end street. Keep going almost to the end. It's the third house from the end, on your right."

"Who owns the house? Nederland?"

"Not exactly. Just listen. The house is in the estate of someone named Ruth Androvette. She inherited the house from her parents before her marriage. It's still in her name."

"Marriage to who?"

"Ronald Nederland, Senior. Now deceased. They had one child, also Ronald."

"So you got him."

"Yes, but there's more you have to know."

"What?"

"Where are you now?"

"Just turned onto Victory."

"Good. Pull over."

"Why?"

"It's better you're not moving."

Beck felt like lying. Like Telling Liebowitz he had stopped while he kept driving, but he decided to listen to Alex. He pulled over and shoved the gear shift into park.

"Okay. I'm stopped."

"Good. Here's the last part. Ruth Androvette Nederland remarried. Her second husband was Charles Lawrence."

Beck felt a cold shock hit him. He hadn't heard that name spoken out loud in over twelve years, but barely a day had gone by that he didn't think about Charles Lawrence – the cop he'd killed with one punch in a stupid bar fight. The punch that sent him to eight years of hell. The punch that had changed his life forever. Now it all became clear. As if a fog had lifted, and he was able to see where he was and where he'd been since this disaster had started. He checked his watch. Almost precisely twenty-four hours since Manny Guzman had disappeared.

He spoke into the phone, but it was as if Beck were speaking to himself.

"Ronald Nederland is the stepson of the cop I killed?"

"He is. The mother remarried when he was four years old."

Beck felt at once liberated and enervated. In the present, he felt as if he had emerged from a dark tunnel but only to have arrived in a paralyzing no man's land.

He muttered into his phone, "Okay. Keep at it. I'll call you."

He broke the connection and shoved the car into gear. He had to move, to act. To find and confront his enemy. Confront how? To explain? To defend? To destroy this specter from his past who was out to destroy him?

Beck accelerated on Hylan, intent on finding Ronald Nederland's house. When he made a sweeping left turn on Victory

Boulevard, as if to drive home the sudden revelation about Charles Lawrence, a large, roiling, black cloud of smoke rose in the sky to greet him.

The black smoke was on his left. James Beck knew immediately that the smoke was coming from. Nederland's house. Who was he burning this time? Manny?

The thought filled Beck with a disorienting mixture of horror and dread and rage. He pressed the accelerator, pushing the car to race forward and confront his dark fate, dark as the oily smoke in the sky, dark as the churning center of his chest.

He had the Nissan up to nearly ninety miles an hour. The only traffic on the boulevard was a slow-moving step van delivering newspapers. He raced around it as if it weren't there. When he flew by the strip mall where the gym was located, he took his foot off the accelerator but didn't brake. He kept glancing to his left, trying to spot the source of the dark smoke in the dawn sky. The wind was blowing the smoke eastward, making it difficult to estimate the location.

He flew past two streets and braked, looking for Burke. He almost passed it, hit the brake pedal harder, and turned. The back end of the Nissan fishtailed as Beck fought the steering wheel, accelerated, willing the Nissan to straighten out.

Burke Avenue was a narrow street with enough cars parked on both sides to force Beck into the middle of the road. There would be little chance of avoiding a crash if a car appeared coming toward him. Beck didn't care. He accelerated, driven by the fear that Manny might be in that fire. The houses on either side turned into a blur.

He saw flames leaping into the bottom of the dark cloud. Five seconds later, he slid to a halt in front of the burning house.

Beck killed the engine, shoved the car into park, grabbed the Sig-Sauer P220, and ran toward the fire. He pushed through the scraggly hedges, sprinted across the small lawn, and jumped the three steps onto the front porch. Beck barely paused. He lowered his undamaged shoulder and smashed open the front door, stumbling into the burning, smoke-filled house. He wanted to shout for Manny but didn't dare take in enough air to do it. He turned back toward the open doorway and filled his lungs with clean air, shoved the Sig P220 in his waistband, turned, and ran toward the stairs.

The gasoline that Nederland had poured upstairs had seeped through the wooden floor, igniting the ceiling on the first floor. Beck ignored everything and bounded up the stairs with his mouth and nose buried in the crook of his arm, his eyes burning, tears flowing down his face.

Five steps up, a wave of heat hit him. He had to take a breath and almost gagged when the horrible stench of burning flesh and gasoline hit him like he'd run into an invisible wall. He kept going, hunched over, dreading what he was going to find. If there was any chance to save Manny, he had to take it, but the moment he made it to the second-floor landing, he despaired at the thought that his friend and partner might be in the roaring inferno on his right.

Ducking, squinting, his eyes streaming from the smoke, his skin seared by the heat and flames, he shuffled, bent over, to the doorway and peered into the burning room. Amidst the fire and smoke, he saw a twisted human shape burned black, collapsed into the remains of a smoldering wooden chair. Everything seemed to be on fire – the walls, floor, ceiling. He had to hold his hand up to block the heat so he could see the body. He ducked down lower, trying to see under the smoke and flames.

The burned corpse both horrified Beck and brought a nearly disorienting wave of relief. That wasn't Manny. It couldn't be. Way too big. So big that at first, Beck thought it had to be Ronald Nederland. But his second thought was – no, Brian Bozek. Monster-Boy Nederland was setting up an escape for himself.

Beck turned away from the horror. He ran down the hall, checking another bedroom, a cluttered sitting room, and the bathroom. No sign of Manny.

He had to get out of the house, now. The stairs were obscured by the smoke and flames spreading on the ground floor. Beck could barely see them. He tried to get down as quickly as he could without falling. The searing heat surrounded him. Flames crawled along the wall next to him, sucked upward by the inferno on the second floor. It felt like the left side of his head was on fire.

Beck's lungs screamed for oxygen, but he didn't dare breathe in the superheated air. He turned off the stairs and ran toward the back of the house, looking in the dining room, rushing into the kitchen. There were no flames in the kitchen, just smoke and heat. Beck kicked open the back door and stepped out so he could breathe fresh air. He turned back into the kitchen, checking again for Manny. He heard sirens approaching. He spotted a door leading down to the basement. He found a light switch on the wall and stumbled down the steps yelling, "Manny! Manny!"

The basement was dim but free of smoke and heat. He found another light switch. Turned it on. Nothing, just assorted junk. He turned to run back up when he heard a muffled explosion outside. He struggled upstairs. Flames had reached the wood door frame to the kitchen. He heard fire trucks arriving at the front of the house. He took a deep breath while standing at the top of the basement stair, ran up the last two steps, and out the back door. He saw the small garage. Black smoke pouring out of every opening.

Beck jumped off the porch stairs just as the propane tank in the garage exploded. The shock wave knocked him to the ground.

If Nederland had kept Manny at this location, he had to be in that garage. And that meant Manny Guzman was dead.

73

Manny Guzman flailed, helpless to stop his fall. And then, with painful suddenness, he landed hard on the cold, dark water of Main Creek, a tributary of the Fresh Kill.

When he hit the water, it felt like a giant icy fist had come up out of nowhere to smash his face and body. The sting of the cold water kept him from passing out, but that didn't prevent him from thrashing and choking. Manny Guzman had never learned how to swim. And now, with his right hand and arm completely useless, he could barely tread water. Somehow, using his left hand and arm, he managed to get himself upright and his feet under him. He was close enough to the bank so that his bare feet touched the bottom of the creek, but as he tried to walk toward the bank, he sunk into the muck. His heart pounded. The adrenaline rush kept him going, but he couldn't keep his head above the water.

He took a deep breath, leaned forward, let his face go under the surface, and stretched out his functioning left arm. The cold water made his head ache as if it were in a vice. Trying to pull his right leg out of the muck made his left leg sink farther. When Manny tried to lift his head to breathe, he found that he'd had sunk too far to rise above the icy water. He fought down the panic. He reached out farther. The urge to breathe almost made him scream. Manny Guzman knew he only had seconds left before the pain, bleeding, trauma, and lack of oxygen would make him pass out. He stopped trying to pull his feet free of the muck. Manny knew he was close to the bank. He leaned over more, sinking deeper, and then, in one last effort, instead of trying to lift his feet, he pushed forward.

His hand felt something.

A root of some sort. Slimy, but hard and grown deep into the creek bank.

He grabbed the root and pulled himself forward with his last bit of strength. His feet came out of the muck. He kicked underwater, let go of the root, and reached higher, grabbing something solid, pulling himself forward. His head banged into the bank. Once more, he let go and reached higher, taking hold of a handful of thick stalks, and pulled his head above water.

He sucked in the life-saving air, trying not to gasp or groan, greedily pulling the air into his lungs so he wouldn't die but not so loudly so that he would be found.

He stayed where he was, clinging to the stalks, his head against the creek bank, his lower body still in the water. He began to shake, fighting the hypothermia chilling him down to the bone. He heard the monster kicking through the wetlands, crashing through the marsh grass, cursing, pushing bushes and tree branches out of his way.

Manny trying to hear despite his pounding heart and gasps for air. The noise seemed to be moving away from him. Slowly, he eased up out of the water, the effort making his broken hand and cracked scapula explode in pain. The fractured shoulder blade made breathing more difficult, but Manny forced himself to keep going until he was out of the cold creek water.

He felt like he was about to pass out from the pain and trauma, but his rage kept him conscious. He shook uncontrollably now, lying in the cordgrass, the wet marsh under him, listening, tensing his body, fighting to stop the unstoppable shaking. His teeth chattering, he slowly rolled onto his left side so he could slide his damaged right hand in between the buttons of his shirt, improvising a sling of sorts.

He heard a muffled splash. It sounded far off. He sat up slowly, staring out into the darkness. He could see far-off lights

317

back where he had entered the cover of the wildlife refuge, but he couldn't see the monster. He couldn't see any movement through the grasses and foliage. He couldn't move. And he could not stop his raging desire to kill that murderous hulk. He stood up, unable to stop himself from looking for his nemesis, but as soon as he rose to his feet, Manny became dizzy and disoriented. He felt everything inside him fall away. His heart fluttered, everything turned black, and he crumpled down to the ground.

74

Beck jumped up as soon as he hit the ground, standing back from the bloom of smoke and flames that had burst out of the garage door.

He moved toward the blown open garage door, his arm in front of his face to shield himself from the heat and smoke and flames, but as he approached the fire, the heat was too intense to get close enough to see anything. Beck dropped down and crawled under the smoke and flames. He edged far enough forward to see inside. Most of the smoke inside the garage had risen to the ceiling. Everything in the garage, the walls, the ceiling, everything but the floor was on fire. There was nothing on the floor except a small mound of melted and burning plastic, too small to be a body.

Hope made Beck believe it. And then, hope bloomed stronger.

Crawling had given Beck a chance to see bloodstains on the grass leading away from the garage. He had no idea if the blood belonged to Manny, but it was his only lead, so he followed it, bent over, walking slowly in the dawn light, tracking the blood left by Manny's broken and bleeding hand. There were times where he lost the trail and had to walk back and forth to pick it up. Behind him, Beck heard firetrucks pulling to a stop in front of the house, their sirens dying off in a slow grumble. There were shouts, sounds of doors slamming, equipment being pulled off the fire trucks, but Beck ignored all of it and stayed on his trail.

It was the fire that saved Manny. At first, it was the smell of smoke that roused him from his unconscious state. And then the light of the fire. The light and flames rising into the sky, telling him ahead was warmth. And the sounds of sirens telling Manny help was nearby.

He rose up on his left arm, but he didn't trust his feet to hold him. And he wasn't sure he could stand the pain or keep his balance if he tried to walk. So, he crawled. He crawled on one hand and his two knees, his mangled right hand stuck inside his shirt.

Manny had never envisioned crawling with one hand. It was possible but horribly slow. Left hand forward, trying to find a spot on the ground that would cut or damage his only functioning hand. Then move the right knee, then the left. Hand forward, one knee, then the other. Again and again. Carefully, so as not to cause enough excruciating pain to make him pass out. Or cause more bleeding. Manny felt the warm blood trickling down his back, warm blood that quickly turned to join the frigid temperature on the rest of his body.

Despair began to overcome him, driven by the fear that he might not get close enough for the firemen to see him. He cursed at the idea he could pass out and bleed to death in this fucking swamp within walking distance of safety. He kept going, hand, knee, knee, hand, knee, knee – shuffling, pushing himself over the rough, overgrown ground.

Beck followed the faint trail of blood out behind Nederland's garage into the backyard of the house behind. Thick hedges separated the yard from the street behind Nederland's house.

Beck hustled over to the hedges, trying to pick up the blood trail, but the area was too dark and overgrown. He had no choice but to keep going, hoping he was going in the direction that Manny had gone.

Desperate now, Beck hurried out onto Shelby Street, the street that ran parallel to Burke Avenue. Beck turned back for a moment to look at the fire, hoping maybe it would illuminate the street a bit more. Lights were appearing in the houses nearby as the fire woke up the neighborhood.

Beck scanned the asphalt, trying to find blood on the dark, rough surface of the street. There were too many dark spots and stains. Beck looked ahead and saw the end of the road marked by a battered guardrail and a yellow sign mounted on a green U-channel signpost. The sign said END.

If Manny had made it this far, he had a good chance of escaping into that forest or wetland or whatever the hell it was.

Beck ran forward, skirted the guardrail, and plunged into the thick brush and scrub forest, almost overwhelmed by the effort required to push his way through. He emerged from an overgrown area to find himself at a drainage ditch. It was nearly dry. He clambered across it and came face to face with even thicker foliage, but the area to his right looked less overgrown. He headed in that direction, giving up any notion that he could find a trail of blood in the wetlands and just kept going, heading for a clearing in front of him.

Manny felt his strength waning. He looked up, trying to gauge how far he had to go to get back onto a street. The effort of crawling had warmed him but drained him. He thought about dying. Just lying down and dying. This wasn't a bad place. Quiet. Part of nature. For someone who had lived his entire life on the rough streets of New York's worst neighborhoods or inside the bleak, soul-draining walls of prisons, this wildlife refuge felt like its name – a sanctuary, a place safe from all that had tormented him. Manny Guzman had always figured he'd die on the street. Or maybe in a bar or a shithole apartment. Once he'd gotten out of prison, thanks in large part to James Beck, he knew he wasn't going to die in prison, not even in a dingy, stinking prison hospital bed. He'd never really allowed himself to fully imagine dying in a clean bed on Conover Street. Surrounded by his friends and partners, with Beck there and D and Ciro. Maybe even Willie

Reese and some of his boys from the Red Hook neighborhood. All his relatives had either abandoned him or died, one in particular by his own hand, but he still had Beck and his crew.

Manny had never lingered on that dream of being with friends at the time of his death. He had pictured it once or twice. But not for long. Too far-fetched. Nice shit like that didn't happen to guys like him. But this wasn't so bad. At least it was peaceful. Cold. Wet. Muddy. But you could hear birds and smell the salt air.

Except for the goddamn fire. That damn dirty, oily fire set by that goddamn maniac that should die before I fucking die.

Manny reared up and yelled, "Fuck! Fuck, fuck, fuck!"

And then, as if he were dreaming, Manny heard a voice answer back.

"Manny? Manny!"

He knew that voice.

He couldn't believe it.

Was he already dead or hallucinating?

"James."

"Manny!"

"James!"

Beck answered, "I'm here. I'm here. Keep yelling. I can hear you. Where are you?"

"Over here. Can you hear me?"

"Yes."

It sounded like Beck was closer now. Manny was out of breath. He could barely stay upright on his knees.

Manny gasped out, "Over here, James. Yo, over here," and then he collapsed.

75

Jablonsky had the lights and sirens going full blast on the big Chevy Tahoe as he raced along Victory Boulevard toward the smoke darkening the dawn sky over Staten Island.

They had been hearing sirens and monitoring the fire on the FDNY radio channel. When they turned onto Burke Avenue, a glut of fire department equipment filling the narrow street. There were fire engines from two companies, a hook and ladder engine from the local volunteer fire company, and an FDNY pumper truck. Two patrol cars from the NYPD 123rd Precinct were parked at the top of the block to close off access. Two uniformed cops stood by the vehicles, two more uniforms had taken up positions near the fire to keep neighbors and onlookers away from the scene of the fire.

Brennan said to Jablonsky, "Drive around the patrol cars and pull up where that cop is standing.

When Jablonsky arrived near the patrolwoman, Brennan said, "Park here. Let's go."

Jablonsky followed a few paces behind his boss as she approached a slim, dark-haired woman in her early thirties. Her patrol partner stood on the other side of the street. Brennan took in the crisp cut of her uniform and the shine on her shoes. She walked straight to her, ignoring the other cop. She held up her identification and said, "Officer, my name is Dianne Brennan. What's yours?"

If a deputy inspector showing up at a house fire in Staten Island surprised the patrolwoman, she did a good job hiding it.

She answered, "Douglas. Maureen."

"Tell me what you know, Officer Douglas."

Douglas gestured toward the nearly destroyed house. "Don't know a whole lot. The fire was mostly out by the time we got here." She pointed toward Victory Boulevard. "There's a volunteer firehouse over on Victory. And an FDNY house is about three blocks east. I think the volunteer guys got here first."

Brennan glanced at the house. "Even so, looks like a lot of damage was done."

"I heard the fire guys talking about accelerants."

"Anything else?"

Douglas pointed toward a cluster of firemen in front of the house. "They're waiting for a fire marshal to show up."

"Because it was a suspicious fire?"

"Yeah. And if you get closer, you'll smell the other reason."

Brennan turned toward the house. "I can smell it from here."

It was the same unforgettable, nauseating odor she had smelled in the abandoned Red Hook grain terminal. Brennan frowned. She assumed the odor came from the corpse of Manny Guzman and that they had found Ronald Nederland's house.

Brennan turned back to Douglas and nodded. "Okay, thanks. Call your sergeant. Tell him to notify the exec at your precinct that I'm here, and I want him to call me." Brennan handed Douglas her business card. "On that cell number. Right away."

"Yes, ma'am."

Brennan headed toward a group of three firemen gathered in front of the burned wreck that had once been Ruth Androvette's house. Jablonsky followed close behind. One of the firefighters, a tall man, seemed to be doing most of the talking. Two pairs of firefighters were still hosing down the burned remains of the house. Gusts of wind sent smoke and steam wafting around the area. The stench of a burned human body mixed with the acrid smells from the extinguished fire was more intense now.

As Brennan approached the men, the conversation stopped. All three turned toward her, but none of them stepped aside to give her space to enter the group. Brennan stopped a couple of feet from the firemen. She held up her identification and kept her voice and manner neutral.

"Dianne Brennan. NYPD. Deputy Inspector working out of One PP. Who's in charge?"

The tall firefighter, his face streaked with soot and sweat, pointed to the man on his left. He was older, heavier, the commanding officer of his engine company.

The fireman said, "That would be me. For the moment."

"What can you tell me?"

"We're waiting for someone from the Bureau of Investigations."

"Because?"

"The fire was intentional, and there's a body in the ruins."

Brennan nodded. She motioned toward Jablonsky, "This is William Jablonsky, my executive assistant."

There was a pause as the three firefighters absorbed that information. It had the effect Brennan wanted. They were to understand they were dealing with a higher-up.

The senior firefighter said, "I'm Captain Jim Maloney." He pointed to his two men, "Firefighter Second Class Joe Field, Third Class Israel Hernandez."

There were nods all around, but no handshakes.

Brennan asked the taller firefighter, "Field, I take it you were inside."

"Just long enough to search the premises. The fire was still running pretty hot in there."

"What did you see?"

"Signs of accelerant on the floors and walls. A burned-up corpse collapsed in the remains of the upper floor along with the remnants of a chair. I assume the deceased seated himself in the chair."

"He was in a chair?"

"Yes."

"A male?"

"Yes. Too big to be a female. Much too big."

Field pointed toward the heavily damaged second floor. Most of the roof was gone, and the second-floor wall on the north side was mostly gone.

"Fire started on the second floor. It's too soon to say anything definite, but you ask me, it looks like a suicide."

"A suicide?"

"Again, real preliminary. The victim soaked himself in flammable liquid, lit himself up. Remains of a twenty-liter gas can was still in the room."

"How do you know?"

"That corpse is the center of the fire. That's where the fire started, moving out from there."

Brennan asked, "And there was nobody else in the house?"

"Nope. We cleared the premises. I did the above-ground rooms. Hernandez, the basement."

Maloney said, "My guys also cleared the garage. Nothing in there except signs of arson, including a tank of propane lit on fire that exploded. It's a wreck. When we're done hosing everything down, we'll turn it over to the bureau. They'll determine the identity of the presumed suicide, verify the origin and cause in both locations, and so on."

"You're sure he lit himself up?"

"I'm confident the bureau investigators will confirm that."

"How'd he do it?"

Hernandez broke into the conversation. "Amount of accelerant around that body, it wouldn't have been hard. A match. A lighter."

Brennan asked, "And you said the victim was an adult male? Way too large to be female?"

Field answered, "Definitely. I'd estimate well over six feet. My guess, looking at the remains, easily above two hundred pounds."

Brennan asked, "How much of the body is intact?"

"Most of it. Some of it is skeletal. Feet are burned to the bone. Hands, too. Portions of the skull. Mouth and teeth are intact. Legs and torso are there, blackened and burned, of course. It's gonna take time to ID the corpse. We don't even know who owned the house."

"Who called it in?"

Maloney said, "Neighbor in the house behind. Volunteer fire guys got here first."

Brennan said, "Is there any chance I can get in there to look at the body?"

Maloney asked, "Mind if I ask what your interest is here, Inspector?"

Brennan knew she had been asking all the questions, and the firemen had been forthcoming. She had to say something, but she thought for a moment before she spoke.

"We believe the person you think committed suicide is involved in multiple murders we're investigating."

Field said, "You don't want to go in there, Ma'am. Even if you had boots and proper clothing, the bureau would go apeshit if we let you in."

"We've got some sort of jurisdiction, I'm sure."

Field reached into his fireman's coat and pulled out a small digital camera. "I don't think you have to. He handed her the camera. Here. You can see almost as much as if you were in there."

"Oh," said Brennan, "thanks."

She started clicking through images. She already knew the fireman's description didn't fit Manny Guzman. By the second shot, she was convinced the corpse was a match for Ronald Nederland. Field's report didn't convey what the pictures showed. The remains were quite large. Grotesque and misshapen, completely blackened, but the sheer size of the body convinced her that Ronald Nederland had committed suicide. But why? Did he know they were closing in? How?

Brennan handed the camera back to Field.

He said, "Is the guy you're looking for that size?"

Brennan decided there was no reason to be secretive. She said, "Yes."

The firemen waited to see if Brennan had anything else to add. She didn't.

Maloney said, "Well, if you were looking to arrest him or question him, I guess he decided suicide was the better option."

Brennan said, "Yes. It appears to be the case. I appreciate you all for being cooperative. I guess it's obvious the NYPD doesn't usually send a deputy inspector to house fires, but everything is too much in flux to say anything more."

Maloney said, "Understood."

Brennan was about to leave when a voice called out, "Hey."

Brennan and Jablonsky saw Beck first because the others had their backs turned to him. He staggered toward them, coming from between the house and the garage with a nearly comatose Manny Guzman slung across his back in a fireman's carry.

After a few moments of confusion, the firemen, Brennan, and Jablonsky hurried toward Beck. Seeing them, Beck slowly went down on one knee, relieving Manny of the pain caused by carrying him across his back. The firefighters surrounded Beck. Maloney took charge. He stripped off his fireman's coat, laid it on the ground, and said, "Joe, help me get him on the ground. Cover him with your coat. Israel, go get the medical kit, the portable stretcher, and blankets."

Beck said, "He's been shot. Right shoulder blade. Right hand is mangled. He's soaking wet."

Maloney was already on his radio, calling for an ambulance.

Beck knelt next to Manny. He grabbed Manny's left hand and arm. "Hermano, you're okay now. You made it."

Manny grabbed back with surprising strength and pulled Beck toward him, trying to speak into Beck's ear, "You find that fucking monster, James. You find him, and you kill him. Kill him, or he's going to kill all of us."

328

Beck whispered into Manny's ear. "Rest easy. Say nothing. Wait for Phineas. I'll be with you when it's over. Just hang in. Okay?"

"Yeah."

Hernandez appeared with the medical kit and stretcher.

Maloney gently nudged Beck aside and said, "Give us room."

Beck stood up and stepped back. He watched as the firemen rolled Manny onto his side. Maloney cut open the back of Manny's shirt and applied a wound dressing to the area gouged out by the 12-gauge ball of shot. Manny didn't make a sound as Maloney applied a large adhesive bandage. They cut open Manny's shirt and sleeves and gently pulled it off him, taking care not to hurt his grotesquely swollen and bloody right hand. Then they wrapped Manny in a blanket and laid him back down.

As they worked on getting Manny's wet pants off and wrapping him in a second blanket, Beck walked over to Brennan. She said, "Guzman?"

"Yes. Somehow, he got away. I found him out there in the wetlands."

"He was here?" Brennan asked.

"Yes. I couldn't get much out of him, but he told me Nederland had him handcuffed to a chain in that garage. Didn't get any details on how he got away. Part of it was, he busted up his hand so he could squeeze out of the handcuff."

Brennan winced. "Jeezus."

"Yeah. Can't imagine it."

"Did you look for him in the house? Was it burning when you got here?"

"Yes."

"How'd you find it?"

Beck said, "Property records."

Brennan waited for more of an explanation, but that was all Beck was going to say. "Did you see the body?"

"Yes."

"Why do you think Nederland killed himself?"

Beck answered with a shrug. He wasn't surprised Brennan thought that the burned corpse was Nederland. He wasn't going to correct her.

"I don't know. Maybe when Manny got away, he figured it wouldn't be long before you found him. And once he lost Manny, he didn't have any leverage on me."

"But did he know Manny was alive?"

"He never found him. I guess he assumed Manny was alive."

Brennan thought that over for a moment. "Maybe. But why didn't Nederland just run for it? Disappear?"

"Who the fuck knows what a juiced-up maniac was thinking? I don't know a goddamn thing about the guy. How much do you know?" Beck asked.

"Not much. I do know the address of that house is the same as the address of the cop you killed."

Beck tried to look surprised and confused, even though he wasn't.

"Charles Lawrence?"

"Yes. I presume Ronald Nederland was related to him somehow. Maybe a stepson or something."

Beck said, "Who was his mother?"

Brennan said, "No idea."

Just then, Alphonse Grimaldi and Dave Metuchen appeared coming toward Beck and Brennan. Jablonsky had been standing back. He joined Grimaldi and Metuchen. Grimaldi had heard Beck's question.

"We just heard from Solowitz that his mother was someone named Ruth Androvette. We called Nina to catch up on the way over here. She found the property records. Ruth Androvette was the owner of this house. Inherited from her parents. She was married to somebody named Ronald Nederland. They had a kid. The first husband died. Androvette remarried to Charles Lawrence. Nina's still trying to nail down exact dates."

Brennan turned back to Beck. "I guess that explains the motive."

Metuchen looked beyond the burned-up house and saw the firemen still gathered around Manny.

"Who's that?"

Beck said, "Manny Guzman. He escaped. Got shot in the process."

Grimaldi said, "By Ronald Nederland Junior, I presume."

"Yes."

"Where is he?"

Brennan said, "In the house. Burned up. Firemen are calling it a suicide."

Metuchen said, "That's convenient. How'd you ID him?"

Brennan said, "Size. Firemen said the corpse is huge. We'll have to wait for confirmation."

"Even burned up, he could tell?"

Brennan pointed toward Joe Field. "That tall fireman has pictures. Unless there's another six-seven muscle man connected to this house, I'm going with Nederland. Until the medical examiner's office tells us different."

Grimaldi asked, "How long is that going to take?"

Brennan said, "I don't know. I'm sure the fire department's Bureau of Fire Investigation will want the body first. I don't want to get into a big jurisdictional fight. Once the body goes to the ME, we can follow up on it."

Grimaldi was exhausted but didn't argue the point. "Sure. We'll stay on it."

Beck turned to walk back toward Manny, who was now on a stretcher wrapped in blankets, an IV drip in his arm. He'd found out everything there was to know from Brennan and her men. Time to cut loose. At some point, they would find out it wasn't Ronald Nederland burned up in that house, but Beck figured he'd have at least a day or two, maybe three.

Brennan told her men, "I'll be back in a second."

She caught up to Beck and asked, "What are you going to do now?"

"Make sure Manny gets to a hospital and is taken care of. After that, I don't know. Clean up. Eat. Sleep."

"Where?"

Beck hesitated. "Oh, shit. Forgot I don't have a home anymore. I guess a hotel somewhere."

Brennan looked at Beck. It seemed like something had gone out of him. The anger. The relentless drive to find his enemy. Or maybe it was just exhaustion.

Beck said, "Can you do me a favor?"

"What?"

"When the ambulance comes, I don't want to get into an argument with the driver. Can you make sure they take Manny to Staten Island University Hospital?"

"I don't think it'll be a problem. I assume that's the nearest hospital."

Beck said, "My lawyer is there. And a friend who's a doctor. They'll take care of him. Once that's done, I can stand down."

"Okay. I'll tell whoever shows up. How are you going to get there?"

Beck said, "I have a car. What's your next move?"

Brennan took a deep breath and exhaled.

"I have to hang in here. It's a crime scene. I want to make sure it stays my crime scene." She nodded toward the smoldering house. "I'll have to deal with the fire department investigators. I'll get the commissioner involved if I have to. I'll be herding paperwork for weeks."

"He should be pleased with all you did. You ought to get a medal or something."

"I get to keep my job. You only get a medal if somebody shoots at you and you shoot back. And preferably hit them."

Beck looked at her sideways. "Nobody shot at you during this whole thing?"

"Not yet."

"Well," said Beck, "maybe you're not trying hard enough."

Brennan smirked at Beck but didn't say anything.

Beck said, "Well, I got to head over to the hospital."

"Okay. I'm sorry about all the shit that happened to your friends."

Beck said, "Thanks."

Brennan said, "Just one more thing."

"What?"

"When I let you go after our meeting, Roth wasn't too happy with that. He put it on me to make sure you didn't do anything that would bounce back on the department. I can likely smooth over the thing at Montello's house, but that will pretty much use up my chips."

"I understand."

"Understand what?"

"No more get-out-of-jail-free cards."

"Understood."

Beck reached out to offer a handshake to Brennan but saw that his hand was covered with Manny's blood and muck from the wetlands. He lowered it.

"We don't have to shake hands on it."

Brennan said, "No. That's all right."

"Or promise each other we'll have lunch soon. Or a drink. Or whatever bullshit normal people sling."

"No. All I need from you is to tell me this is over."

Beck circled a finger in the air. "This, is over."

He turned and headed for the Nissan. Brennan watched him get in the car. It was then she saw the outline of the Sig Sauer at the small of his back. It was then that she realized she wasn't sure what Beck meant when he pointed around with his index finger and said, "*This*."

Brennan hurried over to Grimaldi and Metuchen.

"Alphonse, Dave, me and William have to stay here and deal with FDNY investigators. Beck seems to be standing down, but

I want to make sure. I want you guys to keep tabs on him. Get over to Staten Island University Hospital. Confirm Beck is there. And get me a status report on his men."

"Baldassare and Jones?"

"Yes. Baldassare was shot, and Jones stabbed. Let me know what's up with them."

Brennan saw the curious looks from Grimaldi and Metuchen, but she didn't explain how she knew they were injured.

"And Guzman is about to be transported there now. Find out everything you can about what's going on and let me know."

"Understood."

"The local precinct will probably be sending detectives to interview Guzman because he's been shot. Maybe you can find out if they learn anything, although I doubt it. Beck's lawyer is there."

Grimaldi said, "We'll ask, but we already know the answer."

"I know. Don't worry about that. Your main job is to keep tabs on Beck. I want him out of the picture until I close out everything with Roth."

A fire department ambulance arrived and slowly drove up the overgrown dirt driveway that led to the garage. Paramedics jumped out and unloaded the gurney. Maloney and his men helped lift Manny onto it.

Metuchen said, "We'd better go."

Brennan said, "Stay in touch," and headed toward the ambulance to make sure they took Guzman to Staten Island University Hospital.

76

Ronald Nederland parked his Ford F-150 in one of five parking lots that were part of an apartment complex eight miles from his now destroyed house on Burke Avenue. He'd parked a second car, a tan eight-year-old Subaru Outback purchased two months earlier, in another lot behind a different building.

A month earlier, Nederland had signed a ninety-day lease for a furnished one-bedroom apartment using an altered Alabama driver's license that identified him as Wayne Rosenberg. Nederland liked using a Jewish name. It made him feel disconnected from himself. When the rental agent told Monster-Boy he needed to check his credit, Nederland paid the full ninety days in cash.

The complex consisted of five brick buildings separated by lawns and walkways. Each of the buildings held four units. Each building had its own parking lot in the rear. Nederland's unit was on the second floor of Building C facing the lot, a one-bedroom with a modest kitchen. An open counter connected the kitchen to a sitting area not large enough to be called a living room. A short hallway led to a bathroom that was almost too small for Nederland to use and a bedroom with a twin-size bed definitely too small for him. The carpeting was inexpensive. The furniture was basic to the point of being expendable.

Nederland carried a backpack and a duffel bag up the rear steps and into the apartment, then stashed them in the bedroom. In the confined space, he smelled the acrid odor of oily smoke clinging to him.

Ronald stripped off his shoes and clothes. There was a combination washer/dryer in the kitchen. He stuffed everything into the washer, found a detergent pod, selected heavy-duty, and started the machine. He didn't intend to wear the clothes again but wanted to get rid of the smell.

He was tired, hungry, and thirsty. He'd stocked the refrigerator with eggs, packaged ham, and milk. He grabbed a Brita water pitcher and drank out of it, draining half of it.

Still naked, he walked to the sitting area and began doing pushups. He did a hundred of them, followed by a hundred sit-ups, followed by a hundred curls using two of the stools pushed against the counter.

He showered, injected himself with his daily intake of drugs, then treated and bandaged his cuts. There was nothing he could do about the bruises on his face.

He dressed in khaki work pants, a long-sleeve t-shirt, and a gray XXXL waffle-knit thermal shirt.

Nederland made a mess of the kitchen trying to scramble a bowl full of sliced ham and eggs in a too-small frying pan. He wolfed down the food standing up, drinking milk from the carton. He dropped the bowl and frying pan into the sink. Nederland had no intention of washing them.

He checked his watch. 8:35 a.m. He needed to locate Beck, but not now. Now he needed sleep. His contact probably didn't know anything yet anyhow.

Monster-Boy made his way to the bedroom. Shut the cheap blinds and crawled under the polyester blanket. He curled into a fetal position, the only way to fit on the too-small bed. He imagined the drugs and the food revitalizing him. He felt himself getting an erection. He stroked his cock through his pants, mostly for reassurance and a flutter of pleasure. Now would be a good time to have the Worm around. Too bad.

Monster-Boy comforted himself by thinking about the final reckoning. And what he would do to James Beck. Tie his wrists and ankles, hang him up, and start cutting. He'd cut him to shreds. He'd cut off his ears and nose and lips. He'd use him for a punching bag. Then a kicking bag. He'd hit him and break him and let him bleed out, and then light him on fire and watch him turn into a burnt, blackened thing that he would leave strung up like a dead animal.

Monster-Boy fell asleep, hearing Beck's screams and smelling the burning flesh.

77

Beck couldn't wait to get into his car and be on his own.

He drove off quickly. He had no intention of going to the hospital. Brandon Wright and Phineas Dunleavy would do more than he could. As would Willie Reese, Joey B, and the men they'd gathered.

Beck also had no intention of staying connected to Dianne Brennan. As far as he knew, she had treated him fairly, but now he needed to be free of her. By murdering and burning Brian Bozek, Nederland had bought time for himself and for Beck. How much time, Beck didn't know. Even if Bozek's girlfriend reported him missing in the next day or so, nothing would connect him to the house on Burke Avenue. It might be days before the medical examiner's office identified the corpse.

It didn't matter. Beck knew that until Nederland killed him, Monster-Boy wasn't going anywhere.

Beck thought about what had propelled Ronald Nederland onto his path of revenge. He thought back to the bar in Brooklyn where he'd gotten into the altercation with Charles Lawrence, Ronald Nederland's stepfather. A cop. A detective. A loudmouth out getting drunk with his cop buddies. Beck himself hadn't been entirely sober. He'd been nursing a shot of bourbon and a lager at the time, waiting for a hamburger. Charles Lawrence had been mouthing off. Doing a loud, annoying interpretation of Al Pacino in *Scent of a Woman*. "I'm in the daaaaark here!" Yelling. Acting like he and his two cop buddies owned the place. At first, it was just annoying. But when their bullshit went on and on, it pissed him off. Why? The entitlement. The fact that those cops didn't give a shit about anybody else in the bar finally got to him.

Beck had gone through what happened next hundreds of times. Maybe thousands. During his arrest, when the other two cops pinned him to the bar and put him in handcuffs. Sitting in the precinct holding cell with detectives and cops threatening him. Waiting and waiting because they delayed his paperwork. Waiting to call a lawyer. Waiting until his bladder almost burst before they let him go to the bathroom. Waiting in the court holding cell to be arraigned. He'd become obsessed with that one moment in time. He'd thought the thirty-six-hour ordeal was punishment enough for one punch.

In the bar, when Detective Charles Lawrence wouldn't shut the fuck up, Beck had finally said to him, "Hey. Why don't you give it a rest?"

The result was predictable.

"What did you say to me?"

"I said, why don't you give it a rest?"

"Why don't you shut the fuck up, asshole."

Beck stood up. The cop leaped off his barstool and came right up to Beck. Then the chest bump. Then, in an instant, without thinking about it, with no thought of the hell that would ensue, Beck punched him. A fast, hard, angry uppercut. Caught him right on the chin.

That's all it took. One punch. The fatal moment that started a nightmare, beginning with thirty-eight hours they had locked him up until his arraignment. Then seventy-five-hundred dollars for a lawyer that drained Beck's savings. Then months of negotiations that went nowhere. More money evaporating. A trial. Endless days in court. The judge overruling his lawyer on every motion. The DA's office withholding testimony. The arresting officer lying on the stand. Beck helpless to change the course of his slow, steady slide into hell.

And then, unbelievably, the verdict. Guilty. Second-degree manslaughter. Fifteen to twenty-five. Twenty-five fucking years.

At the sentencing, the judge came down on him with both feet. Assigned him to a maximum-security prison on a second-degree manslaughter charge. The victim was a cop. Beck had killed a cop.

And then those first days in Dannemora where proving himself sent him into the lonely, horrible, hallucinatory days during his first stretch in solitary confinement. That was when Beck would have made a bargain with the Devil to change that moment in that Court Street cop bar. Beck had finally admitted to himself that he could have just pushed the man back. Made it a shoving match. The kind of bar alteration where somebody stepped in and broke it up. Settled it down. Beck admitted he had been angry. Something snapped. He would not be bullied.

He'd asked himself thousands of times if he really believed the drunk cop was going to hit him. Did he? Yes. No. Probably. Beck had always ended up in the same place. The place he'd believed in eventually. He didn't start it. He certainly didn't intend to kill the man. The cop shouldn't have died. It was luck or fate or karma that he had hit his head on the edge of the bar going down. And then on the tile floor. The skull fractured in three places. And who knows if the doctors had botched his treatment? Three days later, Detective Charles Lawrence died. That was the only final, unarguable truth that mattered. And Beck had gone to prison. He spent years finding a lawyer that would take his case. More years appealing the verdict. Even then, his prospects were bleak until Phineas Dunleavy found out that the over-zealous DA had withheld the testimony of the one cop who'd told the truth.

Eight horrible years that had made James Beck into who he was today.

And apparently, had somehow made Ronald Nederland who he was. How had Nederland ended up in an Alabama prison? What had happened to him there? It wasn't hard for Beck to picture what had turned Ronald Nederland into a monster. A young, white northerner, first-time offender, in an Alabama prison? How many times had Ronald Nederland been beaten, raped, extorted, shanked, terrorized before he had earned the name "Monster-Boy"?

Had prison turned Beck into a monster, too? Someone willing to kill. Maybe even eager to kill?

Did it matter? Did any of it matter?

Whatever had come before, Beck knew the final reckoning was coming now. Ronald Nederland had tried to kill his friends, the closest thing Beck had to a family. Now he was going to try to kill him. To beat him, cut him, torture him, and burn him.

So be it, thought Beck, but now, right now, nothing happens until I eat and sleep.

Fatigue and the situation he found himself in hit Beck all at once. He pulled over, located the closest hotel on his phone, and tapped the hotel icon to bring up driving directions.

He took a deep breath, pulled back onto the road, and followed the mechanical voice on a path that led to a Ramada Inn.

He drove into a parking lot running alongside a gray, squat, bunker-like building. Beck could see outdoor lights and cameras mounted on corners and walls. He parked in the first empty spot he found, shoved the Sig into his waistband, covered it with the down jacket Joey B had provided, and walked around into the hotel.

There was a young man at the desk who looked like a high school student. Long, black hair hid some of the adolescent acne that marred his jawline and cheeks. He wore a white shirt and dark pants. A minimalist version of business wear.

Beck checked the analog clock mounted on the wall to the right of the counter. 9:02 a.m. The hotel décor featured wood tones, faux marble, and modern wall coverings. A cut-rate attempt to appear luxe. But the ceilings were too low and the lighting too harsh to pull it off. Cheap didn't get covered over so easily.

The young man seemed to take a long time finding a room on the hotel's computer. All the clicking and mousing around gave Beck the impression the young man didn't know what he was doing. Nor did the hotel clerk seem to notice the blood on Beck's shirt collar, the bandage on his ear, and the lack of luggage.

Finally, the young man said, "Uh, the only room I have ready right now is the jacuzzi room."

Beck blinked back his fatigue. First, he couldn't believe the place was full. More likely, the kid couldn't find the inventory, with all his farting around on the computer. Beck didn't have the energy to argue about it. But he had to know, "What does that mean? The jacuzzi room."

"Uh, there's a jacuzzi in the room."

"I got that part. But with a bed and bathroom and all the usual stuff?"

"Yeah. A king-size bed."

"Okay, fine. I'll take it."

Beck didn't bother to ask what floor it was on. There were only two floors in the motel. He did ask, "Is there any food available? A restaurant?"

"No restaurant, but we are serving breakfast. And our pantry is open."

"Okay," said Beck, thinking that serving breakfast without a restaurant is a good trick and wondering what the boy meant by the pantry is open.

Beck used his Thomas Eaton driver's license and paid cash for one night. He got his room card and wandered into the serving area wincing at the décor, the cheerful colors, the furniture, an attempt at what? Cheerfulness? Business casual?

Breakfast foods were laid out on top of a long counter at the end of a room with four tables.

Beck navigated passed the assortment of cheap carbs – pastries, muffins, bread, cereals, juices – and picked out two hardboiled eggs, two cartons of milk plucked from a bowl of melting ice, two small cups of yogurt, flabby slices of processed ham, and a wan slice of unidentifiable cheese. He added two pieces of rye bread and stacked everything between two plates so he could carry the fuel to his room. He didn't have the heart to check the *pantry*, whatever that was. Clearly, they had built this motel on the DIY principle.

Despite the warning, Beck could hardly believe what he saw. A giant jacuzzi filling half the goddamn room. A massive black plastic tub surrounded by a black base, not in the bathroom, but right next to the bed. What the fuck, thought Beck.

He set his food on the edge of the tub, the only available horizontal space in the room other than the bed and a tiny nightstand.

The room was in the back section of the motel. Beck pulled aside a green polyester curtain. There was nothing much to see except the parking lot.

He sat on the edge of the bed and used the corner of the jacuzzi as a table, eating his food methodically, washing the mash down with swigs of milk from the pint cartons.

He didn't even think of getting into the jacuzzi. He was sure he wouldn't be able to stay awake long enough for it to fill. Leave that to a honeymoon couple or the next whore and businessman who rented this room.

He ate as much as he could stomach. Then went back outside the motel, got into his red Nissan, and pulled it out of the lot. He drove around the corner and parked the car on Willowbrook Road. If Brennan's cops remembered his vehicle and were looking for him, he didn't want them to see it in the motel parking lot.

As he walked back to the hotel, he spotted a side entrance facing Willowbrook. He used his key card to reenter the hotel and return to his room.

In the bathroom, he methodically stripped off his clothes and showered in the pre-molded plastic shower stall. The two so-called bath towels were just enough to dry himself, way too small to wrap around his waist. Beck pulled the blackout curtains closed, turned on the wall unit hoping it would bring in outside air, and crawled into bed naked.

He told his phone to call Alex Liebowitz.

Liebowitz sounded as tired as Beck felt.

Liebowitz answered, "I'm here."

"Alex."

"Yeah."

"You okay?"

"My stomach can take a couple more Red Bulls before I crash. How are you doing? Did you find the guy?"

"Almost. Your information panned out. More important, I found Manny."

"No shit. Tell me he's all right."

"Banged up. Shot. His right hand fucked up. Long story, but he'll survive. Unfortunately, the bad guy got away."

"Okay, tell me the details when you can. You sound beat."

"I am. I'm gonna crash for a few hours. Anything I should know?"

"We're compiling a lot of information about Ronald Nederland. Obviously, there's a hole during the time he spent in Saint Clair Correctional. We haven't been able to hack into his prison record yet. For all I know, the records aren't digitized. For sure, that joint is a very fucking dangerous place. Most murders of any prison in Alabama."

"Shit."

"Yeah. Lots of blood on those floors. Anybody coming out of there should be considered dangerous and probably insane."

"How much time did he do there?"

"Almost six years. On a drug charge."

Beck listened but didn't have the strength to query Alex further.

"Okay, Alex. I'm not sure what's going to lead me to him. It might help to find men who were in prison with him. He's had help. At least one guy. The guy who stabbed Demarco. Probably another con. You know what to do."

"We're on it. Family, friends, relatives, relationships. This guy might be a loner, but there's a connection to somebody, somewhere."

"Right. Like to Charles Lawrence. If you need to crash for a couple of hours, switch off with that woman you've got working. Or get Ricky and Jonas to help. They still around?"

"Absolutely. Ricky is catching some sleep. Jonas is working with me and Lucille. You want me to call and wake you up?"

Beck said, "Yeah. Good. Three hours. Keep calling until you wake me."

Beck remembered hanging up. He remembered placing his phone on the pillow next to him. He didn't remember falling asleep.

78

Grimaldi and Metuchen made the twenty-two-minute drive to Staten Island University Hospital in eighteen minutes. They parked their unmarked NYPD ride in a handicapped parking space and went in the main entrance, stopping at reception to show their IDs and inquire about Beck's men. Metuchen asked the questions and listened to the information from reception. Yawning and rubbing his face, Grimaldi trailed after Metuchen as he ran down the locations of Beck's men. All of them were in various parts of the same wing, at different stages of their treatment. None of them were in a hospital room except for Ciro, who was waiting for his surgery to be scheduled, his lower right leg encased in a brace to keep his foot from moving.

They did not find James Beck. They did, however, run into Beck's bulldog lawyer, Phineas Dunleavy, in one of the hallways.

Dunleavy always perked up when confronted by police detectives. He enjoyed putting together a mix of fake Irish charm, senior citizen confusion, feigned solicitousness, and general bullshit. All of which were a prelude to statements about his clients' rights, followed by polite warnings about filing lawsuits in both civil and criminal courts if necessary. This time Phineas dispensed with his threats because he wanted to wheedle information out of Grimaldi and Metuchen.

After telling them that James Beck might be on the premises, perhaps in the cafeteria, Phineas asked, "I wonder if you gentlemen could help me with something."

"What's that?" said Grimaldi.

"Well, maybe you could put in a word to the higher-ups that somebody should coordinate the NYPD visits here."

"What does that mean?"

"Fellas, you two make this the fourth visit from the NYPD. Frankly, it's a bit excessive. Bordering on harassment, I'd say. Especially for innocent and wounded victims."

Grimaldi said, "What the hell are you talking about?"

"Since I've been here, there were two uniformed coppers from the hundred-twenty-third precinct making inquiries. A detective from some sort of borough task force. Two more detectives from the one hundred-twenty-second precinct. And now you two fellas from the commissioner's office. We're happy that victims of assault such as Messrs. Guzman, Baldassare, and Jones are getting attention from the NYPD, but investigators constantly popping in without warning is getting in the way of their medical treatments, not to mention violating their legal rights to have representation. Is there something going on that I should know about? As their attorney."

Grimaldi was about to answer, but Metuchen broke in.

"No."

Metuchen turned and walked away down the hospital corridor, Grimaldi following him.

As they headed for the elevators, Metuchen said, "That lawyer's bullshit is annoying."

"Understood. But what the hell was he talking about? I get the precinct cops showing up, but what did you make out of someone from a borough task force?"

Metuchen said, "Maybe Roth set something up on the borough level. Who the hell knows?"

"If she doesn't know about this taskforce shit or whatever it is, that would be a bad sign."

Metuchen shrugged. "That's up to Roth."

"I'm ninety percent sure that shyster was bullshitting us about Beck, but let's check the cafeteria just in case he's there. I need coffee anyhow."

"I'm a hundred percent sure the lawyer is full of shit. Beck isn't here."

They quickly found the cafeteria on the main floor. It was larger than expected, with few people eating. Most were getting coffee and food to go. They made a quick circuit.

Grimaldi said, "He's not here."

"No kidding. I'll get the coffee while you call her highness."

Grimaldi nodded and speed-dialed Brennan. As soon as she answered, he said, "We're at the hospital. No sign of Beck."

Brennan said, "What?"

"Beck ain't here. We checked everywhere. Located all his men. They're still here. Their lawyer is here. Beck might've come and gone, but I don't think so."

"What did his lawyer say?"

"Said he might be in the cafeteria. He's not. What do you want us to do?"

"Find him."

"Got any ideas?"

Brennan said, "I'm hoping he did what he said he would. Clean up and crash somewhere. He looked wiped out when he left. Start checking motels. Start with the ones nearest to the fire."

"What should we do when we find him?"

"Bring him to me."

"And if he's not inclined?"

"Arrest him. I can't deal with his shit anymore."

"Arrest him for what? Interfering with an investigation."

"Good enough."

"Where are you now?"

"I'm back at One PP. I'm waiting to meet with Roth."

"By the way, you should know something."

"What?"

"Beck's lawyer was complaining about all the cops showing up to interview Beck's guys. Two teams from the local precincts, plus someone who said they were on a borough taskforce, plus me and Dave."

"A what?"

"A borough taskforce, whatever that means."

"Was the lawyer bullshitting you?"

"I don't think so. You think Roth has green-lit something at the borough command level?"

"Maybe. I'll find out. You two concentrate on finding Beck."

Brennan hung up. Grimaldi's call had unsettled her. She'd napped for fifteen minutes on the drive back from Staten Island, but after Grimaldi's call, she felt more tired than ever. And more tense. She sensed events running out ahead of her.

She sipped the coffee Nina had brought along with word that Roth wanted to see her in thirty minutes. That had been twenty minutes ago.

Brennan steeled herself, took a deep breath, and tried to put everything out of her mind. Focus, she told herself.

She had her bullet-point list she'd sent Roth from Staten Island. She held the one page with two hands as if it were a sacred text. She told herself, stick with this. Don't deviate. Concentrate on getting Roth to identify the burned corpse on Burke Avenue asap. Forget about Beck, forget about everything except closing this fucking case.

79

It wasn't his smartphone that woke Beck. It was a word. A realization. Something that had been lurking in the back of his mind for hours but hadn't coalesced into a clear thought while he'd been running full blast for twenty-eight hours.

One word.

Cops.

Beck sat up in the darkened jacuzzi room.

NYPD cops had pervaded every part of this mess.

Beck fumbled for his phone on the pillow. 12:02 p.m. Willie Reese had walked into his bar with news that cops were in the neighborhood at noon yesterday.

Cops.

Then there was the run-in with that cop Grimaldi on the pier.

Then the bad luck of running into him again and his cop partner after he and Ciro had found Catherine Hodge.

Dianne Brennan. A deputy inspector cop in charge of more cops.

All the talk about Beck's past and the gunfight that injured four cops years ago.

The cop on Staten Island, Montello.

That black cop who had manhandled him and tried to arrest him after Nederland had rear-ended him and shot at him.

Monster-Boy's stepfather, Charles Lawrence, the cop Beck had killed.

Beck turned and put his bare feet on the floor.

Almost since this nightmare had started, Beck had been plagued by the suspicion that Nederland had people helping him. Not just another convict who had helped him take out Manny and kill his friends and stab Demarco. There were others. There had to be, and it had finally dawned on Beck that the others had to be NYPD cops helping Nederland.

That's how Monster-Boy was able to set the ambush up so precisely at Montello's house. Maybe even conspire with Montello to have him come to the door with his gun.

And how had that one patrol car appeared so soon after Nederland had rear-ended him and tried to kill him in the park? For that matter, how did Nederland know he was on that isolated dead-end street? Beck tried to remember. He'd assumed those cops were responding to 911 calls about gunshots. But Nederland's shots were sporadic, and he'd fired most of them out in that park. No. That one patrol car arrived too fast, and the black cop had an agenda. He wasn't interested in anything but taking Beck in. If Brennan hadn't stopped him, Beck knew he'd probably be locked in a precinct cell somewhere.

Beck stood up from the bed and headed for the bathroom. He splashed cold water on his face and body and toweled off, questioning himself about what his gut was telling him. Was he being too paranoid? Was the Montello thing a coincidence like Brennan said? Just another cop among hundreds living on Staten Island. Did Brennan really let him go, or were her two detectives keeping tabs on him?

Beck checked himself in the mirror. He'd taken off the bandage covering his left ear and head. It didn't look too bad. The bruise and cuts on the side of his right shoulder looked worse, but the wounds had started to scab over, hopefully enough so they wouldn't reopen and bleed.

Beck began to dress. He had to move. If Brennan's cops had gone to the hospital to track him, by now, they knew he hadn't been there. He had to get out of this motel room. There couldn't be very many motels on Staten Island.

By the time he finished dressing, everything had fallen into place for Beck. He'd gone back to the first question he and his men had asked. How did their enemy find out where Beck lived in the first place? Knowing his address, let Nederland know where to set up his surveillance camera. And that, in turn, let him figure out how to abduct Manny.

Who knew how to locate him? And then Beck recalled a name – Jeffrey Esposito. The cop who had tried to serve that warrant on him four years ago. Beck had sent an ex-NYPD detective, Walter Pearce, to warn Esposito that he would be walking into a dangerous situation, but it still had turned out to be a bloody confrontation with the two criminal gangs who had come to kill Beck and his men. Beck had made an enemy of Esposito. Esposito worked out of the Seven-Six. The precinct that covered Red Hook. Beck killed Charles Lawrence in a bar located in the 76th precinct. A bar known to be a hangout for cops. What were the odds that Esposito knew Charles Lawrence? For Beck, high enough to be a certainty. Did that mean Esposito knew Lawrence's stepson, Ronald Nederland? Why not?

The dots began connecting, and the connections spread from Esposito to Charles Lawrence, to his stepson, Ronald Nederland, to Brennan, Grimaldi, Metuchen…all of them.

But the first dot had been Jeffrey Esposito. It was time to go back to the beginning.

Beck left the drapes drawn in his room and slowly opened the door to the corridor. The lobby was a short distance down the hallway and to the left. Beck heard voices in the lobby, one of them belonging to Alphonse Grimaldi.

Shit.

He assumed Metuchen was with him. Probably waiting outside. Or maybe covering the parking area in the back.

Beck stepped out of his room and moved quickly out of sight down the hallway that led to the motel's back exit. He hustled along the corridor that ran parallel to Gannon Street, checking his pockets: Phone, wallet, key fob, and the Sig Sauer P220 that Joey B had provided stuck in the small of his back, covered by the jacket Joey B had given him.

He approached the exit door and slowly pushed the release bar. He cracked open the door. No sign of Metuchen or police vehicles. In five seconds, he was out the door and down the steps. Ten steps took him to Willowbrook Street. He turned right and walked to his car, quickly, but not running.

Beck and the Nissan were gone before the high school desk clerk opened the door to the "jacuzzi" room for Grimaldi and Metuchen.

80

Beck drove as if he were invincible, cocooned in a shell of rage, dread, and determination. He weaved in and out of traffic without regard for speed limits or traffic, like a bullet fired into an unwavering path. For a man who usually thought five steps ahead, Beck now had only one singular focus. Find Jeffrey Esposito. Break him down. Find out what he had done.

Beck found himself on the Verrazano Bridge without much awareness of how he had arrived there. He exited onto the BQE, weaving in and out of traffic, almost missing the exit onto Hamilton Avenue, cutting in front of two cars to make it off the expressway.

The traffic lights on Hamilton forced Beck to stop, which helped him focus. By the time he turned onto Union Street, he was able to drive slowly, noting how police vehicles and personal cars belonging to cops had taken over the entire block. They were parked side by side on both sides of the street. Beck didn't even bother looking for an empty slot. He stopped the Nissan just past the front of the precinct, turned on his flashers, and reached into the back seat where he had tossed the NYPD Tact Squad Jacket Brennan had given him. He stepped out of the Nissan, put on the jacket with its array of NYPD insignia, and walked straight into the precinct, right up to the desk sergeant. A fit, uniformed officer with close-cropped salt and pepper hair stood behind the counter that dominated the lobby. A uniformed Hispanic female PO sat to his right. Behind him, another uniformed cop shoved folders of paperwork into a set of file shelves.

Beck ignored the civilians waiting in the area and tapped the counter to get the desk sergeant's attention.

"Yo, sarge, sorry to interrupt. I'm looking for Detective Esposito. Jeffrey Esposito. Is he in the house today?"

Beck had entered the precinct with such purpose and entitlement that when the desk sergeant looked up and saw him standing in front of him wearing the NYPD jacket, he assumed Beck was a cop.

"Yeah, he's in today. Who should I say wants to see him?"

Up until that moment, Beck hadn't really thought about the answer to that question. For a second, he thought about using his name. That would bring Esposito to the lobby, but most likely with his gun drawn and reinforcements. Beck answered, "Officer Montello. Richard Montello."

The sergeant was about to pick up the phone to call down Esposito when Beck said, "Can you tell him I'll be right outside? I'm double parked."

Double parking on Union Street didn't need any further explanation. The sergeant said, "Sure. No problem."

Beck turned and hustled outside. He stood five feet away from the bottom step leading up to the precinct entrance. This gave him an angle on whoever came out and let him watch his car in case anybody needed it moved.

Beck knew he had never seen Jeffrey Esposito, but he didn't think identifying him would be much of a problem. How many Hispanic detectives would be coming out to find somebody?

Beck checked his watch. Ten minutes after one. He wished he had a cigarette. He'd given up smoking decades ago and didn't want one now. It just felt like he should be smoking. Cops were always smoking when they were hanging around.

Beck spent ten minutes that felt like thirty watching people come in and out of the precinct when a tired-looking Hispanic man stepped out, stood on the top step, and looked around.

Guess that's Esposito, Beck thought.

Beck slipped the Sig from the small of his back into the right pocket of his NYPD jacket and walked over to Esposito. Beck figured the next few moments would be the most dangerous. Trying to persuade an armed NYPD detective to get into a car with someone he didn't know while standing in front of a police station. Beck couldn't think of a better way to get arrested. Or shot, if he pulled his gun.

Beck thought about shoving the muzzle of the P220 into Esposito's back and threatening to put a bullet into his spine, but he knew he wouldn't do that, which meant Esposito probably wouldn't believe him.

Instead, Beck decided to simply tell Esposito who he was.

He said, "Detective Esposito." When the man turned toward him, Beck said, "I'm the one you and Ronald Nederland are looking for. I'm James Beck."

"No shit. You think I haven't seen a picture of you?"

"Yeah, I suppose so," said Beck. "I'm not exactly at my sharpest. How about you get in my car, so I don't have to shoot you."

Esposito said, "And why would I do that?"

"Like I said, so I don't have to shoot you."

"You're not going to fucking shoot me. You don't look like you want to commit suicide. Although maybe you should."

"What?"

"Get your hand off the fucking gun and get in your car."

Before Beck could respond to that, Esposito stepped down to the sidewalk and headed toward the Nissan. For a moment, Beck was too surprised to move. Then he hustled after Esposito and slipped into the driver's side as Esposito took the passenger seat.

Esposito slammed his door shut and put on his seatbelt.

Beck did the same. He turned off the blinkers and sat unmoving.

Esposito said, "Where are we going?"

Beck looked at him, resisting the urge to punch Esposito in the face.

Esposito said, "You have no idea what the fuck is really going on, do you?"

"Apparently not."

81

Dianne Brennan finished delivering her report to Warren Roth on the progress she'd made since the last time they had met. Or, more accurately, reciting the report. Something had diminished her motivation to tell it.

Roth had listened without interruption, proof to Brennan that Roth was taking it in but thinking about something else. She'd become accustomed to seeing Warren Roth listening to her while thinking about other things. But this was different. Something was wrong. It felt like Roth had already come to his own conclusions. Like he didn't need to hear what she had told him.

Well, she thought, whatever is going on, there's nothing more for me to say.

After a pause, Roth asked, "So where is Beck now?"

"He was bunked at the Ramada Inn on Staten Island. He told me he was going to crash. I had Grimaldi and Metuchen check it out. Apparently, he left before they got there."

"So, you don't know where he is."

"No. You want me to guess?"

"Why not?"

"I think his next step will be to check on his crew at Staten Island Hospital."

Roth nodded. "That would be convenient."

"Why?"

Roth picked up a folder from a pile on the left side of his desk. He dropped it in from of him but didn't open it.

"I've got warrants issued for two of Beck's crew." Roth opened the folder and referred to a page to make sure he had the names straight. "Uh, Ciro Baldassare and Demarco Jones. I'm waiting for arrest warrants on Guzman and Beck. So it would be convenient if Beck were there, too."

Brennan tried to conceal her surprise. "Warrants for what?"

Again, Roth looked at the pages in front of him. "Assault and battery on persons and property, possession of firearms, possession of deadly weapons, murder, discharging of weapons." Roth closed the folder. "Whatever else the DA wants to come up with. There are a lot of dead and injured people connected with Beck and his partners. Plenty of charges to go around."

Brennan waited, but Roth didn't elaborate. Didn't specify who would be charged with what. It didn't matter. The hammer had come down. Or was about to. The suddenness of Roth's decision left her reeling, unable to figure out how she fit in.

Roth saw the look on her face. He said, "Listen, Dianne, these men are associated with years of criminal activity. I want them off the street. Especially James Beck. I want him off the street most of all."

Brennan knew it wasn't a good idea to press Roth about how he thought he could make the charges stick. And then she realized he didn't have to. Some of Beck's crew were probably still on parole. Roth had enough to violate them back to serve the rest of their terms. That alone could mean years in prison. It was Warren Roth's system, and he was going to use it whatever way he wanted.

Brennan stammered, "What about Ronald Nederland?"

"You said he was dead. A suicide."

"To be confirmed. But I mean, what about what Nederland did?"

"What did he do?"

"For starters, killed those two men in Red Hook."

"Based on what? The videos Beck showed you?"

"What about Guzman? He's alive. He can testify?"

"About a dead man. Maybe it was Guzman who killed those two. Maybe Nederland's death wasn't a suicide. We both know Beck wanted to kill him. I think Beck did kill him."

There it was. Like a slap on the side of her head to wake her up to what was going on. Roth could see the light go out of her eyes.

"I don't have time to go through all my thinking right now, Dianne. You did good work. You've helped us solve a lot of problems."

She nodded but said nothing.

"Last thing before you move on, what can you do to find Beck and help us arrest him?"

Brennan couldn't respond. She hadn't seen this coming. She'd been too busy running nonstop with Beck trying to solve the Red Hook murders to keep up with what Roth had been doing. The scope of it, the fact that Roth had decided to use Nederland's crimes as an excuse to take down Beck and had done it with such matter-of-fact brutality stunned Brennan.

Roth said, "Dianne. C'mon. Catch up. Where are you? What can you do to help us track down Beck? Call Grimaldi and Metuchen. Get on this. I need it done."

Brennan scrambled to respond.

"Yes, yes. Of course. I'll find Beck. We'll find him. I know how to contact him. We'll get it done."

"Good. Get copies of the warrant on Beck from Nina. Keep in touch."

And with that, Warren Roth dismissed Brennan by reaching for his phone. She stood up to leave, barely realizing that Roth had manipulated her into agreeing to betray James Beck as if it were entirely expected of her.

Dianne Brennan walked out of Roth's feeling like she had lost a part of herself. Or maybe she had lost it long ago and just now realized it.

82

Beck and Esposito ended up in a Mexican restaurant/bar on Columbia Street, not because Esposito was Hispanic. Beck didn't give a shit if Esposito liked the place or not. They ended up there because Beck had found a parking space nearby.

Beck hadn't spoken during the short drive. He knew what he wanted from Esposito. But he had no idea what the hell Esposito wanted from him.

Beck had been in the restaurant before. There was a bar on the ground floor and a restaurant on the second floor. The downstairs bar suited his tastes. Old wood floors, a substantial wooden bar with a brass footrail, dark enough inside to feel like a haven. They took a table near the back. The restaurant kitchen wasn't open, so when the waiter asked if they wanted guacamole and taco chips, Beck said yes. He ordered a Negro Modelo to go with the chips. Esposito ordered the same.

When the waiter left, Beck studied Esposito for a moment. The cop looked like Beck had imagined him. Medium height, medium build, the expected cop's paunch from years of irregular meals and perhaps too much alcohol. Clearly Hispanic. A thick salt and pepper head of hair with a mustache to match. It was Esposito's eyes that Beck hadn't expected. The eyes were confident but also revealed a man resigned to his situation. Why was that? Because Esposito knew what the fuck was really going on and Beck didn't?

Finally, the detective broke the silence.

"Where the hell did you get that damn jacket?"

Beck had forgotten he was wearing the NYPD Tact Squad jacket. Perhaps that's why the guacamole, beer, and chips arrived so quickly. He took off the jacket, dropped it on the chair next to him, and then unzipped the down jacket Joey B had given him.

As they poured their beers, Beck said, "I got it from a deputy inspector who works for the commissioner."

Esposito nodded, frowning.

Beck said, "So what's going on that I don't know shit about?"

Esposito rubbed his face trying to dispel fatigue or maybe frustration.

"You know how many times I thought about arresting you?"

"On what charges?" And then he waved away his question and said, "I guess you'd have made some shit up. But why?"

"Because you set us up for an ambush four years ago."

Now that Esposito was talking, Beck heard a slight accent. Latin mixed with Bronx perhaps. It reminded him of Manny's accent. Making Beck even more resentful about Esposito.

Beck said, "Ambush? How could it be an ambush when I sent a retired NYPD detective to warn you?"

"Somebody I didn't know from Adam with a story I had no time to verify."

"Maybe you should have made the time."

"Time I didn't have."

"I guess you didn't have time to verify that the arrest warrant for me was based on complete bullshit, either."

"Fuck off. You know I couldn't do anything about that warrant once it was issued."

"Fine. But why blame me? I didn't send you on that mission. Your bosses did."

Esposito leaned forward. "Hey, however that came down, the whole fucking mess started with you. You were the one involved with those Russian gangs."

"Russian gang. Not gangs. The other group was Eastern European. Bosnian."

Esposito waved off Beck's correction. "Whatever. You should have turned yourself in instead of letting the NYPD do your dirty work." Beck watched the anger in Esposito take over. "Four cops were shot. Four. One guy ended up behind a desk. Turner or Tanner, I forget his name. Any one of those cops or all of them could've been killed. I could have been killed."

Beck's voice rose, fueled by his own anger.

"And so could I. And my friends. Are you telling me we should have risked our lives, risked going back to prison, so you didn't have to do your damn job and arrest a bunch of bad guys? What the fuck are you for, if not that? So you were forced to do your damn job. I didn't open fire on you. You were warned. You should've called in a hundred cops before you went in there."

"Yeah, like I could just snap my fingers and make that happen."

"And that's my fault?" Beck raised a hand. "The hell with it. I'm not going to argue with you. Is what happened that night behind all this shit with that maniac Ronald Nederland? Did you use him to get back at me for that night? A fucking juiced-up meth-mouth murderer who stabs and burns people?"

Esposito sat back. He waved to get the bartender's attention and called out an order for a shot of Don Julio Reposada. He looked at Beck.

Beck said, "Why not?" He'd drink with the cop if it helped him talk.

Esposito held up two fingers. The bartender nodded.

Beck didn't say anything while the bartender brought the drinks to the table. He wanted the situation to cool down.

Esposito downed half his tequila and took a bite out of the slice of lime that came with it. Beck skipped the salt and lime ritual and swallowed a musky gulp of the sharp cactus liquor. He chased it with his beer, inhaling and tasting the combination, trying to let it relax him and tamp down his anger.

Esposito again rubbed his face and said, "Shit is always more complicated than you think."

"What does that mean? You didn't use Ronald Nederland to get back at me?"

Esposito raised his voice. "It means it's not that simple. First thing you have to know is why I'm talking to you. Actually, why I'm talking to you now."

"Why?"

"Because I'm getting out. I put in my retirement papers. I'm done."

"What's the second thing?"

"The second reason is that both of us are in the middle."

"Middle of what?"

"What's going on out there, and what's going on inside."

"Inside meaning inside the police department."

"Yes."

Beck said, "Okay. Where do you want to start?"

"With Nederland. That poor son of a bitch."

Beck had never thought of Monster-Boy Nederland as a poor son of a bitch but didn't argue the point.

"What about him?"

"Well, how about we start with the fact that you killed his father?"

Beck said, "Not his father. His stepfather. What about it?"

"Okay. His stepfather. You don't think that affected the kid?"

"Affected? What the fuck does that mean?"

"Listen, Nederland never had a break. His biological father died when he was around four or five. Apparently, his father didn't give a shit about him. Didn't pay any attention to him. I don't know why. From what I heard, Nederland got pushed around and bullied in school. He was a big fat kid. Maybe dull or a momma's boy. I don't know."

"How is any of that my fault?"

"It isn't. But what came next is. Nederland's mother remarried when Nederland was around ten."

"Charles Lawrence."

364

"Yeah. Lawrence tried to help the boy. Toughen him up a little. Nederland finally had a father who cared about him. After Lawrence died, everything went downhill for the family."

"How old was Nederland when he died?"

"Around sixteen, seventeen."

Beck said, "How do you know all this shit about Ronald Nederland?"

"I knew Charles Lawrence from the Seven-Six. We were there at the same time a couple of years before you killed him. When he died, the mother started showing up at the precinct. You know, people tell the bereaved – if there's anything we can do, blah, blah. Nederland's mother took it literally. Cried a lot on the shoulder of the precinct commander, who happened to be female at the time. A captain. What I heard was the mother had a drinking problem that got worse after she lost Lawrence."

Beck said, "Ruth Androvette?"

"Was that her maiden name?"

"Yes."

"I don't think I ever heard her maiden name. Anyhow, yeah, things kept getting worse, and she kept looking for help. After Nederland left high school, he fell in with some skels on Staten Island selling meth, pills, whatever shit they could get their hands on. That didn't take long to fuck him up. He got addicted. Lost a lot of weight. Went way off the tracks. I mean, from what I heard, whatever grip he had on life, he lost it. You know what that shit can do to someone. Paranoia, violence, mood swings. Fucks your brain permanently."

Beck nodded. He'd seen plenty of men who had been addicted to meth in prison.

"Anyhow, Ronald ended up getting arrested in Alabama. That's where his lowlife drug crew was getting their supply. Got caught transporting a load north."

Beck said, "I know he went to prison down there. Didn't know what for."

"Possession with intent to distribute. Got sent to a real hell hole. I've heard about guys changing from prison, but this was another whole story."

"How so?"

"I saw him when his mother passed. Word was she basically drank herself to death after everything fell apart. A group of us from the precinct went to the wake. I'd never seen her son. Just heard about him. Then I see this fucking freak sitting near his mother's coffin. I'd never seen anything like him. That guy is in a whole different category. I don't know how many steroids it took or how much iron he lifted in prison, or how many convicts he fought, but he was a beast when he got out. Between the prison steroids and whatever was left of his meth brain." Esposito spun a finger in the air and made a sound like a leaking tire. "Ends up with this shaved convict head, weird, crooked meth-tooth grin. The kind of guy you cross the street if you see him coming. The kind of guy you don't want noticing you, or if he does, makes you damn glad you got a gun."

Esposito paused. He finished off his tequila and shook his head, remembering Ronald Nederland.

Beck was only marginally interested in the history of Ronald Nederland, but if Esposito wanted to talk about it before he got to what he wanted to say, Beck decided to let him.

Beck said, "So then what?"

Esposito refocused. "So, when I saw him, like I say, I thought between the drugs, his stepfather and his mother dying, and whatever the hell he did to survive in that shithole Alabama prison, this guy's hold on reality went out the window."

Beck said, "So why did you decide to have something to do with him?"

"Again, a little complicated."

"How so?"

Esposito held up his empty tequila glass. He looked at

Beck. Beck shook his head no. This time Esposito didn't wait for more tequila to keep talking.

"I'll admit after seeing Nederland, hearing about his background, yeah, I felt bad about what happened to him. But, trust me, I didn't want to have anything to do with him. After the wake, I put him out of my mind."

"What made you change your mind?"

"About a month later, I get a call from him at the precinct. He said he wanted to meet with me."

"Why?"

"He said he wanted to find out more about what happened with his stepfather. He sounded sincere. A little agitated, but genuine."

"And that was enough for you to decide you wanted to meet with a maniac?"

Esposito took a swig of beer before answering. "Hell no. I had no intention of meeting with him. I asked him why he wanted to know more about what happened to his stepfather."

"And?"

"He came up with the usual bullshit. Something about closure."

"And that convinced you?"

"Of course not. I just wanted to get him off my back."

"How?"

"I knew he wasn't the kind of guy who was going to disappear. I pictured that son of a bitch sitting on my front steps waiting for me. I didn't want him anywhere near my family. So I decided I could get rid of him by giving him the files I had on the trial. Your trial for killing his father. Stepfather. It was all public record anyhow. It wasn't anything he couldn't get on his own."

Beck knew Esposito was exaggerating about Nederland getting the trial records on his own, but he didn't want an argument. He wanted Esposito to keep talking, so he said, "How was it you had my trial records?"

"After that goddamn massacre you engineered, I made it my business to investigate you. The higher-ups were walking away from it, but I wasn't. They wanted the whole thing to go away. Didn't want the truth coming out, so they made up that bullshit about it being a gang thing. Two rival gangs attacking each other. It pissed me off."

Beck said, "Two gangs that had nothing to do with Red Hook, Brooklyn."

"Who the fuck knew the difference? The news outlets concentrated mostly on the four cops who got shot. The brass had to come up with something." Esposito's face hardened. "Anyhow, the bosses quashed it. I guess they figured the bad guys got what was coming to them. Nobody gave a shit about you. But I couldn't let it go."

"Why?"

"I didn't like being played. Particularly by a cop killer."

Beck leaned back. Esposito's mask had slipped. It wasn't just that he survived the attack in Red Hook and got away with it. He was a cop killer who survived the attack and got away with it. Both he and Esposito knew what Esposito had done. Esposito had fed Ronald Nederland information to get him off his back *and* point him toward James Beck.

Beck kept his anger in check and asked, "What was in that file?"

"The court reporter transcripts for the trial and the sentencing hearing, and some shit about your civil suit."

Beck noted the part about his lawsuit against the state. If Nederland was angry about Beck killing his stepfather, finding out Beck had been exonerated and paid a financial settlement must have sent Ronald Nederland over the edge.

Beck couldn't keep his voice from hardening. "What else?"

Esposito paused and then said, "Copies of the articles in the Post and Daily News about the shootout. Also a matter of public record."

The way Esposito downplayed everything made Beck want to pull out the P220 and shoot him in the knee. The look on Beck's face made Esposito say, "Yeah, I know. I gave him enough to find you. And yeah, I didn't mind if he showed up on your doorstep. Maybe I figured you owed the guy an explanation."

Beck had had enough of Esposito's rationalizing.

"An explanation? A little heart-to-heart chat with a maniac, ex-con killer would have sent him on his way? Bullshit. You figured that since the NYPD didn't come after me, you'd send Ronald the monster Nederland instead."

Beck could see Esposito's anger and frustration spiraling into defiance.

"So what are you going to do? You going to kill me, too?"

"Not right now. You haven't told me everything."

Esposito said, "Nobody involved in this knows everything."

Beck said, "So what part do you know?"

The waiter brought Esposito his second shot of Don Julio. When he asked Beck if he wanted another, Beck said, "Sure."

"Yeah, well, clearly, I know more than you, asshole. Giving Nederland that information seemed to get him off my back. I didn't hear from him for two or three weeks. Then all that shit blew up near your place with those two murders."

"And the abduction of Manny Guzman."

"Yes. But that part didn't set anybody's hair on fire. The murders got all the attention. My precinct commander was all over it."

"Who's that?"

"Captain Nicholas Fernandez. A body burned up in the grain terminal. Another stabbed, throat slit. That kind of shit tends to get a lot of attention. I suppose for a minute, I tried to convince myself it had nothing to do with Nederland, but I knew that was bullshit.

"I'd been thinking about retiring for at least a year. When things blew up with those murders, that was it. I put in my papers before anybody found out I'd been in touch with Nederland.

Fernandez was pissed at me. The whips don't like guys packing it in. They're all like, congratulations, and I'm happy for you, but it makes life harder for them. They have to adjust. Anyway, Fernandez stuck his finger in my face and told me not to think about checking out or laying low while my papers went through."

"Why'd he need you?"

"To get in good with the commissioner."

"How?"

"Fernandez knew you were my white whale. He knew I had a big file on you. He told me to copy everything I had on you and personally take it to the commissioner's office. Fernandez wanted to be the hero coming up with the goods. He told me to bring every fucking scrap of paper I had on you and take it to Roth's office."

"But you didn't say anything to Fernandez about giving information to Ronald Nederland."

"No. No way. And I only gave Nederland just enough to get him off my back. I had a ton of information on you, your crew, arrest records, all the shit about the gunfight four years ago. All I gave Nederland is what I told you. But even giving him that would've been the end of my pension. At that point, nobody fucking knew that Ronald Nederland was connected to the murders on the pier and in that grain terminal."

"Nobody but you."

"Yeah, but even so, I was just assuming it was him. I didn't really have any proof."

Beck's shot of tequila arrived. Esposito lifted his glass toward Beck. Beck raised his glass but didn't go so far as to clink them together.

Esposito downed half his shot and continued.

"Listen, Beck, I know you think I'm justifying all my bullshit. I know what you're thinking, but you have to listen to me."

"You finally ready to tell me the part that I don't know shit about?"

"Hey, I thought you should know the background."

Beck nodded but said nothing. His patience had run out, and Esposito knew it. He leaned toward Beck and said, "So, you coming for me at the precinct told me you finally figured out Nederland was getting information from our side. You're right. But you gotta understand how this thing went down. The scope of it."

The tequila and beer were having an effect on Esposito. His speech was a bit slurred. His accent more pronounced.

Beck said, "I'm listening."

"Once my files got to the commissioner's office, the focus wasn't just on finding Nederland. The focus was on you, too. Maybe even more."

"More than on a crazed ex-con murderer burning and stabbing people?"

"From what I could see, yeah. I mean, Warren Roth wanted the killer found. But he also wanted your ass pinned to the wall. You know, two birds with one stone. He saw the situation as a chance to nail you, too."

"How so?"

"The way Fernandez put it, Roth figured either Nederland would kill you, and the asshole who had killed a cop and gotten away with it would get what he deserved. Or, you'd kill Nederland, and Roth would put you in prison for it. Fact is, the way Fernandez told it, that's how Brennan pitched it to Roth so he would agree to let her work with you."

Beck nodded but didn't respond. He already knew that's how Brennan convinced Roth to let her work with him because that's how he told Brennan to pitch it to Roth.

"So Fernandez was your source on all this?"

"Not my source. Fernandez was my handler."

"What do you mean?"

"Fernandez knew I'd fed information to Charles Lawrence's stepson about you before."

371

"How'd he know that?"

"Back when I was in contact with Nederland, one of the old lady civilian clerks complained to Fernandez that I made a bunch of copies of my files. Precinct keeps track of that shit. When I put in my retirement papers, Fernandez got suspicious. Figured it might have something to do with all the shit that went down near your place. Fernandez confronted me. Why was I leaving? Did the murders have anything to do with it? What did I know I wasn't telling him? Then he brought up the shit about me making copies of my files on you."

"And?"

"I knew Fernandez wasn't going to let it go, so I told him the truth. I told him about Nederland. I knew Fernandez didn't have enough proof to really nail me. But Nicholas Fernandez didn't really care about that. All he cared about was getting in good with the commissioner. Fernandez didn't get to where he is without being as ruthless as the next guy. He told me, don't worry about it. Told me I could be of use to the department. He went to Roth and said he had a way to communicate with the prime suspect."

"You."

"Yeah, me. Of course, Roth was all for it. Gave him a chance to control everything. Fernandez comes back and puts the screws on me. Says I can kiss my pension goodbye unless I play ball. Help him and Roth with the investigation, and then I can retire."

"Jeezus, Esposito, what the fuck is wrong with you people?"

"You gotta realize how this shit operates, Beck. Everybody got what they wanted. Fernandez got in tight with the commissioner. I got my pension and a way to stick it to you. Roth got to pull the strings, manipulate everything the way he wanted it to go. And Brennan got to waltz around out there like she's hot shit."

"You're saying she was in on it, too?"

"Nah, she didn't know what was going on, but she sure as hell wanted to use you as much as everybody else."

Beck nodded. Esposito was right. It all made perfect sense.

"Where did Roth get his information on what I was doing so he could feed it to Nederland through you and Fernandez?"

Esposito said, "What, are you fucking kidding me? According to Fernandez, from everyone. Brennan was obviously reporting in. Her piss boy Jablonsky was calling into Roth every chance he got. That little sneak has been in the commissioner's pocket from day one. I know Brennan's guy Metuchen chimed in. Maybe Grimaldi, too. And by the way, I'd bet there are more cops than just me who are helping our boy Ronald. If he reached out to me, he could've reached out to other guys involved that night four years back. I'd bet any of the cops that got shot would be willing to help Nederland get to you."

"Did you send word to Nederland when I would be showing up at Montello's house?"

"Yes." Esposito leaned forward. "Look, wherever you were going, whatever you were doing, word got to Roth. He doled it out to whoever he wanted to know about it. The local cops. To Nederland through Fernandez and me. Whoever."

"And Brennan didn't know everybody around her was reporting back to Roth?"

"Hey, if she had more experience, maybe she would've known to keep her guys on a tighter leash. Fernandez and Roth knew she was being cagey with her reports so she could stay a step ahead of everybody else."

Beck nodded. He knew that was true.

Esposito said, "Think about it. Nobody passes up opportunities like this. Brennan wanted to be the one to crack the big case. Roth wanted payback on the cop killer who embarrassed the department. And your crew, if possible. Fernandez wanted to make Brennan look bad and get in good with the commissioner. Precinct commanders and chiefs work their whole careers and never get as close to the top as Brennan did. All the other sniveling snitches wanted to get in good with the commissioner, too."

"And you wanted to retire with your pension and see me go down along with everybody else."

Esposito finished his beer and said, "Yeah. Why not?"

Beck gripped the sides of the table. "And it didn't matter if three guys who had nothing to do with me killing Charles Lawrence went down, too."

Esposito gave Beck a look. "Gimme a break. Your pals ain't choir boys. They been out there running and gunning with you for a long time, Beck."

Beck resisted the urge to smash Esposito's face. He had to make sure he found out everything Esposito knew.

"So after Nederland burned himself up, what was the plan?"

"Last thing I heard from Fernandez was that Roth figured he had enough on you and your crew to get arrest warrants for all of you."

"For what?"

"He was going to charge you with killing Nederland. Your boy Guzman for killing the guys on the pier. Baldassare and Jones for breaking bones at the gym you dropped in on. Fernandez said Roth was just waiting for you and Brennan to find Nederland, then drop the hammer on everybody. How'd you find Nederland's house?"

"Kept following the breadcrumbs he'd laid out. Are they still using you to find me?"

Esposito shook his head. "Nah. I was pushed aside after they found Nederland burned up in his house."

Beck said, "His mother's house."

"Whatever."

Beck took a moment to put everything together. Warren Roth got everything he wanted. All his people played off against each other. The prime suspect for two murders and an abduction dead. Enough ammunition to arrest him and everybody on his crew.

But that wasn't the whole picture. Not by a long shot. Esposito didn't see it, but Beck could see Roth's real end game. Warren Roth had to know that he and his men would beat the criminal

374

charges. Roth knew they would all have first-rate legal representation. Demarco would get off with self-defense. He'd been stabbed twice. The case against Manny was ridiculous. Ciro and his mob pals would eliminate any witnesses from that gym. And even if that had been Ronald Nederland's corpse, they had no solid proof Beck had burned him to death.

No, the arrest warrants were all bullshit. Warren Roth was setting him and his men up for execution. Beck knew when the cops came to arrest him, they'd use it as a chance to gun down a cop killer. Manny, Ciro, and Demarco would make it easy for the cops. They'd all shoot it out before going back to prison.

Beck leaned back. Esposito had most likely told him everything he knew. Beck had just one more question.

"Okay, just one more thing," said Beck.

"What?"

"Why are you telling me all this? Just because you're retiring? Because you want to get all this shit off your chest? Because you're pissed off at the way Roth and the NYPD operate? Why?"

Esposito gripped his empty shot glass, looking like he wanted more tequila. He grimaced and pushed the shot glass aside.

"All of the above. But none of that is the main reason."

"Then why?"

Esposito looked directly at Beck.

"Because you have to face what you did." Esposito reached into the side pocket on his suit jacket. Beck had the P220 out from behind his back before Esposito's hand showed. "Take it easy." Esposito slowly took out a cell phone.

"Everything starts with you, Beck. You killed Charles Lawrence and got away with it. Whatever turned Ronald Nederland into a monster is because of you. That goddamn gunfight we walked into four years ago was because of you. The murders in Red Hook, the stabbing, the burning, what happened to your crew — all of it is because of what you did. The only way this ends is when you face Ronald Nederland."

Esposito turned on the cell phone.

"Ronald Nederland didn't burn up in that house. I don't know who did, but Nederland is still alive." Esposito opened a screen displaying text messages. He held up the phone so that Beck could see the last exchange of texts.

Where's Beck? 12:47 PM

Stand by. Wking on it. 1:13 PM

Work fast. 1:15 PM

"Time for you to face the music, Beck. You want to find Nederland, text him. You want to run, good luck. Nederland's gonna come after you until either you're dead or he is. One way or another, you're going to face Ronald Nederland. And when that happens, pal, my money is on the monster."

Esposito stood up and said, "You sent that guy to warn me four years ago. Now I'm returning the favor."

He set the phone down in front of Beck and walked out of the bar.

83

Monster-Boy had slept almost five hours. He woke refreshed and energized. His injuries were stiff and sore, but that meant nothing to him. He'd been stabbed and beaten so many times in prison that these wounds were insignificant. They might start bleeding, particularly the cut on his arm, but so what.

He sent a text to Esposito.

He wasn't surprised at the answer. He figured Beck was doing the same thing he had done – sleeping and eating. Esposito had said as much in his last text.

He pictured Beck in a shitty hotel room. Maybe waking up right about now.

He picked up his phone and dialed Elliot Tanner.

Monster-Boy said, "It's me. What's going on? You still at the hospital?"

"Right now, I'm in my car. I been keeping track of everything. It's like you figured. All Beck's men are on the same post-op wing. Building L. First and second floors. Or gonna be."

"What does gonna be mean?"

"Oh, you might not know. The spic came in here a couple hours ago. All fucked up. Shot, something about his hand. He's still in surgery. Should end up on the same wing soon."

Monster-Boy grunted at hearing the news. He thought Guzman was lying dead in the wildlife preserve. Tough bastard made it out somehow.

Tanner said, "I also talked to a couple of cops from the local precinct at the hospital. They were there investigating the gunshot wounds on one of Beck's guys. I badged them and told them some bullshit about us being on a borough taskforce. They said there was a private doctor here riding herd on the hospital for these assholes. And a lawyer getting in everybody's face."

Monster-Boy grunted again.

"Also, I spotted some of Beck's pals skulking around outside. Probably looking out for you. There's also a big nig in Jones's room. And a guinea built like a fire hydrant in the mob guy's room."

Monster-Boy smiled at the news.

"Any sign of Beck?"

"I saw him in the emergency room area hours ago. Ain't seen him since."

"When was that?"

"Like five in the morning when I got here."

Monster-Boy nodded to himself. This was coming together even better than he had pictured it late at night lying on his prison bunk, willing it all to happen, seeing the flames of hell devouring his enemies.

"Okay. Where are you parked?"

"In one of the lots where I can see who goes in and out of the main entrance."

"You done good, brother. You can get the hell out of there now."

"No problem. Happy to help with anything that fucks up these guys. One other thing."

"What?"

"The precinct cops told me word around their house is that the Richmond County DA is drawing up warrants for all these guys. So, the next stop for these fuckers is jail. How soon, I don't know."

Monster-Boy checked his watch. Time to get moving. Where the fuck was Beck?

84

Beck stared at the phone Esposito had left on the table. It was a cheap, pre-paid flip phone. Beck grabbed his empty shot glass and took it to the bar.

"I'll have another."

The bartender nodded and poured a generous shot of Don Julio into Beck's glass. He reached for a wedge of lime, but Beck said, "No fruit."

The bartender dropped the wedge back into his condiment tray.

Beck said, "What's the tab?"

The bartender turned to his cash register and rang up the bill.

Beck had his money in hand when the bartender set down the check. $121.78.

Beck looked at the check and couldn't help smirking a bit. Don Julio was a premium tequila, but fourteen bucks a shot in Red Hook? His last pour made it six of them. Each beer was seven. Fourteen and a half bucks for the guacamole and chips. The computerized bill even suggested the appropriate tips in increments: 18% $21.92, 25% $24.36, 30% $30.44.

If this isn't proof that Red Hook is over, I don't know what is, thought Beck. He laid $160.00 on the bar.

The bartender asked, "Need change?"

"No."

For $160.00, Beck didn't hesitate to make a request. "Can you tear me off a piece of Saran wrap?" Beck held out his hands to indicate how much he needed.

The bartender hesitated for a moment, then said, "Sure." The roll of plastic wrap was right under the bar. Beck wasn't surprised. Bartenders were always covering or wrapping stuff with it.

The bartender tore off a piece a little bigger than Beck had indicated but was careful to hand it to Beck so it wouldn't stick to itself.

Beck said, "Thanks. And can I borrow a pen for a second?"

The bartender gave him a ballpoint pen out of his shirt pocket.

Beck thanked him and returned to his table with his tequila, pen, and plastic wrap. He set down his shot and carefully opened Esposito's flip phone using just the tips of his thumb and index finger. Then he laid the plastic wrap on top of the open phone. He used the tip of the pen to scroll back and see if there were any other text messages on the phone. There weren't. Not a surprise. Esposito had erased everything that connected the phone to Warren Roth and Fernandez. At least Beck had a flip phone with Esposito's fingerprints on it and, more important, none of his own.

Beck laid the plastic wrap over the phone, closed the phone, and folded the rest of the plastic wrap around it. He took out his smartphone and called Liebowitz. The voice answering was groggy.

Beck said, "You get any sleep?"

"Couple of hours."

Beck checked his watch. Almost three o'clock.

"How much cash do we have in the local Brooklyn bank account?"

"Quarter of a mill."

"How late is that bank open?"

"Until six."

"That's the branch on Montague."

"Yeah."

"You got a contact there?"

Alex said, "Yeah, we get a private banker with that account. Along with a couple hundred other assholes, I presume."

"Right. Call and tell him you're coming to see him. I don't want you standing in line. Tell him you're going to need ten cashier's checks for ten grand each."

"Cashier's, not bank checks?"

Beck said, "Yes. I want Phineas to be able to make them out to whoever he needs to. And you might as well take out ten grand in cash. It might come in handy."

"Got it."

"Hire a driver and car. Have him wait for you. You're going to take the money to Staten Island University Hospital. Phineas will be wherever they take patients post-surgery."

"Who's he with?"

"Everybody."

"Shit. Everybody?"

"Yes. Thankfully, nobody has fatal injuries."

"Still."

"I know," said Beck. "Hard to believe one guy got all of them."

"But you're okay."

Beck didn't want to tell Alex that Nederland almost got him, too.

"Yes. After I hang up with you, I'm calling Phineas. He'll be waiting for you."

"I'm on my way."

"Wait. Did you find out anything more about Ronald Nederland?"

"We hacked into his prison records. It might be a shithole prison, but their online security is surprisingly good. It took a little time."

"Find out anything interesting?"

"Yeah. Ronald Nederland was in thirteen different incident reports. Details are gory. He's famous for using his teeth on people and trying to burn them."

"Lovely. Anything else?"

"Want to know his nickname?"

Beck said, "Monster-Boy?"

"How'd you know?"

"It stuck with him. Thanks for all the work, Alex. Get on that money thing for Phineas. Then stand down. And watch yourself. Be careful until this thing is over."

Beck hung up and immediately dialed his lawyer. Phineas answered on the first ring.

"James."

"Phin, the forces are about to descend on you."

"Talk to me, lad."

Beck could almost picture the look of determination hardening his lawyer's features. Phineas P. Dunleavy was a man who ran toward the sound of the cannons.

"The NYPD is getting arrest warrants for all of us."

"On what charges?"

"Demarco for killing the guy who stabbed him."

"Absurd. It was self-defense."

"Manny for killing his fishing buddies."

"And then abducting himself? Ridiculous."

"Ciro for assaulting some guys in a gym and shooting off his gun."

"They'll have a hard time finding witnesses who'll testify."

Beck said, "And me for killing Ronald Nederland. But don't worry. I have an ironclad alibi."

"Good. So what's their game, lad? Harassment? Trying to violate Demarco and Ciro back to prison?"

"Phin, I think they're setting up an excuse to take us out. Ciro isn't going to get arrested without a fight. Or Demarco. Manny, too, I suppose. Me, I'm a cop killer. They'll light me up whether I have a gun or not. I don't want the cops getting anywhere near Demarco, Ciro, or Manny, even if they're in the hospital. Between Willie Reese, Joey B, and the guys with them, it could end up with a lot of people hurt."

"Understood. I promise you it won't happen, James."

"You need to pull out all stops on this, right now, counselor. Hire as much help as you need. Get on the horn with the people who have the best connections to Richmond County's DA office. Start negotiations on these charges now. Alex is on his way to you with a hundred thousand in cashier's checks and ten thousand in cash. That should be enough for whatever retainers you need. Or bribes. Whatever. I want a firewall around everybody. Total war, Phineas. The whole thing stinks. It's being controlled by the police commissioner himself. Hire private security people if you think it's a way to go. Threaten lawsuits, civil, criminal. Threaten media exposure. Whatever it takes, Phin."

"I'll start making calls as soon as I hang up with you."

"Good. And call Walter Ferguson. He's Demarco's parole officer, and he knows Ciro's parole officer on Staten Island. See if he can show up and help slow things down. Walter's a good man. He'll do what he can to help."

"I have Walter's number."

"Is Brandon still there?"

"He is."

"Good. I want as many doctors and hospital administrators as he can gather to make the case that nobody should be moved. We'll pay whatever fees they want."

"Done and done. I'll need to call in a couple of other law firms, James. Comrades in arms."

"Do it."

"What about you, James? You've got to lay low."

"Don't worry about me, counselor. Just make sure our guys stay where they are with plenty of protection. No transfers to a hospital with a jail ward. What's the hospital they might try to take them to?"

"From here, it would be Kings County. That's not going to happen. At least not while my heart is beating."

Beck said, "Good man. I'll be in touch."

Beck put his phone in his pocket. Suddenly, the peace and quiet in the old bar reminded him of his place on Conover. This one wasn't as old, wasn't as close to the waterfront, but close enough. He felt his mind wandering to his life just a little more than twenty-four hours ago. He realized that everything he had created over the years was now threatened. His home, his friends, all of it built on a foundation as light and gossamer as the dust motes floating by him in the sunlight of the Mexican bar.

Beck told himself it wasn't all gone. Battered and in parts, broken, wounded, but not gone. I still have my friends and friends of my friends. I still have money. I still have myself. And like Phineas had said, the great, tough, loyal Phineas P. Dunleavy, I'm not letting this go while my heart is beating.

Beck pushed aside the maudlin bullshit he found himself wallowing in. This wasn't over. Not yet.

He took a sip of his fourteen-dollar tequila and scooped up some guacamole with a taco chip. He had a swig from his beer. It all tasted good. He'd be damned if this was the last drink he'd enjoy in the last bar he ever sat in. Fuck that. He pushed aside the sadness and foreboding that had penetrated him. For now, his friends and partners were safe. But they'd all be in danger as long as Monster-Boy Nederland was alive. Esposito had been right. Everything had started with that punch he'd thrown in another bar within walking distance of this one. Time to close the loop. Face what he had caused. End this trail of misery even if it meant unleashing another round of death and violence. If that was his fate, so be it.

But how? How?

Beck came at it from every angle, sipping, thinking. He finished the shot of tequila and bottle of Negro Modelo. The combination of warm tequila and cold beer felt like it had cleared a path to the truth.

Ronald Nederland did not want to kill him from afar. He could have done that at the very beginning. No, Nederland wanted him to suffer. To lose his friends, his home, and then his life in the most painful way possible. Nederland wanted his hands on him. He wanted to cut him, beat him, sink his teeth into him, and set him on fire.

Beck would have to meet the monster face to face.

And that brought Beck face to face with the true, rock-bottom reality.

His chance of surviving a fight with the monster was very slim. Like Esposito said, his money was on the monster. He'd have to shoot him down out of arms reach. But how? And if he did, Roth would undoubtedly arrest him for murder. First-degree, pre-meditated. The State would throw everything and him and likely win.

Not to mention that Beck did not want to bet the lives of his men on the hope that he could take down a six-seven, two-hundred-seventy-pound monster by himself.

The final truth, Beck realized, was that he needed help from the last person he wanted to provide it, from the person who had set him up and used him from the very beginning: Dianne Brennan.

85

After finishing the call with Elliot Tanner, Monster-Boy felt everything quickening, becoming more urgent. He had to move now, while Beck's men were in the hospital and before the police arrested them.

It was the first time since the ambush at Montello's that Monster-Boy wished the Worm were still alive. Having Worm around had made everything easier to do, including getting what he needed for the final reckoning.

They had been shopping for groceries. They parked near a Key Fook in a mall on Arden Avenue when they spotted a compressed gas delivery truck in front of a Subway sandwich shop. The sight of the gas cylinders lined up on the Isuzu truck's flatbed sparked a reaction in Monster-Boy. The cylinders were izn various sizes, many of them nearly six feet tall. They looked lethal to Monster-Boy. Like bombs. He imagined whatever was inside those cylinders had to be dangerous.

Monster-Boy forgot about Key Food and pulled the Ford F-150 a spot where he could keep an eye on the compressed gas truck. After a five-minute wait, the driver emerged from Subway carrying his lunch to the truck.

The driver was a big man, of course not as big as Monster-Boy, but the size of someone able to handle heavy-looking steel cylinders holding compressed gases. The driver wore a blue jumpsuit and climbed into his truck to eat his lunch.

Monster-Boy wanted to steal the truck and its contents then and there, but he waited, watching, staring at the bomb-shaped gas cylinders.

The driver finished his lunch, started the truck, and pulled out of the parking area. Monster-Boy followed as if the truck and its contents were a magnet pulling him along in its wake. They kept watching the truck as it made various stops. The last stop on its delivery route was Staten Island University Hospital. Monster-Boy and Worm watched the driver use the Isuzu's hydraulic rear-end lift and a pair of hand trucks to haul in various cylinders. One hand truck designed to carry two cylinders. The other an industrial, tilt-back hand truck capable of moving cylinders weighing 1,000 pounds.

The next day was much like the first. They picked up the driver at the mall on Arden. Followed it along a route different from the day before until the driver took Lilly Pond Road to the Staten Island Expressway, where the compressed gas truck headed for New Jersey.

The pattern remained the same the following day. Each day the driver stopped in the same Subway shop midway through his route, parked at the far end of the lot, bought the same lunch, and sat in his truck eating it.

Stealing the truck on the fourth day couldn't have been easier.

As the driver sat eating his Italian BMT footlong sandwich, the Worm tapped on the driver's side door. The driver lowered his window.

Worm said, "Hey, did you know you got a rear tire going flat?"

"What?"

"Your rear tire. On the passenger side. It's like almost flat."

Cursing and grumbling, the driver set his sandwich on the passenger seat and climbed out of the Isuzu.

Worm stepped back, giving the driver room to walk to the rear of the truck. As the driver passed him, Worm stayed near the open driver's side door. When the driver turned at the back of the truck to head for the rear wheel on the passenger side, he ran into Monster-Boy, who had been waiting behind the truck. The driver stopped, surprised. During that two seconds of confusion, Monster-Boy hit him just above the bridge of his nose, breaking both nasal bones at the joint, rupturing two vertebrae at the top of the driver's neck, and sending him down onto the asphalt hard enough to crack his skull.

Monster-Boy dragged the driver around to the truck's passenger side and shoved him as far as he could under a Ford Excursion parked in the adjoining slot.

The Worm had already climbed into the Isuzu.

Monster-Boy walked up to the passenger door, pulled it open, and watched the Worm used his knife to search for the tracking device they knew would be hidden somewhere in the delivery truck. Monster-Boy verified the keys were in the ignition as Worm sliced open the sides of both seats, the headliner, broke apart the dashboard, pulled off the speaker covers, and finally located the tracker under the carpet near the truck wall behind the passenger seat.

Worm disconnected the tracking device and said, "Good to go."

Monster-Boy shut the door and walked over to his Ford-150.

Worm drove the stolen truck to a commercial parking lot tucked under the overpass of the Staten Island Expressway, where Monster-Boy had rented a parking space for one month. Monster-Boy following close behind with two large tarpaulins in the F-150 truck bed.

They had the delivery truck parked under the Staten Island Expressway overpass in twenty minutes, the flatbed covered in blue tarps.

Nederland had secured everything he needed for his plan, including four tanks of acetylene used for welding, a dozen thirty-pound tanks of propane, and, most important, a rack of J-size nitrous oxide cylinders, each of them containing 18,000 liters of gas and weighing 253.5 pounds.

86

Dianne Brennan sat in her office feeling a debilitating numbness come over her. Paralyzing her. She felt foolish and naïve. She'd been strutting around for two years as the deputy inspector special assistant to the commissioner of the NYPD, acting like she had a measure of power because of her rank and association with Warren Roth. But now she realized it all amount to little more than being used by a ruthless and decisive man who had real power. She was a glorified flunky. A pretty show pony of a stalking horse.

She'd been chewed up and spit out by Warren Roth and then told to do his bidding. Find James Beck. That is after Roth had used Beck in his scheme to kill Nederland and go back to prison, or be killed and go to hell.

But why the anger and shame? She'd floated that very idea to Roth so that *she* could use Beck in her investigation of the Red Hook murders. Did she suddenly regret treating Beck the way she had? Before she could answer that question, her burner phone rang.

Beck.

She thought about letting the call go to voicemail but decided not to. Why? Because she still wanted to follow Roth's orders? Because she wanted to stay in the game?

Brennan answered and said, "Yes?"

Beck said, "How's it feel?"

"How does what feel?"

Beck said, "I'm assuming you met with Roth."

"Yes."

"How much did he tell you?"

There was a pause before Brennan said, "Enough."

"I'm pretty sure he didn't tell you all of it," said Beck.

"What else is there to know?"

"Quite a bit. We should meet."

"Why?"

"To put an end to this."

"What does that mean?"

"Meet me, and I'll tell you. And, by the way, leave your two detectives behind and take a cab."

"Why?"

"Because you can't afford to let anybody know you're meeting with me."

Beck gave her the address of the bar and hung up. Either Brennan would come, or she wouldn't. He wasn't going to try to convince her.

By the time Brennan walked into the Mexican bar, Beck had downed two club sodas, finished the chips and guacamole, and started on coffee. He was sorry to see the tequila and beer buzz fade away, but the time for drinking had ended.

When Dianne Brennan entered the bar, she quickly spotted Beck and headed toward his table. The sun was low in the sky, filling the room with a golden light that made Brennan's red hair glow. Six more patrons had come into the bar since Beck had arrived with Esposito. Five were men. All five turned to look at the redhead with the athletic body and determined stride moving past them.

As closely as they watched her, Beck doubted any of them had caught the outline of her Sig-Sauer high up on her right hip under her tailored black blazer. It occurred to Beck that Brennan could pull out her gun and tell him he was under arrest. Or grab the police radio on her other hip and call in a team of cops to swoop in and arrest him. Deliver what the commissioner wanted.

She sat opposite him.

Beck asked, "You want something?"

"Coffee."

Beck turned to the bartender. He didn't have to get his attention. He was already looking at Brennan. Beck motioned for another cup of coffee. Milk and sugar were on the table.

Beck said, "You came alone?"

"Yes. In a cab. Why? What's this all about?"

Beck paused for a moment. Partly to look at Brennan in the golden-red light, partly to gather his thoughts.

Beck ignored Brennan's question and said, "I've decided not to hold anything against you."

"Oh, really? Like what?"

"Like you helping Warren Roth try to have Nederland kill me." Brennan was about to respond when Beck held up his hand. "Not intentionally. I'm going to assume you didn't know what Roth was doing."

"I didn't. Assuming what you're saying is true, which I don't believe."

"Why not? You got Roth to agree to let you work with me by floating the possibility that the bad guy might kill me."

"Or you might kill him. So what? As I recall, it was your idea to pitch it to Roth that way. I'm not denying Roth wouldn't have minded seeing you dead. But accusing him of working with Nederland? That's crazy. Is that why I'm here?"

"No. You're here because Ronald Nederland is still alive."

Brennan took a moment to absorb that. "How do you know that?"

"I'll explain in a minute. Since Nederland is still alive, our interests coincide. He's still a danger to me and my men. And you still have a chance to take him down. Which I assume you want to do. As do I."

"Define take him down."

"Arrest him. Shoot him. Whatever it takes to get him off the streets and somewhere he can't kill anybody."

"And you have proof Nederland is alive?"

"I do. That's reason number one. There's another reason you're here."

"Which is?"

"We have another common interest. I want to take down Warren Roth because he wants me dead. You should want to take him down because as long as he's in power, you're in danger of losing everything."

"Why? And why do you think you could possibly take him down?"

"Both for the same reason."

"What do you mean?"

"Look, you know he wants to take out me and my partners, but you don't know how far over the line he's gone to do that."

"What do you mean?"

"He's corrupted everybody involved with this case. He's conspired with a maniac responsible for multiple murders. Not to mention he's going to dump you the first chance he gets. If you have any survival instincts left after sitting so long in that One Police Plaza outhouse, you'll realize what Roth had done could mean the end of everything you've worked for."

The waiter arrived with Brennan's coffee. Brennan waited until he left to ask, "How do you know all this?"

Beck pulled out Esposito's plastic-wrapped burner phone and placed it on the table.

"Christ, again with a phone. It's like the first time we talked."

Beck said, "So be it." And then he explained everything he had learned from Jeffrey Esposito. He laid it all out, briefly and to the point, even as he saw how the corruption and self-dealing and double-dealing hurt and disturbed Brennan.

He didn't exaggerate or hold back. Brennan didn't interrupt. She didn't ask any questions, and she didn't comment or argue.

Beck finished by saying, "I think you believe me, Dianne. Since we met, I may have held back on you, but I never lied to you. And I think you know the truth when you hear it. Roth has been playing everybody and controlling everything. Including you. He's conspired with Monster-Boy Nederland. He's a ticking time bomb."

Brennan had finished her coffee. She turned the cup around on her saucer, thinking. Finally, she looked up and asked her first question.

"Do you really think you can take down the NYPD police commissioner?"

"Let me be more precise. I think we can take away his power to hurt either one of us. And give you the leverage you need to get to a better situation."

"How?"

Beck pointed toward Esposito's phone.

"Esposito erased all the texts except for his last exchange with Nederland. But apparently, he doesn't know that the companies who sell these burner phones keep text files in their systems. Some for a few days. Others for up to three weeks. My tech guy found out that the company for this phone still has copies of the texts. Better yet, he can get copies of those texts. The phone still has Esposito's prints. Between this phone and having the chain of texts from Fernandez to Esposito – Roth is vulnerable. And, if it comes down to it, once Esposito is off the force, I don't think he'll cover for Fernandez and Roth."

Brennan stared at the phone. "I don't know. Even if Esposito is retired, Roth will find a way to threaten his pension. Fernandez will deny everything. Nederland sure as hell isn't going to admit Esposito helped him, assuming we even find Nederland. And assuming the texts say what you think they say."

"None of that matters."

"Why?"

"How do the mayor and the commissioner get along?"

Brennan paused for a moment and said, "They're friends until they're not."

Beck nodded. "I'm sure His Honor wouldn't mind having the means keep Warren Roth in his back pocket. You think Roth wants the mayor to have this phone with Esposito's prints and the texts between Esposito, Fernandez, and a murderer wanted by the NYPD? Or the New York Times? Or the attorney general of New York State? Or all of the above?"

"How are you going to prove the texts came from Fernandez, much less Roth to Fernandez?"

Beck leaned toward Brennan. "Look at it from a slightly different direction. Do you honestly believe that Roth will want to risk his reputation and career on the fact that a double-dealing, brown nose, conniving piece of shit like Nicholas Fernandez won't spill his guts if the Mayor of New York threatens him? Or the attorney general? Or the governor? Fernandez will turn on Roth the second the higher-ups tell him to."

Beck watched Brennan thinking it through.

Beck said, "Brennan, I may not have a place to live or clothes to wear, but one thing I do have is money. More than enough to assemble a small army of attorneys. Enough to subpoena Roth, Fernandez, Esposito, your fucking turncoat detectives and punk-ass driver, anybody who had anything to do with this. I can afford to pay for as many depositions as I need to and all the court hearings necessary to make those depositions happen. I can afford lawyers who'll raise hell with the NYPD Inspector General while other lawyers file lawsuits in civil courts for Esposito, you, and me.

"And while all that is happening, I'll still have plenty of money to hire a fucking PR firm to flog a story about Roth colluding with a crazed murderer in every New York newspaper, starting with the Times. You think Roth or the mayor or the governor want that?" Beck sat back and said, "I have to neutralize Warren Roth, and so do you. Listen, we don't have to do anything but convince Roth of the danger he's facing. All you need to do is deliver the message to him about what I'm prepared to do. It's your fucking job to keep him informed, isn't it? And trust me, Roth will know my threats aren't bullshit. He didn't take me out when he had a chance. He still wants to. He knows I've got nothing to lose."

Brennan nodded. Saying nothing.

Beck leaned toward her and said, "Brennan, are you going to let Roth and Fernandez and all the other assholes who want to see you go down get away with this? Including that supercilious quisling Jablonsky who stuck a knife in your back?

She looked up, and Beck saw the fire in her interesting green eyes.

"No. I am not. And what about Ronald Monster-Boy Nederland?"

"We can take him down, too."

"How?"

Beck said, "Order another cup of coffee, and I'll tell you."

87

Beck opened Esposito's cell phone and showed Brennan Esposito's last text exchange with Nederland.

> Where's Beck? 12:47 PM

> Stand by. Wking on it. 1:13 PM

> Work fast. 1:15 PM

Beck said, "Nederland still thinks Esposito has this phone. All we have to do is make Nederland think Esposito knows what I'm doing. Where I'm going."

"But it has to be believable."

"Agreed." Beck typed in a text and showed it to Brennan. "How's this?"

> He made a deal with the cop. Agreed to turn hmslf in after he sees crew and lawyer at hosp. She ok'd but only if she stays w him. 3:13 PM

Beck asked, "What do you think?"

"Why make a deal with me? And why should I agree?"

Beck rewrote the text.

> D Insp tried to sve warrant on Beck. He agrd to turn himself in after he sees crew and lawyer at

hospital. She ok'd but only if she stays with him.
Prbly wants to arrest them too 3:15 PM

Brennan looked at the text and said, "Better."

Beck said, "It's good enough. All he wants to do is kill me. He'll figure this is his last chance before I go to jail."

Brennan nodded. Beck sent the text. It took seven minutes for Nederland to respond.

When. 3:22 PM

Tell you sn as I know. Shd b soon. 3:24 PM

The trap was set. Brennan and Beck hashed out the rest of the plan. Argued over several points, made adjustments, agreed it wasn't perfect but reasonably solid, mostly because Beck knew one thing for sure. Ronald Nederland wanted to kill him up close and personal.

Beck sent the last text.

Both heading to SIUH. bout 30 minutes out. 5:10 PM

Sitting in his tan Subaru, Nederland checked his watch. 5:15 p.m. Beck and the bitch should be arriving soon. He'd left for the hospital without even waiting for the second text. He'd already finished almost everything he'd needed to do. He drove to the hospital. Parked the Subaru. Took an Uber to the medical gas delivery truck. Drove the Isuzu back to the hospital and hauled in what he needed to the hospital's compressed gas storage room. Left the nearly empty delivery truck in the back lot outside the loading dock and retrieved his Subaru.

Now that Nederland knew Beck would be arriving in about twenty-five minutes, the last thing he needed to do was go back to the storage room and set the timer on his firebomb. But in his steroid-heightened rage and anticipation, Nederland had difficulty focusing his attention. His mind raced too fast to add up the minutes. He had to count in ten-minute intervals. The text said thirty minutes for Beck to arrive. Okay, twenty-five minutes left. Add ten minutes to follow Beck to wherever he parked, beat him into submission but keep him conscious. Break some ribs. His jaw. That would do it. Ten minutes would be enough time. No, make it fifteen. Twenty-five plus fifteen, forty minutes. Add five minutes to get Beck where he could see the explosion. So, forty-five minutes.

Nederland slipped out of his Subaru and headed for the basement door to the utility rooms, going over the times again and again. Twenty-five minutes plus fifteen plus five. Forty-five? But what if Beck took longer than thirty minutes to arrive?

Nederland had so much adrenaline pumping through him, it almost felt like being on meth. An overpowering urge to get high caused a chemical taste in the back of his mouth. Nederland focused again on the numbers. Add ten more minutes in case Beck was late. So, fifty-five. He went over the numbers repeatedly as he walked through the basement corridors to where he had set up his firebomb.

Nederland checked his watch. 5:22 p.m. Shit, another seven minutes gone. So how long now? Fifty-five minutes on the timer? No, forty-eight. He'd burned seven minutes. Seven from fifty-five. Forty-eight. Fuck it, stay with fifty-five minutes. Better to have more time than less.

Gotta get in place and be ready to spot Beck. Shoot the woman cop. Quickly. Beat the shit out of Beck. Get him in the back lot. Slap him around and taunt him about seeing all his men blown to shit and burned up in flames. Make him watch. Boom! Then take the asshole back to the Red Hook grain terminal. He'd have plenty of time there. String him up. Cut him. Use him like a heavy bag. Break bones. Set that piece of shit on

fire. Whatever was left of him. Then adios, cocksuckers. Head
south. Cut down on the steroids. Drop weight. Grow my hair
back, maybe a beard. Lay low in Mexico for a couple of months.
Figure out the next move.

As Nederland hurried into the hospital's medical gases storage
room, he felt an erotic swirl of anticipation and excitement. He
looked at his watch again. 5:24 pm. How many minutes now? The
numbers blurred. Rushing now. The sequence became muddled.
He knelt on one knee to set the timer, suddenly plagued by the
thought – what if Beck gets here sooner?

Most of the plan Beck shared with Brennan had been formulated
while he had waited for her to arrive at the bar. He'd considered
the problems from various angles. Paring everything down to
find a logic that made sense, methodically eliminating anything
that wasn't simple or believable, despite knowing he couldn't
really have much confidence in what a madman might believe.
Mostly, he tried to focus on what he knew for sure and build
everything based on two facts. One – so far, Nederland had
believed Esposito. Two – Ronald Nederland wanted to kill him.
He'd show up anywhere on earth to do that.

Now, Beck sat in a black unmarked, unwashed NYPD Dodge
Charger parked in a hospital parking lot off Olympia Boulevard,
a street that ran the quarter-mile length of the Staten Island
University Hospital campus. His position gave him a view of
where Olympia intersected with Seaview Avenue at the hospital's
main entrance.

Beck had arrived twenty minutes before the text said he was
due. Logic said that Nederland would park on Olympia near the
main entrance so he could spot the red Nissan. Then Nederland
would follow the car to wherever it parked, take out Brennan,
and try to kill him in the parking lot.

There were parking lots on both sides of Olympia Boulevard.
Visitors would naturally drive to the lots nearest the hospital's

main entrance and work their way back until they found an available parking spot. Beck figured that would give him plenty of opportunity to see if Nederland was tailing the Nissan, fall in behind Nederland, and help Brennan take him down.

Simple.

The only thing Beck couldn't confidently predict was when Nederland would arrive. But he'd solved that by having Brennan wait on a side street in the red Nissan until Nederland was in place. Once Nederland was set up, he would tell Brennan to drive onto the hospital campus.

A bit complicated. Further complicated by the fact that with Beck on the lookout for Nederland to arrive, he couldn't be in the Nissan with Brennan. That's what he had texted to Nederland posing as Esposito. That the policewoman would be with him. A woman alone in the red Nissan wouldn't cut it.

Brennan came up with a solution. At first, she'd wanted Grimaldi to take Beck's place in the Nissan. She assured Beck that Grimaldi hadn't betrayed her by communicating with Roth. Brennan believed Jablonsky could have, and also Dave Metuchen. He was the most political. But not Alphonse Grimaldi. Beck would not relent. They finally compromised on the third member of her squad to substitute for Beck – the dapper black detective Phil Harris. Brennan insisted Harris had not been co-opted by Roth because he hadn't known anything he could tell Roth. He'd been out of the loop doing research in the RTCC. After a bit more discussion, Beck and Brennan agreed that with night falling, Nederland wouldn't be able to see Harris's skin color inside the Nissan.

Beck couldn't come up with anything better, so he agreed. He figured two cops armed and ready, with him closing in behind Nederland, would give them their best chance to take down the maniac.

The downside was Brennan insisting Beck give up his gun. He said only if Brennan guaranteed she and Harris wouldn't shoot him. Brennan said she'd try not to, but no guarantees.

Brennan's attempt at being flip didn't put Beck at ease, but he went along with her demand. He knew if Nederland, Harris, and Brennan got into a gunfight, there'd be a good chance somebody other than Nederland would get shot. Adding rounds fired from his P220 would almost guarantee it. So, Beck agreed to give up his gun, but only because he knew he had another weapon. A 3,332-pound car. He fully intended to drive the unmarked NYPD Dodge Charger into the juiced-up hulk the second Nederland got out of whatever he was driving.

There was a bit more arguing about having more men involved, either cops or Beck's men at the hospital, but both Beck and Brennan ended up agreeing that involving more players would risk tipping Nederland off.

It was about as good a plan as Beck could come up with. A plan Beck had no illusions about. He knew all plans could fall apart on execution. He just didn't think this one would fall apart before he even had a chance to put it in motion.

Beck had expected Nederland to arrive from outside the hospital complex. Maybe park out on Seaview Avenue or, more likely, somewhere on Olympia near the main entrance and wait there for the Nissan to appear. Instead, he saw the unmistakable form of the six-seven, bald hulk driving an old tan Subaru Outlook along Olympia coming from *inside* the complex heading toward Seaview Avenue.

That meant Nederland had been on the hospital campus before Beck had arrived. What had he been doing? How long had he been here?

Shit.

Beck grabbed his cell phone off the passenger seat. He speed-dialed Willie Reese's number.

Reese answered on the third ring.

"Yo."

"Willie, is everything all right?"

"Yeah. Everything is cool. Manny's done with surgery. Out of recovery. In his room. I'm with Demarco. Pastor Ben is with

401

Manny. Joey B with Ciro. Nuthin' from any of the guys inside or out. Why?"

"The fucker is here. I just saw him."

"Where?"

"Heading for the exit onto Seaview."

"What the hell's he doin'?"

"I don't know."

Beck got out of his car and tried to spot the tan Subaru Outlook. He couldn't see it until he looked over the roof of the car nearest to him. Nederland had pulled over and parked about fifty feet west of the entrance on Seaview. He was in place, but what the hell had he been doing inside the hospital grounds?

Beck climbed back into the Dodge.

Had Nederland set up his own trap? Planted people in the parking lots?

Beck said to Reese, "Let me check this out. Tell everybody to be on the alert. I'm going to look around."

"Okay. You need me?"

"No. Stay where you are. If he gets past me, shoot him."

Beck pulled out onto Olympia and turned right, heading away from where Nederland had parked. He thought about calling Brennan but rejected the idea. Let her stay where she was. In place and safe.

Beck drove slowly along Olympia, checking the cars parked on the street or in the lots trying to spot anybody sitting in them. Anybody there to help Nederland.

This didn't make sense. Beck was convinced Nederland would think he could take him and Brennan down by himself. Especially since the texts from Esposito's phone had given him the advantage of surprise.

When Beck approached the main entrance of the hospital, he saw that Olympia ran into an intersection. Turning left would lead out onto Mason Avenue, another entrance on the other side of the hospital complex. Shit. Nederland must have had entered on the other side of the campus then driven through to set up at the main entrance.

Beck checked his watch. He'd burned up almost ten minutes. No problem. The red Nissan could arrive ten minutes late. Still time to execute the plan.

Beck was just about to make a U-turn and race back into position when a short distance beyond the main entrance, he saw something in a small parking lot behind two dumpster bins. It was a row of medical gas cylinders, but just the tops. Something about the shape of the cylinders set off an alarm.

He turned into the parking area. Shadows shrouded the small lot. Beck reached for the post-mounted spotlight added to the cop car, turned it on, and drove past the dumpsters aiming the powerful beam back and forth. That's when he saw a flatbed delivery truck. There were five caution signs for compressed medical gases attached to the side of the truck. The flatbed was nearly empty, but in Beck's agitated state, the upright cylinders of compressed medical gases with their oblong caps looked like bombs.

Beck told himself to calm down. Hospitals used compressed gases. But why was the truck parked there? He looked at his watch. 5:38 pm. It seemed late for a delivery. And the truck wasn't parked anywhere near the loading dock.

He got out and ran toward the truck. He saw vertical stacks of ventilating towers lined up on the far side of the lot. Storage sheds and trailers on the other side. Near the loading dock at ground level was a set of double doors leading into the basement. When Beck came parallel to the truck, he saw the diamond-shaped green, white, and red signs attached to the side of the flatbed. All of them displayed the word "flammable." Beck's pulse went up a notch.

He grabbed the side view mirror on the driver's side door and pulled himself up so he could see into the Isuzu's cab. He tried the driver's side door. It wasn't locked. When he pulled the door open, the interior lights went on. Both seats had been slashed open. The door speaker covers ripped off. The headliner sliced. The dashboard next to the glove compartment pulled apart. Somebody had torn up the truck looking for the tracking transmitter.

Nederland. He'd stolen the damn truck. Beck's heart started pounding.

88

Nederland had parked on Seaview Avenue so he could spot Beck's red Nissan arriving from both directions. For the first few minutes, he entertained himself by picturing what he would do to Beck. During his time in prison, Nederland had become addicted to torture and maiming, even to the point where he savored the pain he'd endured in brutal prison fights. Assaults on human beings that would sicken normal people thrilled Nederland. The sound of fists on flesh, weapons breaking bones, shivs cutting muscles and tendons pleased him. Burning any part of the human body exhilarated him. Pain became a fetish. Pain was the balm that assuaged Monster-Boy's rage. The anticipation of having James Beck at his mercy was almost too much for Monster-Boy to handle.

After ten minutes of fantasizing about Beck, Nederland realized his time was running out. He wasn't a hundred percent sure how many minutes he had entered on the timer. Sitting in the car allowed him to think more clearly. Had he set it for fifty-five minutes or fifty? He wasn't sure.

Where the fuck was the red Nissan? Had he missed it? Shit. Something was wrong.

Nederland pulled out of his parking space and turned onto Olympia, driving slowly, trying to spot red cars in the parking lots he passed. He knew he could only see the vehicles in the lots alongside Olympia. Should he turn into the lots and search? Fuck that. No time. But if he'd missed them, he'd have to search the lots and take them down when they left. But by then, the goddamn hospital might've blown up, and he'd miss his chance at Beck. Shit!

And then, halfway up Olympia Boulevard, he spotted something. A light in the darkness ahead. A spotlight of some sort shining into the parking area where he'd left the medical gas delivery truck.

What the hell was going on? If the cops had discovered his firebomb, there'd be dozens of police vehicles. But there were no flashing lights. No sirens. He accelerated toward the gleaming spotlight.

89

Beck pulled out his cell phone and ran toward the double doors leading to the basement. He speed-dialed Brennan. She answered on the first ring.

"We ready?"

"Nederland is parked on Seaview about twenty feet east of the entrance. Drive in and see if he picks you up. And call the bomb squad."

Brennan yelled, "What?!"

Beck ran through the doors and found himself in a corridor sloping down, dimly lit by widely spaced utility lights.

"I think Nederland has rigged up some sort of bomb in the first building after the main entrance. Come in now. If he picks you up, let him follow you, call for backup, shoot him, do whatever the fuck you have to do to keep him away from here, and call the bomb..."

Beck heard his cell phone emit a beep. He looked at it. No signal sub-ground. He didn't know how much Brennan had heard.

He kept rushing down the concrete block corridor. Ahead, he saw a steel door plastered with signs and symbols. MEDICAL GASES, AUTHORIZED PERSONNEL ONLY, NO SMOKING, and three diamond-shaped warning signs like those on the truck outside. FLAMMABLE. FLAMMABLE. FLAMMABLE.

He grabbed the door handle and tried to turn it. Locked. He pulled, and the door popped open. The frame had been bent back so that the lock and deadbolt no longer fit the strike plate.

Beck fumbled on the wall next to him for a light switch. He found one. Bright fluorescent light flooded the twenty-five-foot square room. Dozens of compressed gas cylinders filled racks bolted to the concrete block wall on the far side of the room. More cylinders almost as tall as Beck were chained to the walls on his right and left. There were lines of copper tubing and dozens of gauges attached to the walls with hoses connected to various cylinders. Beck saw markings on cylinders: O2, N2O, N2, 400 KPa, MA7. And in the center of the room sat a bright blue, plastic, 70-quart Coleman cooler. Beck assumed it was filled with gasoline. Six thirty-pound propane tanks were duct-taped to the ice chest. Four J-size tanks of nitrous oxide, each containing 18,000 liters of gas, had been placed around the cooler and propane. Lastly, three #4 size tanks of acetylene were interspersed around the nitrous oxide cylinders. Each one held 145 cubic feet of gas.

The crude assemblage of tanks and cylinders surrounding the blue cooler sent a spasm of fear and dread through Beck that hit him like an electric shock.

And then Beck heard the hissing from oxygen cylinders attached to the walls with their valves opened. The storage area was filling with pure oxygen.

Beck ran toward the grotesque bomb. On the top of the cooler, a digital timer ticked down.

Nederland had screwed up. Instead of setting the timer for fifty-five minutes, he'd set it for thirty-three minutes, mistaking the threes for fives. Beck had spotted Nederland parking on Seaview eight minutes later. It had taken Beck seventeen minutes to search for Nederland, find the delivery truck, and make his way to the storage room. By the time Beck got close enough to see the digital numbers, the readout on the timer showed 08:19.47.

At first, he thought it meant eight hours, nineteen minutes, forty-seven seconds. But when the .47 flashed down to .00 in less than a second, Beck realized the bomb was set to go off in eight minutes, eighteen seconds.

For a second, Beck couldn't breathe. And then he dropped down to his knees, running his hands over the cooler, frantic to find a wire or something to detach from the timer.

The only thing visible was the timer's digital readout. The rest of the timer was covered in black plumber's epoxy. The battery, plug, and electrical cord were all hidden, glued to the inside of the cooler's lid. There was no way to open the sealed cooler. Beck didn't want to smash the timer or try to break open the cooler for fear it would spark an explosion.

He looked around frantically. There were fire extinguishers hanging from the walls and a sprinkler system overhead, but Beck had no idea if they could extinguish whatever was about to explode in that Coleman cooler.

There was only one thing he could do. Get that goddamn ice chest out of the room.

Beck didn't have a knife to cut the duct tape holding the propane tanks to the cooler, so he kneeled on the cooler lid and grabbed one of the propane tanks, pulling, twisting, pushing down on it until he tore the tank free. That's when he noticed the cylinder valve and safety release vent on the propane tanks were all encased in the same hardened epoxy.

Beck remembered the firebomb that had exploded in Nederland's garage. He knew the gas in the propane tanks and cylinders were under pressure. With the safety valves sealed, how long before the propane inside boiled and exploded? What about all the other cylinders? He saw that all the valves had been sealed with the same epoxy. Beck pictured the assembled heap of compressed gas cylinders engulfed in fire, the pressure building in them until they exploded. It looked like Nederland had put together more than enough of them to blow up half the hospital along with every person he loved or cared about.

He ripped the next thirty-pound propane tank free. The readout said 06:12.16.

With two tanks free, the duct tape went slack. Beck began ripping and pulling the rest of the tanks away from the ice chest. He was just about to grab the cooler when the door behind him banged open. The hulking shape of Ronald Nederland filled the entire door frame.

Nederland roared, "You!"

The shock of suddenly seeing the monstrously large man paralyzed Beck.

Nederland pulled a gun and rushed into the room.

Beck grabbed a propane tank and hurled it at the monster. Nederland raised his arms to block the thirty-pound steel tank. It hit with a thud, cracking the ulna bone in his right arm, one of the few spots on Nederland not covered by thick pads of muscle. The impact knocked the gun out of his hand and slowed Nederland just long enough for Beck to grab another tank and hurl it at Nederland's left knee.

Nederland turned away, taking most of the impact on his lower thigh, but the tank hit where Manny's pig shank weapon had created a wound and hit enough of the knee joint to do damage. The hulk almost went down, regained his balance, then lunged at Beck, who ducked under Nederland's reach, just barely avoiding Nederland's attempt to grab him. Beck threw himself at Nederland, grabbing him around the waist, pushing, shoving, trying to take the monster down to the floor. He barely moved him.

Nederland raised both arms and smashed down on Beck's back, breaking Beck's grip and sending him to his knees.

Beck felt like a refrigerator had dropped onto his back.

Nederland grabbed Beck's coat. He wanted to pull Beck to his feet so he could punch and beat on him and sink his misshapen teeth into Beck's face and throat. But even with ribs broken, even with Nederland pulling him upward, Beck rammed a short, vicious, right-hand uppercut between Nederland's legs, immobilizing the monster. Despite the pain, despite one arm broken, Nederland was still able to lift Beck off his knees. He wanted to slam Beck into the rack behind him over and over until Beck was a limp, unconscious heap.

Beck felt himself being lifted. Desperate, he grabbed onto Nederland's injured leg, wrapping both arms around the huge thigh, holding on with all his strength as Nederland pulled him higher. Beck hung on. He didn't try to stop Nederland from lifting him. He did the opposite. He used all the power in his legs to stand and lift Nederland's leg as he drove his shoulder into Nederland's chest.

Nederland toppled backward, landed hard, cracked his head on the concrete, but he still held onto Beck's coat. Beck landed on the hulk's chest, grabbed Nederland's forefinger, twisted and wrenched it downward, breaking the finger and loosening Nederland's grip enough so he could pull free, straddle Nederland's waist, and rise up.

Nederland immediately grabbed the back of Beck's neck with his damaged hand, pulled him down, and reached for his throat with his good hand. Again, Beck didn't fight the monster's strength. He allowed Nederland to pull him down, increasing his momentum as he smashed his forehead into Nederland's face. The impact nearly knocked Beck unconscious, but he reared back, twisted to his left, preventing Nederland from grabbing his windpipe, and jammed his right forearm into Nederland's throat.

Nederland snarled and pulled at the back of Beck's neck, trying to get him close enough to bite him, but the more he pulled down, the more Beck's forearm pressed into Nederland's throat.

Beck was on top now, with his left hand free. With every bit of his strength, he pounded his left fist into Nederland's right temple, jaw, throat, nose, eye socket. Punching nonstop, over and over, despite Nederland's attempt to block the punches or turn away. Each punch gained Beck a bit more room to rear back and punch again. Beck knew he was breaking up his hand, cracking knuckles and bones, but he kept punching and punching, landing blows even as Nederland let go of Beck's neck so he could block the punches with both forearms.

Most of Beck's strikes didn't get through, but Beck wouldn't stop. And wouldn't release the pressure of his forearm on the giant's throat. Putting Nederland on his back had neutralized much of his strength and power, but the giant was still able to rear up and try to throw Beck off. He managed to get Beck's forearm off his throat, but only for a moment. Beck twisted back into his straddle and wailed at Nederland, this time with both elbows and both fists.

He smashed the other side of Nederland's face and head. Alternating now between elbow shots and hammer fist strikes. Finally, Beck felt resistance from Nederland fade. Exhaustion and the need to get that goddamn firebomb out of the storage room finally made Beck stop. Nederland lay unconscious. His face swollen and bruised and bloody. His nose broken. His breaths ragged, wheezing.

Beck pushed himself off the inert hulk and staggered over to the Coleman cooler. With its contents, the cooler weighed almost a hundred pounds. Beck couldn't lift it with his one functioning hand, so he grabbed the handle on the end of the cooler and dragged it across the room and out the door. He staggered and ran toward the exit, this time up the sloping corridor. The digital numbers on the timer flashed 01:58.45.

Hunched over, the ribs in his back screaming with pain, Beck kept going, dragging the firebomb. The doorway seemed so far away. Every step, every gasping breath, hurt. He knew he had broken ribs. He couldn't stand up straight, but he could move his legs.

The readout flashed 01:41.11.

Beck made it to the door that exited to the parking lot. He reached for the door handle. That's when he saw the piece of carbon steel rebar shoved behind the handles and bent into a U to prevent the doors from opening.

Beck screamed a curse. "Fuck!"

He dropped the cooler, grabbed one side of the rebar, and tried to push it straight. Despite his broken left hand, desperation gave him strength but not enough to bend the rebar. How the hell did Nederland bend it? Beck shifted to one side of the rebar and grabbed the top end with both hands despite the pain it caused in his battered left hand. He reared back, pulled, and pulled again, putting all his weight into it.

And then he heard the door to the storage room bang open. He turned and saw the huge shambling shape of Monster-Boy Nederland coming at him. The giant's face and head had already swollen horribly. One eye was swollen shut. Blood poured out of his nose, broken by Beck's head butt. The weird childish face was horribly misshapen and twisted with rage. The was truly a monster coming for him, gaining momentum, moving faster with each lurching step. Nederland growled something that Beck couldn't decipher.

Beck roared and pushed against the rebar. He looked at the cooler. The readout flashed 00:41.16.

Beck had no time left. And little strength. He grabbed one end of the rebar, jammed his foot against the other end, and pulled it with everything he had left, putting his whole body into it. He screamed with pain and effort, feeling the bar move. He stopped, out of breath. He'd straightened the rebar just enough to turn it and slide it free from the door handles.

He shoved the double-doors open. He had to get the firebomb out. He reached down and pulled the cooler up two steps, stumbling away from the building, counting in his head, trying to figure out how many seconds before he'd have to drop it and get away from the blast.

Seven yards away from the door, Beck slipped and fell. He struggled back to his feet. Nederland burst through the open door, staggering after Beck.

Six seconds left.

Beck dragged the ice chest five more feet, his strength giving out. He stopped, held onto the handle of the cooler, lifting and turning like a hammer thrower, holding on, building centrifugal force, lifting the cooler higher, turning one full revolution, Nederland almost on him, screaming at him.

With his last desperate measure of strength, Beck let go of the hundred pounds, sending it flying toward the monster.

The cooler smashed into Nederland's chest, stopping him in midstride. But Nederland absorbed the impact, caught the firebomb, and lifted it over his head.

Beck turned away, tried to run, fell again, thinking as he went down, he's going to throw it at me. I'm going to die.

Nederland roared. Just as he released the Coleman cooler loaded with gasoline, it exploded with a muffled whump, instantaneously followed by a blossoming fireball spreading in every direction.

Gasoline and burning plastic covered Nederland from his head down. Beck had scrambled ten feet away and was down on the ground. Most of the fireball exploded above him but melting plastic and burning liquid splattered his back and legs. He heard shouts. He rolled over, trying to smother the oily, sticky flames burning through his clothes. That's when he saw the terrifying specter of Nederland staggering toward him, covered in flames, arms outstretched, still screaming at him.

Beck didn't try to stand. Nederland was too close. He scrambled backward like a crab. Nederland threw himself at Beck, falling, getting close enough to grab Beck's right ankle. Beck kicked at the burning attacker, kicking at the flaming head as Nederland pulled him closer to the human inferno. He was trapped. Suddenly, Nederland lunged forward and buried his teeth into Beck's shin, grabbing Beck's leg with both hands. It felt like Nederland's teeth were crushing his shinbone. Nederland crawled toward Beck, bringing the flames closer. Beck believed he was going to die. An overpowering wave of anger and regret came over him. He managed to land a heel into the side of Nederland's burning, battered face. And then everything switched off in James Beck. The pain, the panic, the injuries overwhelmed him. He fell back. Unable to breathe. He thought he heard the crack of gunshots somewhere in the din of Nederland's growling and shrieking amidst the dark smoke and oily fire pulling Beck into hell.

90

James Beck didn't end up in a metaphorical hell. He ended up in a living hell – the burn unit of Staten Island University Hospital, pumped up with just enough sedation and painkillers to barely tolerate the intolerable.

Hour after hour, Beck felt mired in a miasma of pain and helplessness that shook him to his core. The IV lines, forced-air oxygen mask, his hand encased in fiberglass cast attached to a pulley, a catheter, the never-ending stream of doctors and nurses covered in required masks and clothing to prevent infections, all of it made Beck feel trapped and confined.

His friend, Doctor Brandon Wright, worked nonstop to keep Beck alive. The list of medical problems Wright confronted rolled on and on, each one complicating and affecting all the others. Wright worked with the hospital medical staff and con-sulted with his own experts when needed. One of them, Jess Yang, was a brilliant hand surgeon who examined the x-rays of Beck's left hand and ruled out surgery, insisting he could set two broken phalanges in Beck's little finger and ring finger and a broken metacarpal bone in Beck's little finger. Yang also insisted on casting the fingers himself to make sure everything stayed in place and supervised construction of the rigging over Beck's bed that would keep Beck's battered hand elevated to reduce the inevitable swelling.

Beck's burns were mostly second degree. Rolling over in the parking lot smothered the gasoline enough so that the liquid didn't completely burn through his clothes. The burns on his ankle and leg where Nederland had grabbed him were all third-degree. Nerve damage and loss of pigment were inevitable. Fortunately, the third-degree burns were small enough to be treated with sheet skin grafts. Beck had undergone six of them.

Nederland had died with burning hands gripping Beck's ankle and calf, as well as his deformed teeth sunk into Beck's shin. As a burn patient, Beck was already at high risk for wound infections. Having Nederland's misshapen teeth bite into his skin and bone greatly increased the odds of infection, which meant Beck had to endure high doses of antibiotics and anti-microbials.

Beck had been right about the broken ribs in his back. Three of them. They would heal. Painfully.

The big problem, the problem that could kill James Beck, was inhaling the super-heated air and contaminated black smoke from the burning gasoline, plastic, and flesh. Brandon Wright kept tabs on everyone from the pulmonary department resident to the attending physician in charge. He carefully monitored Beck's regimen of forced oxygen, bronchodilators, pentoxifylline, and heparin. It wasn't Wright's area of expertise, but he consulted with colleagues and pulmonary specialists he knew and read the literature. His most challenging negotiation involved a difference of opinion about the industrial-strength doses of steroids a resident physician had prescribed to delay the pulmonary edema that threatened to kill Beck. Brandon won the fight to reduce the dosages as well as the argument for administering aerosolized versions of heparin and acetylcysteine instead of via IV.

Brandon's persistence, combined with his unthreatening manner, helped. As did Phineas Dunleavy's veiled threats to initiate personal injury and malpractice lawsuits against the hospital, its administrators, and physicians if they defied Beck's primary care physician.

On the other legal front, Phineas shielded Beck from the NYPD's and district attorney's demands to interview him, not hard to do since he could claim Beck was too sick and couldn't talk. More difficult were the negotiations for immunity from prosecution that Phineas pursued.

Phineas and seven other lawyers he had hired had successfully fended off the arrest warrants Roth tried to serve on Beck and the others. The Richmond County DA's office was no match for them and backed off despite pressure from Roth.

None of Beck's men were allowed to visit him, but Brandon let Beck know they were all recovering and would soon be discharged to live in a house on Staten Island Ciro had procured for them. Beck took comfort in that, but it also made him feel more alone and isolated than ever.

Lying in his hospital bed, immobilized, isolated, dealing with the incessant pain and treatments, plagued by all the damage done to him and his men, Beck could not shake the realization that the price paid for his past sins was incalculable. His partners had survived but were all permanently changed. The building he had so painstakingly restored would also never be the same. His prized Mercury Marauder was now junk. Lost, too, was the comfortable feeling of isolation and anonymity Red Hook had afforded him and his fellow ex-cons.

After five days, Beck fought his way back to consciousness, staying awake for most of the daylight hours before they sedated him into a restless, tortured sleep during endless nights. On the sixth day, alone and brooding, Beck saw Dianne Brennan approaching, wearing the mask, gown, and gloves required in the burn unit, none of which concealed the long legs, athletic stride, and red hair that made it clear who had come to visit him.

She sat in the chair next to Beck's bed.

"How are you?"

Beck would have preferred to see her without all the protective garments, particularly the face mask. The coverings did, however, force him to look more closely at her eyes. He'd have to rely on the captivating green eyes flecked with gold to convey whatever Dianne Brennan was thinking.

Beck pulled aside his ventilator mask and said, "You look like a goddamn doctor in that getup."

"Good thing you didn't say nurse."

"Nah, I like nurses."

"Glad to see you're getting back to your usual self."

"Thanks."

"Christ, you sound like somebody shoved a Brillo pad down your throat."

"Feels that way, too. They say if my lungs don't shut down, I probably won't die. I guess I should thank you for being alive."

"And Phil Harris. I wish we'd gotten there sooner."

"Me, too. What happened after I called you? How much of it did you hear before I lost the signal?"

"I think most of it. Caught the part about a bomb and which building it was in. We drove into the hospital grounds, but nobody followed us. So we headed toward the building after the main entrance, like you said. We saw a glow from the spotlight on Phil's unmarked. Headed for it. Then boom, a huge fireball went up. We pulled in, saw Nederland biting you and holding onto your leg. We fired on him. At his body, because we didn't want to hit you. Six rounds didn't seem to do much. I finally got close enough to put one in the top of his spine. That was it."

"Thanks. And, again, thank your partner for me."

"I will. Phil is the one who dragged you free."

Beck paused to breathe through his oxygen mask before he asked his next question.

"How'd you play it with Roth?"

Brennan leaned forward in the chair and spoke softly.

"Blackmailing the Commissioner of the New York Police Department isn't something I'd want to do again."

"Understandable."

"It helped that your lawyer raised all sorts of hell. Particularly with threats to go to the media."

"Phineas loves doing that kind of stuff."

419

"The fact that you saved half the hospital from blowing up also helped."

"Did I?"

"Pretty much, although the bomb squad guys are still debating it."

"Why?"

"Well, the bomb, or whatever you want to call it, was put together by an insane person. So the experts weren't eager to say it would've worked. The debate is about whether the way Nederland sealed the safety valves on the propane tanks and gas cylinders would have prevented them from releasing the pressure."

"Looked like some sort of plumber's epoxy."

"Yes. That's what he used. There would've been a chain reaction. The firebomb would've created enough heat to make the gas inside the propane boil. That would have exploded the tanks, assuming the safety valves didn't pop. The propane would have burned at thirty-five hundred degrees Fahrenheit, twice what gasoline burns at. That would have exploded the acetylene cylinders, which burn at forty-five hundred degrees. And that would have blown up the nitrous oxide which would have taken down that whole end of the hospital."

"How do you know all this?"

"I read the reports. But here's the kicker. Everything would have burned hotter and faster because there was a shitload of pure oxygen in the room. Apparently, our friend Mr. Nederland opened up the oxygen tanks in that storage room."

"Yeah. I heard valves hissing when I went in."

"Most medical gases aren't that flammable, but the heat would've caused enough pressure inside all those compressed gas cylinders to make them explode."

"So, it would've been explosions, not fire."

"Well, both. But mostly explosions. Massive explosions. Particularly the big nitrous oxide tanks. It would have been a goddamn disaster. Nobody wants the word to get out about it."

"Not surprising."

Brennan leaned closer. "I know you're not talking to anybody, but there's a couple of things you should know."

"Okay."

"I was at the scene because I had a lead on you and went to the hospital to arrest you – as per Roth's orders."

"But I don't know anything about any of that."

"Exactly. Also, if it comes to it, you should say you drove to the hospital in the Nissan. Phil Harris agreed to say we were in his unmarked. The precinct cops, fire department, bomb guys, they all arrived after us, so no one knows anything different."

"Got it."

"When you get your voice and strength back, we can firm up the details. If you want."

If I want, thought Beck. He liked the idea but wasn't sure if it was a good idea. He responded with a noncommittal, "Okay." And then said, "So, did you make it clear to Roth what I have on him?"

"Clear enough. I came at it like you said, playing my usual role, you know, providing him with information he should have."

Beck put his ventilator mask back on and nodded for Brennan to continue.

"I told him you called me and let me know what Esposito said to you. Not too many details. Just the basics. I said I had no idea how you and Esposito got together. This was all on the phone. I never met with you."

Beck nodded.

"I told Roth you may have the burner phone Esposito used to text Nederland."

Beck asked, "Did Nederland have a phone on him?"

"Yes. But it turned into a melted blob."

"Good."

"I didn't say anything to Roth about what was on Esposito's phone. Roth already knows what's on it and how it got there.

But I did mention that I did a little research and found out the companies that sell burner phones keep records of texts for a few days up to a couple of weeks."

Again, Beck nodded his approval.

"I advised the commissioner that I didn't think it's worth going after you, or your guys, considering what information might be in your possession."

Beck pulled his mask aside, "Information that proves he collaborated with a homicidal maniac so he could kill me or put me in jail."

"Yes. In so many words. Don't worry, Roth got the message. By the way, we're connecting Nederland to the murders of three drug dealers between here and Alabama. All three fit his M.O. Beaten and burned."

"I guess that's how he financed his scheme."

Brennan said, "Looks like it. All the more reason for Roth to bury any association with Nederland."

"Roth should be delighted you're looking out for him so well."

Beck couldn't see the smirk under Brennan's masked as she said, "Yeah, right."

"After you laid it out for Mr. Roth, what did he say?"

"Not a goddamn word. But he took the folder on his desk with copies of the arrest warrants for you and your crew, tore it in half, and dropped it into his wastebasket."

"Then unless Roth does something stupid, the cell phone with Esposito's prints on it along with a printout of all Esposito's text messages to Ronald Nederland will stay locked up in my lawyer's safe."

Beck watched Brennan blink.

"You got all the text messages?"

Beck nodded.

"Your tech guy must be good."

"Didn't need much tech. Just needed to find out who to bribe."

Brennan's eyes showed she was smiling.

"And your charming lawyer has everything."

"He does."

"I'll let the commissioner know I found that out."

Beck said, "Isn't that why you came here?"

"That's why Roth thinks I'm here."

"So, Inspector, where do you come out regarding Mr. Roth and the NYPD?"

Brennan paused before she answered.

"For the moment, I'll stick around to make sure Roth buries everything and moves on to other problems. Take my advice, Beck. Warren Roth has a long memory. If he gets a chance to do you harm, he will."

"Then you'd better convince him he has no chance. Even if he kills me, even if he kills all of us, the information will go to a P.R. firm that will flog the story to every news outlet and social media platform. Relentlessly."

"I'll make sure he knows that."

"Good. What's next?"

"For me?"

"Yeah."

"I'm not sure."

"Of what?"

"I have a feeling Roth admires me because I'm playing the game as ruthlessly as he does."

"Good."

"But that doesn't mean he isn't just waiting for the right time to chop my head off."

"I don't think Roth will risk firing you. When the time is right, let him know you'll take a promotion and be on your way."

"Except, I'm not sure I want to stay with the NYPD."

"Why leave? You're pretty damn good at what you do, Brennan. And I doubt the NYPD is much worse than any organization with fifty-thousand employees."

"Fifty-five. And what do you mean *pretty* good?"

"Well, you did have to go outside the fifty-five thousand to solve the case."

Brennan pulled down her face mask so she could smirk at Beck. He pulled his oxygen mask aside so he could smile at her.

She said, "By the way, when we pulled in behind that building, I heard Nederland screaming something at you. What was he saying?"

Beck breathed through his forced oxygen mask for a few moments. The answer to Brennan's question wasn't something he wanted to recall. But she had been through all of it with him, right to the end, and she had saved his life. Brennan deserved to know.

Beck pulled aside the mask and said, "He kept screaming at me, 'you killed my mother.'"

"His mother?"

"Yeah. Not his stepfather. His mother. Seems it was all about her."

Brennan nodded. It made sense.

"Ruth...?"

"Androvette."

Brennan nodded again. Ruth Androvette. The crucial link in the chain of causes.

"Boys and their mothers, huh?"

"Even monster boys and their mothers."

She nodded and then said, "So, what's next for you, James?"

Beck noted she had used his first name. Maybe for the first time. He took another breath from his oxygen mask before he spoke.

"First of all, not die."

"That's a start. And then?"

"Well, some things will have to change."

"Like what?"

Beck made a circular motion with his right hand.

"Like whatever I did to end up like this."

Brennan said, "You'll figure it out."

Beck said, "Hopefully."

AUTHOR'S NOTE:

Every novel has a boilerplate phrase on the copyright page, pointing out that it is a work of fiction, as does *Death Comes Due*. However, please note that the descriptions of firebombs and explosives made by the villain, Monster-Boy, are definitely fictitious. It's all made up, albeit based on a few logical assumptions. Emphasis on assumptions.

AND A REQUEST:

If you enjoyed *Death Comes Due*, would you mind taking a moment to post a review on Amazon and let other readers know that you like it? Books live and die by the number of Amazon reviews they receive. The Amazon algorithms only measure the number of reviews and star-ratings, so you can be as brief as you like.

It's easy to post a review:
- Go to the *Death Comes Due* product page.
- Click where it says **"ratings"** next to the stars.
- Under "Review this product" click on **Write a customer review.**

Thank you.

For more information on my other books, publishing schedule, blog posts, and more, visit www.johnclarkson.com

CPSIA information can be obtained
at www.ICGtesting.com
Printed in the USA
LVHW012251080121
676100LV00003B/612